Todd and Danielle —

Thank you for
your leadership.

Blessings,
Ed Young

"Ed Young epitomizes creative leadership. His style and depth, coupled with congeniality, has made his church a tower of influence. His book will mentor a generation."

Bishop T. D. Jakes Sr.
The Potter's House of Dallas, Inc.,
and Best-selling Author

"Ed Young is one of the most creative leaders of one of the most creative churches around. This book is not only out of the box and outside the lines; it's on another page altogether."

John Ortberg
Teaching Pastor,
Menlo Park Presbyterian Church;
and Best-selling Author

"Ed Young Jr.'s *The Creative Leader* reveals the spontaneously innovative heart of Fellowship Church. Its dynamics of actuating change to God's glory creates a spellbinder with application to churches and organizations of any size. Get it!"

John W. Reed, PhD
Director, Doctor of Ministry Studies,
Dallas Theological Seminary;
President, The Association for Doctor of Ministry Education

"Along with pastors throughout the country, I have been inspired and challenged by the leadership and ministry success of my friend Ed Young. In *The Creative Leader* Ed reveals the principles that fuel and inform his unique approach to leadership. Complete with illustrations, graphics, and real life Q&A, this is more than a book. This is a manual on how to lead and do ministry in the new millennium."

Andy Stanley
North Point Ministries
and Best-selling Author

>>The Creative Leader

Unleashing the Power of Your Creative Potential }

ED << YOUNG

BROADMAN
&HOLMAN
PUBLISHERS

NASHVILLE, TENNESSEE

13-digit ISBN: 978-0-8054-3177-3
10-digit ISBN: 0-8054-3177-2

Published by Broadman & Holman Publishers,
Nashville, Tennessee

Dewey Decimal Classification: 303.3
Subject Headings: LEADERSHIP

Unless noted otherwise Scripture quotations are taken from the Holy Bible,
New International Version, copyright © 1973, 1978, 1984 by the International
Bible Society; used by permission of Zondervan Publishing House; all rights
reserved. One Scripture quotation is taken from J. B. Phillips' *Translation of
the New Testament*, HarperCollins Publishers Ltd., Religious Books Division;
all rights reserved.

Any emphases or parenthetical comments within Scripture are the
author's own.

The case studies on Walt Disney and Christopher Columbus are summaries
of Bob Thomas, *Walt Disney: An American Original* (New York: Simon and
Schuster, 1976) and Samuel Eliot Morison, *Admiral of the Ocean Sea: A Life of
Christopher Columbus* (New York: Time Inc., 1962). The other two case studies
were adapted from http://www.gore.com/en_xx/aboutus/index.html and www.
proicehockey.about.com/cs/miracleonice/a/miracle_legacy_p.htm.

1 2 3 4 5 6 7 8 9 10 10 09 08 07 06

To Dr. Ed Young . . .
Dad, mentor, and friend.

Thank you for being the kind of leader who inspired me
to dream big and invest my life
into the greatest thing going and growing,
the local church.
I am eternally grateful for all you have done
and continue to do for me.
This book could not have been written
without the wisdom, encouragement, and
creative leadership you've imparted to me
throughout my life.

Contents

Acknowledgments   xi

Introduction: A Call for Change   1

SECTION 1 Forming a Creative Foundation   5
A Case Study in Creative Leadership: Walt Disney   7
    1. Why Creativity?   9
    2. The Creative Payoff   21
    3. The Creative Constant   35
Creative Q & A: Section 1   57

SECTION 2 Enhancing Your Creative Environment   63
A Case Study in Creative Leadership: W. L. Gore & Associates   65
    4. Creative Church Culture   69
    5. Creative Worship   89
    6. Creative Communication   107
Creative Q & A: Section 2   131

SECTION 3 Positioning Your Creative Players   139
A Case Study in Creative Leadership: Miracle on Ice   141
    7. Creative Staffing   143
    8. Team Creativity   171
Creative Q & A: Section 3   195

SECTION 4 Overcoming Creative Obstacles   205
A Case Study in Creative Leadership: Christopher Columbus   207
    9. Creative Cramps   211
    10. Three Things They Didn't Teach Me in Seminary   225
Creative Q & A: Section 4   249

    11. Go Fish!   255

Is It Worth It?   269

Contents

Appendixes   271–90

    1a and b. Easter Invitations   272–73

    2a and b. Christmas Direct Mail with Die-cut   274–75

    3a. "Retro" Series Graphic   276

    3b. Satellite Campus Promotion   277

    4a and b. "Tri-God" Series Graphic   278–79

    5a. "Multiple Choice" Series Graphic   280

    5b. Example of Guest Registry Form   281

    6a and b. "Thread—Tailor Made" Mind Map   282–83

    7. "Juicy Fruit—Faithfulness" Mind Map   284

    8a and b. "In the Zone—Creature from the Cash Lagoon"
            Sermon Notes   285–86

    9. "In the Zone" Series Graphic   287

    10a. and b. Christmas Invitation   288–89

    11. "Character Tour" Series Graphic   290

About the Author   291

Acknowledgments

This book is the culmination of many years of sweat and toil in the trenches of church leadership. And it is impossible to write a book like this without depending on the gifts, talents, insights, and dedication of many people over many years of ministry. Each one of the leadership principles in this book comes out of real ministry run by real, live, dedicated staff. I owe a debt of gratitude to all of the people, too numerous to name, from Fellowship Church who helped make this book possible.

I do want to thank, however, three gentlemen in particular at Fellowship who helped directly in the research, writing, and editing of the manuscript. To Cliff McNeely, Chris McGregor, and Andy Boyd: I could not have completed this huge undertaking without your able assistance. Thank you for the late nights, for your tenacious dedication to detail, and for your creative drive to get the job done.

I also want to thank several people who have been with me for many years at Fellowship Church. To Preston Mitchell, Owen Goff, and Doris Scoggins: Thank you for walking side-by-side with me during the best and worst of times. Fellowship Church would not be where it is today were it not for your dedication and loyalty to the vision God gave us on that hot July day back in 1990. It's been an honor to take this exciting ride with you and to unleash our creative potential together. And, of course, to my lovely wife, Lisa, who has been with me from the very beginning: I can't imagine a greater partner and friend with whom to take this journey.

In addition, to Preston, Cliff, Andy, Troy Page, Pace Hartfield, and Laura Strickland—the regulars on my creative team—thanks for your valuable insight week after week as the weekend waves come crashing onto the shore. Teamwork like this is the bedrock of creative leadership.

Thanks to Tracy Barnes, Vanessa Whitwell, Preston, and Troy for reviewing the manuscript prior to publication and making sure the book is the best it can be.

Finally, thanks to Len Goss and Lisa Parnell at Broadman & Holman for your editing skill and to Jeff Godby for your flexibility and creative direction in the cover design.

INTRODUCTION

A Call for Change

In 1990, a core group of Christ followers in Irving, Texas, came together and asked one simple question: How can we reach people *today* with the life-changing message of Jesus Christ? We didn't know where that question would take us, but we knew for sure that we had to be willing to do things differently than what we had experienced in the past.

As the newly appointed leader of this fledgling church, I wanted to approach that question from the perspective that culture is always changing. We could not rely on the methods of the past to reach the emerging generation. A changing culture demands that we too must change to meet our culture head-on.

Fellowship Church was essentially a mission church birthed from a traditional church. But I was not looking to duplicate the mother church by creating another traditional church for traditional church-going people. I wanted an environment that would communicate God's unchanging truth in such creative and compelling ways that it would connect with anyone, regardless of their church background or lack thereof. I wanted to reach all people, whether they had attended church all their lives or had never darkened the door of a church before.

I was not content to feed the already-fed. There were enough churches doing that, especially in the Dallas–Fort Worth area. That was neither my passion nor the thrust of this core group of believers.

Out of that desire emerged another question: How can we keep God's unchanging truth the same while communicating it in a radically different style? It would take a mammoth effort to keep the church relevant within a constantly changing culture, while remaining anchored to the fundamentals of our ancient faith. To be quite candid, that is the never-ending challenge of the church.

Stepping up to this challenge would require a massive infusion of something missing in many churches today: *creativity*. In fact, this fundamental element of leadership is hard to find in many organizations, whether church, parachurch, or business. Yet this one quality separates extraordinary organizations from the mundane and ineffective ones.

Cutting-edge creativity also marks the lives of the men and women who are true difference-makers in these organizations and the world around them. These leaders don't try to keep pace with cultural change; they set the pace. *Creative leaders are trendsetters for creative change, anticipating people's changing needs within their dynamic environments.*

This book is for the person who wants to be that kind of leader, especially in the local church. If you are a leader in business, education, medicine, law, government, the arts, or any other sector of society, this book will be helpful in your particular calling. If you're looking for a book that will help you maintain the status quo, this is not it. If you are looking for a few buzzwords or shortcuts, you won't find them here either. But if you're looking for a book that can help bring a sense of vitality and excitement to both your life and your organization, keep reading.

I will be writing from the vantage point of a pastor, and most of my insights and illustrations come out of my experiences in the church. I have been in the ministry for more than twenty years—fifteen of those at Fellowship Church—and my heart beats loudly for the mission and mandate of the church. If you are a pastor struggling in the trenches of leadership, this book is definitely for you. I wrote this with you in mind. Whether you pastor a church of 50 or 50,000, my prayer is that this will help you fulfill the unique ministry vision God has given you.

As we begin this discovery of creative leadership, we will take a deeper look at some of the benefits of being a creative leader. Keeping creativity at the forefront of your leadership portfolio will stretch you in ways you never thought possible. Thinking creatively is one of the most exhausting exercises you will ever encounter. And taking those creative thoughts and implementing them into creative solutions will take everything you have and more. The benefits, though, are well worth the expended effort.

Being a creatively driven leader within a creatively driven organization is an exciting ride. This approach to leadership will not only change your outlook on life, your ministry, and your work; it will also infuse those around you with the same passion for creativity and innovation.

In the first section of the book I offer some of the payoffs of creativity in leadership. I answer some questions that are beginning to surface in your brain: "If I begin to implement creativity into my life and my organization, what will happen? How will creativity positively impact my ministry, my business, my department, my school, or my practice?" If you are going to sign on to any approach to leadership, you need to know the potential payoff. Unless the payoff is worth it, the effort is wasted.

In the second section, I demonstrate why your environment is crucial to creative leadership. What does the creative church culture look like? How do worship and communication flow from and contribute to that creative environment?

The third section deals with where and how to place your team players. Learn to leverage your committed teammates for a bigger and better future.

The fourth and final section of the book looks at the obstacles to creative leadership. I share candidly how God has shown me great ways (often by trial and error) to overcome these obstacles and use them for success.

This book offers real answers to real questions that leaders like you face in the trenches. To that end, check out the Q & A after each major section of the book. Compiled from the most common questions I've been asked over the years, these Q & A provide some very practical insight from my own leadership struggles.

But first, why creativity? Of all of the other qualities of leadership, why fill an entire book focusing on this one quality? You may have read books or attended seminars on time management, principled leadership, participatory management, goal-setting, or other leadership topics. To the question, Do we really need another approach to leadership? the short answer is Yes. Stay tuned for the long answer.

Over the next few pages, I share the basis for my emphasis on creativity in leadership. As a Christian pastor, this passion for creativity comes from the many years I've invested studying and teaching God's Word. This book was born from my team and me working on the front lines to make a lasting impact for Christ within the framework of a creative and dynamic church. My understanding of Scripture as it relates to the character of God and the fundamental needs of people drives my creative pursuits as a leader in the church.

And while I write primarily from my perspective as a church leader, the concepts presented in this book can be applied in many areas of leadership within any organization or institution. With that in mind, the first chapter answers an important question, Why creativity? After that, we dive into the next important question in chapter 2, What is the payoff of creative leadership?

Section 1

*Forming a Creative
Foundation*

A Case Study in Creative Leadership

WALT DISNEY

FOLLOWING HIS STINT IN WORLD WAR I, Walt Disney stepped into the American entertainment business with dreams of becoming a cartoonist and animator. Despite setback after setback, Disney persisted with his vision to produce groundbreaking entertainment through the creative medium of animation.

After years of perseverance, he was the first animator to produce a "talkie" cartoon feature or a Technicolor release of a moving cartoon. Disney turned down deals to work for big-name entertainment firms because they would involve sacrificing his vision, his pursuit of excellence, his attention to meticulous detail, and his creative rights. He recognized that film studio committees would stifle the creative process and vowed early on that he would not work for anyone else, insisting instead that he would maintain control of his own work.

Disney embodies the creative ideal. He worked harder than his competition, fought diligently for his dreams, aggressively protected his work, and would not let anyone dissuade him from his vision. He was constantly thinking of ways to stay ahead of the trend. He inspired creative potential in others around him and continues to inspire many today. Above all, he never, ever gave up. Eventually, his vision propelled the Disney Corporation into a multi-billion-dollar entertainment company. There is nothing easy about being creative. Walt Disney worked hard, giving his life to animating talking animals on celluloid to make people laugh. One question, though, begs to be asked: How much harder should we work at giving our lives to building the creative church, a spiritual enterprise that connects people to the living Lord?

It is not easy to stay ahead of the cultural curve in reaching people for Christ. But the nature of our calling compels us, our creative potential demands it, and hungry people cry out for it. We can and should do no less as Christian leaders. We should work no less vigorously, pay no less attention to detail, be no less inspiring, and dream no less than Walt Disney himself.

His greatest claim to fame in my opinion is not the world-wide enterprise, but that he was an ordinary man with the guts and foresight to forge ahead with his creative vision and achieve it—against all odds.

So God created man in his own image,
in the image of God he created him;
male and female he created them.

GENESIS 1:27

CHAPTER 1

Why Creativity?

The young student was lonely, frustrated, and homesick. A thousand miles from home, he found himself drowning in the fast and furious tide of college life. Sex, drinking, and drug binges were the norm. He thought he knew a lot about the world, but in reality, he had grown up in a sheltered environment. The girls, the parties, and the Mardi-Gras lifestyle provided many temptations and distractions, but by the grace of God, he remained faithful to Christ and resisted the pressure to roll with the college tide.

Nonetheless, he felt like his relationship with God was on pause. He wasn't doing anything bad, but he wasn't doing much good either. His spiritual passion was flaming out.

One lonely night, he knelt in his dorm room, rested his elbows on his rackety air-conditioning unit, looked out over the darkened parking lot, and began to pray. But for some strange reason, he didn't pray for himself. Instead, he found himself praying for a friend named Scott.

The intuitive mind is a sacred gift and the rational
mind is a faithful servant. We have created a society
that honors the servant and has forgotten the gift.

ALBERT EINSTEIN

Scott was handsome, tall, and athletic—full of natural ability and potential. Unfortunately, he also carried around a lot of baggage from his past. His parents' marriage was shaky at best. His relationship with his dad was distant, partially due to his father's heavy travel schedule as a college basketball coach. At an early age, Scott began his downward spiral, experimenting with drugs and shoplifting. His experimentation inevitably led to harder drugs. His rebellion continued to escalate when the high he received from shoplifting was replaced with the rush of burglarizing homes. He didn't need the money; it was just something to do. Because of his influential family and his status as a star athlete, he was never arrested or made to pay for his crimes.

One afternoon, Scott was walking to class with this college friend who had been praying for him. Scott suddenly turned and said, "Something is different about you. You have something that I don't have. What is it?"

Scott's statement stopped this young man in his tracks because he had been praying for just such an opportunity. That evening in Scott's dorm room, Scott's friend led him in a prayer to enter into a new relationship with Christ.

I was that college student. More than two decades ago, I prayed with Scott in his dorm room—an event that has changed both our lives. Scott began his journey as a Christian that day, but my own journey into the pastorate also began that very same day. Through my interaction with Scott, I sensed God leading my life into the pastorate. My call to ministry and my vision for the local church began thanks to my interaction with Scott and others like him in college.

Trying to influence my friends for Christ helped me see the need for doing church in a radically different way. Scores and scores of Scotts out there need not only a radical Savior but a radical church to meet them where they are.

After Scott bowed the knee to Christ, I invited him to the church I was attending. And for the first time, I began to see the church through someone else's eyes. The terminology was confusing. The music was tired. The overall feeling was lifeless and just plain boring. *If I ever go into church work*, I thought, *I will do whatever it takes to provide a biblically driven, compelling, and creative experience that someone like my friend Scott could understand.*

I wish I could tell you that Scott is doing well, but the last time I heard from him, he was still floundering. Though he isn't struggling quite as much as when I first met him in college, he remains disconnected from the local church. That breaks my heart.

What if a creative and compelling church had been there for Scott when he first came to know Christ? What if there had been a place where Scott could have connected with others like himself and developed a relationship with his Creator? I'm convinced he would be a different man today.

I am fortunate to pastor a church like that—to put into practice the vision God gave me years ago. Our vision for Fellowship is simple. We bring people into the church by *reaching out* (that's evangelism) in creative ways that relate to real life and contemporary culture. Then we work hard to provide an exciting and God-honoring environment for *reaching up* (that's worship) to connect with God. Finally, we teach our people to grow up into full-court followers of Christ by *reaching in* (that's discipleship) and moving our people from spectators in the stands to the game of active service.

If we want to reach the Scotts out there, we have to get involved up to our elbows in the subject of this book: creative leadership. This requires a tag-team effort. I'm a team member and you're a team member. Together, we must work tirelessly in cooperation with the power of the Holy Spirit to accomplish Christ's bold mission for the church. We cannot let the Scotts of this world fall by the wayside, because of laziness, apathy, or an affinity for the status quo.

The status quo should never, ever describe the dynamic reality that is the Bride of Christ. If the local church is not the most creative, innovative, and alive place on the planet, we are failing as its leaders. My prayer is to avoid this failure by realizing the incredible potential of creative leadership within ourselves and our churches to help unleash the power of the gospel to a needy world.

Realizing Our Creative Potential

I love the local church. I cut my teeth on the pews of Southern Baptist churches where my father served as pastor (across the South and now in Texas). The first time I remember spelling my name was with stale macaroni in vacation Bible school. As a pastor's kid, I really never did anything wild or crazy growing up—except maybe getting drunk on Kool-Aid and smoking a couple of crayons. That was the extent of my rebellious lifestyle. After attending Florida State for a couple of years, I graduated from a Christian college in Texas and headed off to seminary. After seminary, I served on my father's church staff in Houston then came to Dallas to start Fellowship Church.

Throughout that time, I rubbed shoulders with a lot of Christian leaders and saw the collective creative potential in the Body of Christ. Unfortunately, I also watched far too many leaders falter with their creative potential. Too many churches get stuck in a rut, doing the same routine, day after day, week after week, month after month. In the name of tradition and old-time religion, these churches are content to follow the same well-worn path, unaware that the reason the path is so worn is because it is a vast but predictable circle.

Excuses, Excuses—I Hear Them Every Day

One of the reasons we ignore our creative potential is a gnawing sense of inadequacy in the creative realm. Rather than giving God our best creative efforts within the church, we often give Him excuses. We compare ourselves to others, convinced that we can't possibly do it as well as this or that person. We say to God, "I'm not creative. I can't sing, dance, or act. I don't have an original bone in my body." Creativity, we think, is reserved for those extraordinary speakers, actors, writers, and artists who have captured international attention because of their talents and abilities. You know, people like Bill Hybels, Rick Warren, T. D. Jakes, John Maxwell, Thomas Kinkade, Michael W. Smith, the Newsboys, Max Lucado, and John Grisham. Surely, God cannot expect that output from us.

But these excuses ring hollow in the ears of our creative Creator. We are made in His image and, because of that, He desires and expects our participation in the creative process. He wants us to make His nature and character known through our lives by impacting those in our sphere of influence. Intuitively, we are all aware of this basic truth. We understand, as Christians, that God created us and that we are made in His image. We also understand the concept of stewardship. Unfortunately, we often neglect to live out this reality when it comes to realizing our creative potential.

Our creativity is linked to our uniqueness. Our external uniqueness is evident in each person's voice, fingerprints, retinas, and so on. Let's not stop with physical distinctions. Consider the intellectual, emotional, and spiritual distinctions of each individual. No two people have the same intellectual capacity, emotional makeup, prior experiences, gifts, passions, or interests. Because God has endowed each of us with a unique combination of attributes and talents, our creative response will also be unique.

Creative Cramps

Most people have trouble realizing their creative potential, because at some point along life's journey their creativity was beaten out of them. Most of us suffer from a creative cramp somewhere during the course of our lives. Early on in life, creativity is natural and even encouraged as we develop. In our childhood years, our lives are filled with creative thought and potential. Studies reveal that children in the one-to-six-year-old age group score in the ninetieth percentile of creative ability. Those same studies also show that once these children hit age seven, they experience creative cramping that drastically lowers their creative score.* Sadly, these creative cramps continue to squeeze the creative potential of these children as they move into adulthood.

Let's process this hard data to understand why so many of us have lost the unique creative edge God intended for us. What happens to children between the ages of six and seven that causes them to plummet in creative potential? One word: school. Don't get me wrong; I'm all for education. However, there is something about the educational system that beats creativity out of us.

Somewhere along life's journey, at about seven, eight, and nine years of age—when the rigors of education start to heat up—we begin to trade our creative thought for other things we are told are more important for our development as productive people in society. At a crucial time in our creative development, we trade the artistic for the analytical. We trade our imaginations for memorization. And we trade laughter for logic. Pretty soon we find ourselves in prison cells of predictability. We want our life to have meaning and purpose and power. We want things to happen. We want to have adventure and excitement. But when we take a long look at our lives, they seem mundane and boring. After creativity is driven out of us, we realize how stale life can be without the Technicolor excitement that creativity affords.

Obviously, I'm not saying that we need to go back to preschool or kindergarten and start playing with finger paints and Play-Doh. What I am saying is that we need to rediscover something that we lost in childhood. We need to rediscover the joy of trying new things simply to shake up the status quo. We need courage to push the boundaries of tradition from time to time. We need to spend time in reflection and imagination to awaken our dormant creativity.

---

* Marlene D. LeFever, *Creative Teaching Methods: Be an Effective Christian Teacher,* rev ed. (Colorado Springs: Cook Communications, 1996), 46–47.

Reviving creativity may be as simple as savoring the excitement of seeing something for the first time or in experiencing something we've seen a thousand times before in a completely different way. We need to find new pleasure in the beauty and diversity of creation, the arts and the worship of God. Regular time each day in creative activities will help us rekindle our creative flare and rediscover an aspect of our humanity that has been severed since childhood. I'm not talking about going back to crayons and finger paints (necessarily), but I am suggesting that you find those things that get your creative juices flowing. Perhaps it's journaling or listening to music. Maybe it's simply staring at a tree for an hour. It might just be finger painting for you. I don't know. But whatever they are for you, these exercises will not only enhance your personal and spiritual life; they will enhance your ability to lead others more effectively.

The Creative Trinity

At this point in the discussion, it's important to delve into a theology of creativity within the framework of something I call the "creative trinity." When we observe how creativity flows directly from the character of God, we are compelled to mimic God's creative character in our own lives. God alone—not cultural expectations, the educational system, or even church tradition—then becomes the benchmark for creative thought and action. I love J. B. Phillips's paraphrase of Romans 12:2—"Don't let the world squeeze you into its own mould." When you get squeezed into the world's "mould," something inevitably gets squeezed out. For many of us, that is our God-given and God-driven creativity.

God Invented It

The first part of the creative trinity is that you and I should be creative because *God invented creativity*. God thought it up; it was His idea. Creativity is woven into the very fabric and framework of who God is. Look at the fifth word in the Bible in Genesis 1:1—"created," as in "In the beginning God created." God started the creative ball rolling, and it has been rolling ever since.

If creativity is so central to the character of God, how can we claim to be connected to the God of the universe and still be so boring? Ephesians 5:1 tells us to be imitators of God. We are to mimic God by being people of love, compassion, hope, vision, and, yes, creativity.

Consider the diversity and innovation all around us. When was the last time you took a good, hard look at the beauty, wonder, and diversity of God's creation? Does the natural world wow you like it did when you were a child? When was the last time a thunderstorm made you feel helpless? Have you ever stood at the mouth of an endless body of water and felt really small? Let me challenge you to allow experiences like these to drive you to worship God and to stimulate your creative potential. Sadly, our man-made homes of bricks and mortar, mechanical engines, miles of asphalt, and offices of concrete and steel can tend to distract us from appreciating the sheer brilliance and wonder of God's creation.

Think for a moment about human beings. God didn't make one human and then clone him six billion times. Wouldn't it be boring if everyone else looked exactly like you, talked exactly like you, and thought exactly like you? For some of us in the ministry, we may think we want more clones (especially on our leadership staff), but such a world would be unthinkably predictable and dull.

What about other aspects of creation? He didn't create one type of flower and spread that same seed all over the earth. He didn't stop creating animals with one species of mammal, reptile, or bird. God's creation is unique and unpredictable; just when we think we have it all figured out, we are confounded again.

If God wasn't content to make a bland, predictable world, why are we content to make church that way? Why do we come up with one way of doing things and become content to do that same thing over and over again? Why do we not challenge our thinking and move to greater heights of innovation?

Jesus Modeled It

The second part of the creative trinity is *Jesus modeled creativity*. Matthew records that Christ "did not say anything to them without using a parable" (Matt. 13:34). Jesus was the most creative leader and teacher that ever walked the planet. He spoke from hillsides, boat bows, and beaches. He drew in the sand, used a Roman coin, cursed a fig tree, and picked up a piece of bread. He divided fish, turned over tables, and put a child on His knee—all to illustrate important lessons. Jesus was all about delivering His life-changing message in dynamic and creative ways to meet to His listeners' needs and backgrounds.

When we analyze all of the words of Christ recorded in the Gospels, we find that 72 percent of them were based on application. They were words of cultural relevancy that answered the "so what?" question (that is, "What difference does this teaching make in my life?"). If we communicate biblical truth without addressing the specific difference it should make in the lives of our audience, we are not modeling the ministry of Jesus Christ.

Jesus understood something 2,000 years ago that we are just coming to realize—we are visual and even multisensory learners. He constantly used visuals and never used the same approach twice. Everything He did was unique. Every approach was different, based on the type of people and circumstances around Him at the time. It is not hard to make the connection between Jesus, the master communicator, and Jesus, the master of creativity. Being a good teacher and a creative person go hand-in-hand. As church leaders, we need to continually look to Him as a practical model to emulate in creative leadership.

The Spirit Empowers It

The third part of the creative trinity is that the *Spirit of God empowers creativity.* He is the One who gives supernatural abilities to the church (and its leaders) to truly be the magnetic bride of Christ. He empowers creativity in the life of the believer because people have been designed to respond to this creative element. People are wired for and yearn for creativity. Why do you think the entertainment industry is so successful and popular? Actors, musicians, and entertainers of all varieties capture the imaginations of all ages with their creative gifts. Hollywood, Nashville, and New York are meeting the deep-seated need that people have for creativity, adventure, and excitement in their lives—a need the church should be filling through the creative power of the Holy Spirit.

Spend some time reflecting on the way God creatively communicated truth through the men and women of Scripture. For example, God used a piece of fruit to communicate through Adam and Eve. He used an ark to communicate through Noah. He used a ram to communicate through Abraham, a rod with Moses, the carcass of a lion with Sampson, five smooth stones with David, a big fish with Jonah, and fire with the apostle Paul. Ultimately, He used a despised crucifix to communicate His amazing grace to the world.

The Church's Mandate

So why should we implement creativity in leadership? God invented it. Jesus modeled it. The Holy Spirit empowers it because people need it. If we church leaders are going to live out the challenging mission that God has laid out for the local church, we must unleash the creative potential available to us, develop it, and use it to communicate the most compelling message ever given to mankind. Creativity is not an option for the church; it is a biblical mandate that flows from the very character of the Creator.

As we begin this journey toward creative leadership, let me challenge you to start doing things uniquely and unpredictably. Do it in a way that is both biblically driven and communicated with excellence. Then sit back and watch the results. Watch the body language of the people you teach. Watch your staff. Watch your lay leadership team. They will be riveted as your God-given creativity is used to connect their hunger for creativity with their hunger for the truth of God.

We could talk about a lot of different areas where creativity can and should take place—in your marriage, your relationship with your children, your recreational pursuits, or in the corporate world and other professional arenas. And many of the concepts we'll discuss translate to these other arenas of life. However, we are going to talk about creativity in the local church, that entity which is dear to the heart of God, that colossal collection of Christ followers known as the Body of Christ.

They Sure Know How to Say It

Several years ago, a man walking through the lobby of Fellowship Church stopped me and said, "Ed, I know you like sports a lot. Have you ever been to a professional boxing match before?"

"No, I haven't," I answered. "Why do you ask?"

"Well," he said, "there's going to be a huge prize fight in Las Vegas and I'll get us some tickets."

I thought he was just saying that. You know how people say "Let's do lunch" or "Let's play golf one day," and it never happens? Well, this actually happened.

Several weeks later he told me, "I got us tickets." I don't remember the exact date, but it was when Mike Tyson was fighting Evander Holyfield for the World Heavyweight Championship. Sure enough, he secured plane tickets for us and we flew to Las Vegas to watch this fight. I have been to a lot of sporting events in my life, but they all pale in comparison to the feverish level of excitement and energy at this professional prizefight.

The boxing match, however, was not the only thing that caught my attention during that once-in-a-lifetime experience. As we were walking the streets of Las Vegas before the boxing bout, I was overwhelmed by the signage. The massive billboards, the neon lights, the flashing marquees—everywhere I looked in every possible marketable space was a sign of some shape, form, or fashion. If you want to see people that know how to do signage, go to Las Vegas, Nevada. *Man,* I thought, *these people here in Vegas don't have very much to say, but they sure know how to say it!*

And then another sobering thought flashed across my mind: *The local church has everything to say, but we don't know how to say it.* How tragic. The church has the greatest, most hopeful message known to humankind; yet too often, that message fails to connect with the masses of humanity passing by your church and mine.

That's why creativity should grace everything that touches our leadership and ministry. When the church meets together, the creative juices should be flowing, the ideas shaking and baking. People should say, "Wow, when these Christians get together, it is phenomenal. I've never seen such creativity!" When is the last time someone said that about your church? But it should be that way, because we are connected to the Father, we have the perfect model in Jesus Christ, and we are empowered by the Holy Spirit.

Christians should be leading the charge on creativity, because we alone are given the task of spreading the life-changing message of Jesus Christ. We need to get serious about unleashing our God-given creativity for His glory to the people who so desperately need it.

*Whatever you do, work at it with
all your heart, as working
for the Lord, not for men.*
COLOSSIANS 3:23

CHAPTER 2

The Creative Payoff

What's the payoff? That's a valid and worthwhile question. If you are reading this book, you are most likely a leader in some capacity. And as a leader, you're not likely to embark on a journey without knowing at the outset where it will take you. That's smart thinking. You should know, as you start down this road of creative leadership, what the benefits will be for you and your organization. If you were to implement creativity into your life and leadership, what would be some payoffs to such a commitment?

Let me list ten amazing results that happen if you get serious about implementing creativity. Time and time again, as I've been in the trenches of leadership, these things have kept me going. And they can do the same for you when life is kicking your tail.

Creativity Will Make You into God's Kind of Leader

Creativity is a great catalyst for leadership development. That's really what this book is all about—finding your God-given

*One of the advantages of being
disorderly is that one is constantly
making exciting discoveries.*
A. A. MILNE

creative bent that can propel you forward in your leadership journey. Creativity is in our DNA. If we are not striving to develop our creativity as leaders, then we are failing to truly exemplify the high calling of being made in the image of God. I cannot be the kind of leader God wants me to be if I do not own the challenge of creativity. If I choose stagnation, I will cease to function as God made me and will not be the kind of leader who Jesus modeled.

Again, creativity and leadership are linked. Those who work alongside the Holy Spirit to develop their own creativity will be stretched and used in ways that honor God and reap lasting spiritual fruit. Creative people can see what others can't. They make it where others miss. They are ahead of the curve.

Creativity will not only propel your leadership to the next level but will also lead you to new spiritual heights. It's a lifestyle, not a buzzword. Taking the creative plunge will force you to see yourself and the world around you in new ways. It will force you to look long and hard in the mirror and reevaluate your life and ministry. It is a one-of-a-kind adventure that will deepen your faith, challenge your paradigms, and remold you into a leader who truly embodies the character of Jesus Christ.

Creativity Will Deepen Your Dependence on God

Creativity is immensely difficult and especially taxing on the leader. My own journal is a great testament to this principle. When I look back on all of my journal entries since college, I find numerous entries showing my frustrations and requests to God for more creativity.

I have seen many problems in the church and am constantly challenged to look at these problems in a new light. That means being willing to do things differently—something that requires not only a strong work ethic but an infusion of strength and inspiration that can come only from our creative God. Because it requires tremendous commitment, the pursuit of creativity has driven me to my knees more than any other leadership task. What could be a greater asset to a leader than a lifestyle of dependence on his Creator? Nothing I have done in leadership has given me greater frustration or a greater sense of God's presence than pursuing creativity for His kingdom. I know that your own journey in the creative realm will drive you to deeper dependence on the One from whom all creativity flows.

Creativity Will Perpetuate Your Learning Curve

A constant characteristic in the dynamic leaders I have studied is a commitment to lifelong learning. Creative leaders are never content with the status quo. Creative leaders never stagnate. They are always developing and searching for new ways to address old problems. Looking for new answers takes leaders out of their comfort zone and into the realm of the unknown, growing them in and through the creative process.

Status-quo leaders, on the other hand, experience little growth, because they are content to call upon their old education, old experiences, and old methods to address new problems. Sooner or later, the dynamic culture will pass them by and their effectiveness will completely dissolve. Their commitment to tradition and ritual, rather than innovation and excitement, will lead to a cold, dispassionate life and ministry.

That's not what God wants for you and me. He wants us to continue learning and growing. Leadership is not a destination; it's a never-ending process. The moment you stop learning is the moment you stop being an effective leader. Throughout this process of pursuing creativity, we must keep a perpetual thirst and hunger for discovering new and dynamic (that is, changing, fluid, and cutting-edge) ways of doing things. That should be descriptive of everyone who aspires to creative leadership.

Creativity Will Help You Meet Change Head-On

Speaking of change and fluidity, isn't it astounding how fast things are changing these days in technology and communication? The issues and challenges we face will only come faster as time advances. Will you be able to address these changes? Will your organization respond effectively to your changing culture? Creative Christian leaders must have a pulse on the ancient world and on their own culture as well. They need to know the timeless principles found in the Bible but also the critical issues on the cultural horizon. The creative leader understands the past, lives in the present, and anticipates the future. This kind of leader will be most able to proactively lead people, not simply react to a changing world.

Creative thinking helps you deal with change as it's happening. It keeps your radar tuned to the next big thing. It gives you greater insight as you sift through current and upcoming cultural trends. Creative thinking allows you to recognize the impact of those tides as they are emerging, not after they've passed you by.

Creativity Will Give Wings to Your Vision

Though the creative process itself is difficult, one of the results is a renewed vitality for a leader's God-given vision. When a breakthrough emerges after an especially difficult creative process, the leader emerges with a sense of victory, reminded again that the reward is well worth the commitment. When the vision begins to take wings and soar, new territory is conquered—a feeling similar to the "rush" artists feel the first time they see their masterpiece emerge before them. The work always provides ample frustrations, but the result far overshadows these difficulties.

Leaders need these "wins" to continue to fuel their vision. Without seeing positive change occur, the leader is simply treading water. The most dynamic leaders continue to push the limits because they remember the incredible successes achieved through prior creative experiences.

Creativity Will Energize Your Staff

Let's face it: Few people would commit to a vision that is stagnant and tired. A creative leader provides a roller-coaster adventure that is exciting and compelling. As a leader consistently models dependence on God and demonstrates a commitment to seeking solutions on the cutting edge, the staff—who are the hands and feet of the leader—rally around the vision of that leader.

As staff members see new solutions and develop new methods, they become energized as they contribute in helping leaders carry out a vision that is living and breathing. I discuss this further in section 3.

Creativity Will Mobilize Your Volunteers

No words can describe how energizing it is to see the volunteers of Fellowship Church in action. On an average month, we have more than 3,000 volunteers serving at least once a month at all four of our current campuses. At a time when many churches are experiencing difficulty mobilizing the troops, we have seen an increase in the participation of our church body in every area of service. While this is certainly a God thing, I firmly believe that a lot of this has to do with God honoring our commitment to creativity. Because our people see creative leadership in worship, preaching, and ministries across our church, they are motivated to become partners in that dynamic vision.

Making full-court followers of Jesus Christ is always a challenge, but a dynamic vision moves people out of the bleachers and into the game. Many people come through our church doors without a personal relationship with God or any lasting foundation to their lives. While they are often looking for a quick fix for whatever problems they face, we want to give them a place around which to orbit their lives. We want them to discover that church can and should be their epicenter. We also want them to know that their contribution to the local church makes all of us more Christlike. I have found that our commitment to creativity has helped make this happen. Because they want to be a part of something that is exciting and growing, these kinds of people have been mobilized into full-court followers of Jesus Christ.

Creativity Will Infect Your Communication with Excitement

Thinking and leading in a creative fashion will inspire the people we lead and bring a sense of vitality to our own attitude and outlook. This vitality will spill over every time we speak, every time we teach, every time we communicate in private or in public. Whether we are working with kids or adults, it makes a definite impact on us and everyone we come in contact with.

Creativity will keep your communication skills fresh and unpredictable. I don't care if you have a seeker-driven, white-collar boomer or buster mentality, you cannot allow yourself to become predictable or you will lose your ability to communicate effectively with others. Try saying things in different ways. Use different word choices, different illustrations, and different metaphors that will reach out to different people. You may even try pushing away from the two-ton wood pulpit and use a simple stool once in awhile.

We can't say, "Well, I've got this little package down. I'm going to do the same thing the same way and expect great growth to occur." In my book, that's the classic definition of insanity: doing the exact same thing and expecting different results. If you want to grow and consistently reach out to your community, you must examine your communication methods. And if you really want those methods to improve, infuse your communication with creativity.

Creativity Will Give Your People a Fuller Picture of God

I have found that most people carry around incomplete photo albums of the nature and character of God. They have a little album in their mind with just one picture of God and that's the one they come back to time and time again.

Some people carry around the Grandpa God photograph. Grandpa God is graying like I am, but a little bit older, sweeter, and kinder. He always says, "Come over here. Sit right here on my knee. That's right. I love you. Everything is going to be OK. You are great. Don't worry about a thing. That sin thing? Don't worry about that. Grandpa's got it covered."

In your church do you have people who see God like that? For some, that's the only image they have of our heavenly Father. These kinds of people don't want to hear about sin, repentance, or judgment. Grandpa God is more to their liking.

Another picture people have of God in their little photo album is what I call the Candy-Land God. The Candy-Land God is really perpetuated by certain televangelists. They paint God as the Candy-Land God who just rains candy and money down from heaven. They say, "God doesn't want you in that Mazda. He wants you in that Mercedes-Benz. All you need is a Mercedes-Benz faith." Don't get me wrong—God does want to bless His children, but giving material gifts is just one way He does that. And looking exclusively at God as the Giver of good things is a limited and incomplete picture of God.

Another photo we carry around of God is the Man-Upstairs God. This is the deistic deity who is detached from our everyday lives. The only time we call on Him is when we get into a tight squeeze, then we call the heavenly 9-1-1 service and God comes bounding down the staircase of heaven to rescue us. That's a very typical view of God. As we've seen in the post–9/11 era, our country doesn't pay much attention to God until there's some kind of national disaster or traumatic event. It's only during these radical times that we start praying.

Others have a picture of the Supreme-Court God. They picture Him as an austere man in a black robe, proclaiming, "You're guilty! You are going to hell!" The love of God is missing in their picture; they only see severe justice being doled out.

We can also talk about the Emotional God photo that many carry around. The say, "Well, I have not really worshipped until I have cried, had the tingle up and down my spine, or the quiver in my liver." They have a limited view of God as some sort of feeling or experiential trip that carries their mind and emotions to a transcendent place. Sometimes God does choose to work in this way, but it does not represent all that God is or does.

All of those pictures of God have elements of truth about His nature and character. But by themselves, these photos are one-dimensional and extremely limited. Our goal at Fellowship Church is to give people a complete photo album of the essence, nature, character, and work of God. Every time we think about our programs, messages, videos, dramas, teachings, small groups, and classes, we should consider how to give people as broad and accurate a photo album of God as possible. We must ask ourselves how we can give people a complete, balanced view of the nature and character of our creative God. God is multidimensional and multifaceted, so the way we communicate Him should also be multidimensional and multifaceted. We are doing a disservice to God and to our people if we don't.

Where else will people get a balanced photo album if not in the local church? We need loads and loads of creativity to give people this kind of balanced approach, so they know who God really is. It takes innovative programs, new ways of saying things, and creative ways of thinking through deep theological issues to help people get a small but accurate glimpse of a great big God. We won't know Him fully until we see Him face to face. However, we can give strategic glimpses to people right now, if we are willing to make a commitment to thinking and working in dynamic ways. Because God is marked by creativity, we must leverage the creativity He has given us to communicate to our people who He is and what He does in the world.

Creativity Will Help Change Lives

Several years ago I was dropping my daughter off at elementary school and noticed a man getting out of a BMW. He had long hair, an earring, four gold chains around his neck, and looked to be about fifty-five-years-old. I could tell by looking at him that he was spiritually lost. I could just sense by his actions and his attitudes that he was outside the family of God. And I don't know why, but God spoke to my spirit and said, "Ed, start praying for that man." Without even knowing his name, I began to pray for him.

About three months later, I was picking up my daughter from school again and ran into him. I said, "Hi, how are you doing?" He introduced himself as Peter and told me he was in the commodities business and was from Brooklyn, New York. We had a casual conversation about sports. I asked Peter about his Beemer and we talked for several minutes about the usual guy stuff. Surprisingly, he never asked me what I did for a living during that brief encounter in the parking lot.

About a year later, my family moved to a different city and school district, so I lost contact with Peter. Then one weekend I saw his wife and children at one of our church services, but he was nowhere to be found. A member of our church had been inviting this woman to visit our church, and she finally came to see what it was all about. I stopped to talk to her and asked how her husband was doing. She confidently told me, "One day I'm going to bring my husband to church."

That day finally came. Peter and his family attended our Fall Festival, which was a big outreach event for families in the community. We met once again in a parking lot—this time in the church parking lot, where all of the tents and games were set up. He recognized me from our kids' grammar school years ago and said hello. Then he asked, "What are you doing here?" But before I could answer, his wife interjected, "Honey, that's the pastor of the church."

"You know," he said, "I haven't been to church in a long, long time and I'm still not sure about all this stuff. But my family loves it. My wife and kids can't wait to come to church every week."

Two months went by, and I still didn't see the father of this family in a weekend church service. Yet during that time, I continued to pray for him. The first weekend in our current facility in Grapevine, Texas, I was preaching and looked out over the crowd. I looked out into the fourth row, and there he was. *Wow!* I thought. *This is incredible! Peter's coming to church!* So I talked to him afterward a little bit, and we agreed to meet for lunch the next day.

During our lunch appointment, Peter said, "For the first time I understand why my wife and kids love your church. I understand the music, I understand the videos you show, I understand what you're talking about in your messages. I get it."

"Well," I responded, "I'd like to tell you something. I've been praying for you for four years and I want to ask you a question. If this waitress were to walk up to you and ask, 'How do you get to heaven?' what would you tell her?"

Peter began to shift in his seat a little bit and broke out in a cold sweat then said, "I guess I would tell her I'm a good guy. I'm a nice person."

"Those are good words," I replied, "even nice words. But that's not going to get you where you want to go. That's going to take you straight to hell." I explained to him the good news about Christ and what it meant to follow Him, and as I explained it, he began to fall under conviction.

"Ed," he interrupted me, "how do I make this decision? Tell me how to do this."

"Well, Peter, we can do this deal right now. Let's just pray." So we bowed our heads in the restaurant, and he prayed the prayer to ask Christ to come into his life.

After that, we made a little contract together. We wrote a binding contract indicating that by faith, he and Jesus Christ had just entered into an eternal relationship. "OK, Peter," I said, "you deal with commodities and different kinds of transactions, so you know what contracts are all about. Go ahead, sign on the dotted line and date it, and I'll sign as your witness. And you keep this as a reminder of what happened today."

After he signed the contract, he said, "Man, I can't wait to tell my wife that I made the ultimate score today!"

I agreed with him, then we finished lunch and drove back to the church. When he dropped me off at the front of the church, I thought, *You know what, this is worth it. This is absolutely worth it.* It's because of the Peters out there that we are so committed to creativity. That is why we do what we do.

That's how it all begins. That's how lives are changed. There was no earth-shattering event that caused this man to reevaluate his life and come to church. This man's story could be told by a thousand different individuals in a thousand different churches. God used a series of seemingly insignificant events and wove them into something very significant. He impressed upon me the need to meet this man and pray for him. And He guided a tenacious and committed woman to bring her friend to church. He used the creativity of our children's and youth ministries to help draw Peter's kids into the family of God. And then He eventually used that avenue to pique the father's curiosity to find out what had made such an impact in his family's life.

Where would this family be without all these people working together? And where would hundreds and thousands of individuals and families be without the commitment of churches all across the country and around the world to creatively reach others for Christ?

The church is all about being "salt and light." Though the Spirit of God can use any church at any given time, I believe He is especially pleased with the church that takes this creative challenge head-on to win people to Christ and develop them into His full-court followers. Churches that simply stay the course or accept the status quo do not grow and do not energize their people.

Churches that are committed to doing whatever it takes to reach our lost world will raise their share of critics, but they will also turn people into passionate pursuers of Jesus Christ. One of my favorite things as a pastor is to hear stories of how God has used the creative ministries of the local church to rescue people from a Christless eternity and turn them into energetic and active servants for Jesus. I can think of no other pursuit in the world that is more difficult or more rewarding than leading a church that is committed to creatively changing lives for the glory of God.

The really exciting news is that we all know people within our sphere of influence who are just like Peter. Our churches are going to attract different people because we're in different places, but regardless of where you are or the kind of people you reach, the issues are the same. Do the people coming to your church have a full picture of God? Are your events truly impacting your community? Are people made to feel welcome? Are they being challenged through the creative programs of your church to make the most important decision in the universe—the decision to enter into a personal relationship with the living Lord?

It's my prayer that as you read this book, you make a commitment not only to creativity but to the many names and faces in your community that desperately need the life-changing truth of the gospel. I hope and pray that your creative leadership will be used to impact your corner of the world to connect these lost people with the hope of Christ. Implementing creativity has many great benefits, but salvation is the real and lasting payoff.

CHAPTER 3

The Creative Constant

One summer day I got in touch with my feminine side when my wife and I took a day trip to the world's largest flea market, held in Canton, Texas. I watched in amazement as thousands of shopping fanatics frantically pushed their shopping carts from booth to booth in hopes of finding the deal of a lifetime. The fact that they did this in a crowd in triple-degree Texas heat with perspiration dripping off their noses was even more impressive.

After two or three long hours on the quest for the ultimate flea market find, Lisa was gracious enough to say, "Honey, let's break for some lunch." Grateful for the reprieve, I accepted her offer and headed off for some refreshment. The food area consisted of a group of rickety wooden picnic tables strategically huddled around several food stands.

We bought a couple of chicken sandwiches at one of the restaurants and sat down at one of the tables. After a few minutes, Lisa looked over my shoulder and said, "Baby, check that out." I expected her to point out yet another rare piece of art or some bargain that

Most people give up just when they're about to achieve
success. They quit on the one-yard line. They give up at the last
minute of the game, one foot from a winning touchdown.

H. ROSS PEROT

we had somehow missed. However, as I turned around, I noticed an employee of the restaurant carrying a tray of samples. Normally, a restaurant would hand out samples to *potential* customers. But this girl was weaving in and out of the picnic tables, handing out chicken-sandwich samples to those of us who were already stuffing our faces with these same chicken sandwiches.

"Ed," Lisa said, "that's hilarious. I mean, all she has to do is walk about fifteen paces and offer those samples to the people who haven't eaten yet." Hundreds of starving shopaholics were nearby, but she was obviously content to feed the already-fed.

And that's when it hit me like an NFL linebacker. "Lisa, that's it!" I said. "That is the local church in a nutshell."

Many church leaders are so content weaving in and out of the church aisles handing out samples to the already-fed that we have missed the countless opportunities to offer the food, the very Bread of Life, to a lost and dying world.

We are missing opportunities to reach people for Christ because we've got to get a little bit dirty to get out there among the people who are truly hungry. You have to perspire a little bit when you weave through the long lines of starving seekers. It takes a commitment to working harder and smarter than you've ever worked before. You might even discover that you will have to completely revamp the way you have done church for a long, long time.

But we are commanded to get out there among the people. We're also charged to challenge the already-fed to push away from the table, get off their rears, and to share the Bread of Life with a hungry world.

Jesus said in John 6:35, "I am the bread of life. He who comes to me will never go hungry, and he who believes in me will never be thirsty."

Do you believe that we, as the church, have the best meal in town? Do you believe that Christ is the only One capable of satisfying the deep spiritual hunger and thirst of humanity? If so, then

I think you will also agree that the ultimate food demands the ultimate presentation.

I believe the church is an eating establishment. As such, it must serve the food in a creative and compelling way. That means we have to put away the plastic forks and spoons and shelve those paper napkins and cups. I'm talking about bringing out the fine china, the embroidered napkins, and the polished silver. No half-baked presentations. No skimping. We've got to do the best with what God has given us. To do that, we must continually think of new and creative ways to present the ultimate food, so that people will be compelled to come to the table to eat and then share the food with others.

Keeping Creativity a Constant

As I previously mentioned, I grew up in a Christian home and my father is a pastor. I attended Florida State for a couple of years and then, after receiving God's tap on the shoulder to prepare for ministry, transferred to Houston Baptist University. After graduating from college, I worked at my father's church in Houston, Texas, in several different positions while attending seminary. And then in 1990, I helped start Fellowship Church with a handful of people.

Why am I reciting my leadership résumé? Well, during all that time, I thought I knew a good bit about leadership. I was pretty confident that I would be ready to launch out on my own, having observed fine leaders at close range.

But I was wrong.

When I became a senior pastor, I began to realize just how clueless I really was. My confidence dissipated as I was blindsided by one major reality (along with other senior-pastor surprises that are discussed in chap. 10). It was something I had never picked up on as I watched my father's growing ministry. I had also missed it while studying in college and seminary. I even missed it while working on a church staff before coming to Fellowship Church.

What ambushed me when I became a senior pastor is the reality that *creativity must remain a constant.* While this thought doesn't seem very profound, its implications are huge. I began to realize that the church must remain consistently inconsistent to be truly effective in the midst of a rapidly changing culture.

Being consistently inconsistent means the church has to be committed to change and willing to take risks. We are talking about life and death, aren't we? People's lives are hanging on the edge of eternity. Will they spend it with their Creator or be eternally separated from Him? Having one creative idea a year doesn't cut it. It must be a 365-24-7 type of commitment.

The eye-opening part of this realization wasn't just the need for creativity in the church but how difficult creativity was to practice day in and day out. It's one thing to understand the need for creativity in an academic sense; it's quite another to implement it consistently on the rugged plains of reality.

Nothing is more grueling or rewarding than thinking and working in a creative way. It's the hardest thing I do and it's the hardest thing you will do. You won't learn this in seminary. You can observe a creative leader for years and still not get it. There is only one way to discover how difficult and yet fulfilling creative ministry can be: by doing it. You have to get down and dirty in the trenches of creative leadership. That's what this book is about: helping you realize the creative genius within and letting it out of the box.

Reaching the Drive-Through People

Drive-through people fill our churches today. They pull up every weekend and expect an inspirational McMessage, fun-filled McChildcare, heart-warming McMusic, sensational Mc-Programming, and then they're off. The exhaust fumes fill the air as minivans, cars, and SUVs bolt out of the parking lot in rapid-fire succession.

As church leaders, we have a big challenge before us. We have to take these drive-through people and turn them into disciples. We've got to take the McChurched and turn them into the mature. We are tasked with the responsibility of growing God's church in a McChurch culture. And that's a huge challenge in today's entertainment-driven, A.D.D, serve-me world. In fact, it's a bigger challenge than most are willing to admit.

If we're going to take these drive-through people and turn them into disciples; if we're going to get out of the shade and into the heat to serve the ultimate food to the hungry hunks of humanity passing by; if we're going to motivate believers to push away from the table, our leadership must be marked by creativity. We must make creativity a constant in our lives and in our ministries.

Having come to the conclusion that creativity must remain a constant, we have to ask one simple question: How? How do we unleash creativity in our lives and in the organizations we lead? How can we as leaders be marked by innovation, creativity, and vitality? We'll attempt to answer those important questions in the remainder of this chapter.

The Marks of a Creative Leader

What does a creative leader look like? Anyone can talk about leadership theory, but what does it look like in the trenches? Allow me to share the good, the bad, and the ugly when it comes to my personal leadership experience. Most of these principles were discovered as I dropped the ball somewhere along the leadership journey. Other principles have been observed firsthand from top leaders. All of them can revolutionize the way you lead your team and lead Christ's church.

Pray a High-Risk Prayer

We can talk a lot about leadership theories and the best way to implement them in our ministries, but all the greatest principles in the world aren't going to change the world. Ultimately, only God can do that. If we believe that, then we should be willing to humble ourselves as leaders and go to the Source of creative leadership.

Let me challenge you right now. *Ask God to enhance your creativity*. God has wired you for creativity and desperately wants you to leverage it to reach others. Pray that prayer without ceasing as Paul challenged us. Pray that prayer as you begin this chapter and as you face the challenges in ministry that seem to have no solution. If a commitment to prayer is the only thing that you get from this book on leadership, it will change your life.

How do I know that? Praying for creativity has been my greatest asset in unleashing the creativity of God in my own life and ministry. Not long ago I looked through my prayer journal. I have been journaling my prayers since I was seventeen and was surprised at how many times I prayed for creativity. "God, give me creativity. God, unleash your creativity through me. God, I don't have a good read on this text or on this sermon, on this program or this giving campaign. I don't have it, God. Give me your wisdom and insight. Enhance my understanding, God."

You might wonder how or what to pray as an aspiring creative leader. Begin by asking God to unleash the creativity that He has already given you. Remember, the Father started the ball rolling, Jesus modeled it, and the Spirit empowers it. You have miles of creative potential woven into the fiber of your being. Pray that He will use your particular creative bent to serve Him better.

Let me add a word of caution here: This is a high-risk prayer. If you truly want God to use your creative bent, you will be stretched in ways you never thought possible. Buckle up!

Take Action

Secondly, as you trust God for His guidance in the creative process, you will be *called to action* to unleash the creativity within you. Creativity and hard work (not shortcuts) are inseparably linked. When I consider God's creative genius, it always seems to involve hard labor. It says in Genesis that God worked hard for six days and then rested. What about the Son of God? Do you think that it was easy coming up with new methods to teach hard-hearted sinners?

Anyone who has invested any length of time in communicating God's Word knows the challenge of trying to connect the world of the biblical writer to the world of the contemporary audience. Jesus did it so effectively because He was in tune with the Father through prayer and diligent about creative communication. Reflecting God's creation always involves hard work.

People sometimes say, "Ed, I really like what you have done here at Fellowship. How can *I* be a more creative person like you?" They expect me to impart some great secret or give them a magic pill to swallow that can instantly transform their ministry. One secret I will share is that there is a reason why the most creative and talented leaders out there make it look easy. The secret is called hard work.

It takes time on your knees and time getting your fingernails dirty. The most creative people I know are those who are not only willing to spend the time to ask God for help but are also responsible for putting the plan in motion. Without working out the plan to completion, all you have is an idea. The world is full of good ideas. Leaders are those who are willing to put in the time it takes to make these ideas a reality. It is tough, but believe me, it's worth it.

Where would the world be if Thomas Edison said, "I wonder if it would be possible to create artificial light," but then never brought that dream to reality? What if Henry Ford dreamed about making the horse and buggy obsolete but never did anything about it?

Where would the world be if God the Father said, "I really need to do something about this sin problem—perhaps a mediator would work, someone who could take away the sins of the world," and then just sat on the idea and never implemented it? He could have said, "Oh, I've got a good idea. I'll send My only begotten Son, Jesus Christ, to die on the cross for their sins. He'll then conquer death by rising again. He will be the link, the only way to redeem these lovable losers," and then just left this brilliant plan on the shelf? He could have said it was just too complicated. He could have said it was just too expensive, since His only Son would be required to pay the ultimate price for this group of rebels. We would all be in a world of trouble, wouldn't we?

Creativity takes labor. In fact, the creative cycle is similar to the birthing cycle: There is the conception, the pregnancy, the labor, and the delivery. Some leaders conceive these fabulous ideas and then it just ends. They don't want to go through the pregnancy, that difficult labor, or the uncertainty of the birth. But ideas are only as good as the results they yield. Only a constant commitment to the creative process will yield the results that God desires for your ministry.

Creative ideas die two ways. Sometimes while meeting with your creative team, an idea of yours will get trashed (a scenario discussed later on in the book). Usually that is for the best. Most of the time, however, an idea dies due to a lack of courage to follow through with it. If we leaders don't follow through on these creative ideas, our congregations and God's kingdom will suffer.

So take action.

Connect with Creative Geniuses

Another mark of creative leaders is that they draw inspiration from other creative leaders. They surround themselves with other creative people. To get my creative juices going, I have to rub shoulders or hang with other creative geniuses out there. Initially, you might have to go outside your own church walls for inspiration. In due time, you'll be able to connect with people in your own environment that will challenge and sharpen your creative edge.

God has put some creative people around me and I really feed off them. If you don't know who these people are for you, ask God to show you some creative geniuses in your area who can sharpen your vision and enhance your abilities. That is why I love going to conferences, listening to other speakers, and talking to other pastors. Simply immersing yourself with creative leaders during an annual conference will go a long way. It will expose you to new ideas and help you build a community of creative geniuses that can help you keep accountable to the vision God has given you.

(And, speaking of conferences, this is the first of my shameless plugs in this book. If you have not attended a Creative Church Conference [C3] at Fellowship Church, what are you waiting for? Toward the end of January every year, we host a conference on our campus in Grapevine that will give you a ton of fresh and creative ideas for doing church. I'm not bragging on myself; I'm bragging on God and the team He's surrounded me with. Come to this conference every year—we're constantly changing it—and see what new ideas God has for your ministry. Go to edyoung.com to find out more.)

When I say you should surround yourself with creative geniuses, I am not saying that you should reject anyone who has not yet realized his creative potential. You might be used by God to encourage a fellow leader during a difficult season of ministry or inspire others to come alongside you on the creative journey. Watch and learn from others who are excelling at what you want to be doing. We have to be intentional about connecting with creative people who will help us continue moving in new directions.

Build in C. T.

Another important mark of creative leaders is that they know creativity is not a gimmick, but a lifestyle. The best and brightest creative leaders have regular time scheduled for creative sessions. They build in what I call *C. T.*, or Creativity Time. Creativity emerges from order. During these sessions, creative leaders prepare to communicate God's Word in an innovative manner, plan for the upcoming calendar year, or brainstorm a new initiative for the church.

Here's another secret: these leaders know what time of day they are clicking on all of their creative cylinders. It may not be best to schedule creativity time on Monday, the day after four emotionally draining weekend services. Many pastors call this phenomenon the "holy hangover." You know what I'm talking about. Your head hurts, you don't remember what you said the day before, and you can't remember your own name. Basically, you are just plain exhausted. Find out what days and times are the sweet spots for your creative juices. Once you figure this out, block them out on your schedule, so you and your team can really fly. Be very strategic about these creative sessions.

For my team and me, our best ideas come on Tuesday and Wednesday. This is our sweet spot. We begin doing some research earlier in the week, so those ideas can marinate in our minds. But the real creative energy begins to flow when we come together in the middle of the week.

Often in these meetings, our staff will just sit back and talk about a new idea. We will take the idea and turn it, trying to look at it from every angle. Sometimes I will intentionally play the opposite side of the issue just to generate some conflict and hopefully some clearer thinking.

You've probably noticed that I've talked a lot about my staff in the whole creative process. We do a lot of team-creativity work.

If you look around these days, team ministry is the way to go. I believe in it so much that I've included an entire chapter on the dynamics of team ministry for maximizing all of your creative leadership potential. You will not believe the ideas that are generated by even a few committed players on your creative team.

A case in point is a series we did several years ago called "Animal Planet." I had the idea for the series, but it was just the conception part. So I put it on the back burner for awhile. Several months later, we were doing some creative brainstorming in our creative team meeting and I resurfaced the idea. We decided to really go with it, and the structure for the whole series came really quickly. We were all fresh and firing on all cylinders as a team. It turned out to be one of the most dynamic series we've done for our church. We took the animals that are mentioned in the Bible and talked about what they can say to us, because we are a lot like animals sometimes. The first weekend, I did a message called "Sick as a Dog." The next weekend, it was "Fly Like an Eagle." After that, the message was called "Camel Filter." The final message was "Harmless as a Dove."

Creativity time can be excellent on a staff retreat when you are laughing and playing through eighteen holes of golf together. Or you could prefer sweating it out by yourself with a glass of lemonade under a shady tree in your backyard. You could try rafting down the Colorado River with your team—whatever works best.

During one particularly stressful season of ministry, I told everybody to just wear some jeans and meet at my office. Everyone piled into a few trucks and we had a fishing tournament. We bought everybody a cane pole and some worms and had our staff meeting while watching our rods and basking in the sun.

Build in regular and strategic creativity time. Do it together with your team and do it by yourself. Once you figure out your sweet spots, your ideas will flow like the rushing rapids of the Colorado River. Ideas begin to flow for me while I'm sipping

Starbucks coffee, driving in my truck listening to music, or fishing with my son on the lake.

This past Easter, my team and I had been working through the Easter message for a couple of weeks, and I had come to a place where I knew I needed some distance from the message. I had been thinking too long and too hard. I needed to give my mind a break and find a way to get my creative juices flowing again. On the Tuesday morning of Easter week, my son, another staff member, and I went fishing. I spent the morning in a boat, just casting and enjoying some downtime.

When I came back the next day and met again with several members of my creative team (including the one who went fishing with me) to talk again about the Easter message, I couldn't believe the ideas that began to emerge. It was like God had opened the floodgates in our minds. We had so many great ideas that the entire application of the message changed.

What really puts wind into your creative sail? Find out what it is in your life that really gets those creative juices going and flowing and return to those activities often. You won't believe what will happen.

Become a Pastor Caster

As I just mentioned, fishing is one of the primary activities that really gets my creative juices flowing. I love to fish. If it has fins and scales—or even no scales, like the shark and the catfish—I'll go after it. Fishing is, after all, a biblical sport. The disciples fished, and Christ asked His followers to "become fishers of men." So you gotta love fishing.

Obviously, you can't catch any fish unless you practice casting, as not many fish will just jump into your boat while you sit there. And the same goes for casting your vision for the church. Leaders, and especially senior pastors, have to cast the vision and the mission of their church over and over and over. No matter what situation or stage of ministry you find yourself in, eventually your people will lose the vision God has given to you. And you can't expect them to just jump into your boat—you first have to cast the vision to them.

I've heard it said that vision leaks over time. We've got to say it, (and if you're like me) spray it, wheel it, and deal it. One of the biggest mistakes that I've made as senior pastor is that I did not talk about the vision enough during the first few years of our church. People really didn't know why we were doing what we were doing and frustration set in. We have to remember that God has given you, if you are the primary leader, the vision for your ministry. It is your responsibility to communicate this vision to keep your teammates focused and your followers energized. These days I preach at least one sermon series a year just on the vision of our church.

One year, I did a vision series called "Still Counting." It was built on the premise that math matters to God—addition, subtraction, multiplication, and division. The focus of this series was to keep the congregation committed to reaching people in our community for Christ. It was a reminder of the reality that God is always adding, subtracting, multiplying, and dividing certain things to expand our impact in the community.

I've also done a vision series called "The Table." I compared the local church to a restaurant and said that our mission is to invite people to the table to eat with us. At the table, we should serve the Bread of Life in creative and compelling ways. When we come to church, we should not only get fed, but we should also push away from the table to feed the hungry hunks of humanity passing by. The focus of this series was to remind our people that the church should be made up of thirds: one-third should consist of mature Christians, one-third baby Christians, and one-third seekers. And I challenged them to get involved in building believers and serving seekers.

Even though these series on vision are essentially communicating the same core principles and vision, our creative team strategically asks, How can we communicate the vision in a different way this time? Let me ask you the same question: How can you hammer home to your people—in a way you've never done before—the reason why you are doing what you're doing? What technology, drama, or other medium will help captivate your audience and give new light to the vision God has given you?

If you don't focus and motivate your people with your vision, they will become introspective navel gazers. Their spiritual bellies will become so big from gorging on the food and not sharing it with others that their Bible belt will be on its last hole. These navel gazers will turn inward and think only about themselves, their close-knit friends, and their holy huddle. And once they hunch over and form that huddle, the only thing a lost world will see is their rears. So, become a pastor caster. Cast the vision strategically, regularly, and creatively; it will be one of the best things you will do for your church.

Maintain a Vertical Vision

One of the toughest challenges for visionary casters is to keep their lives and ministries on track by *maintaining a vertical vision*. That's the next mark of a creative leader. If you're going to cast a vision for your people, it better be a vertical vision from God; because if you're not continually going vertical for your vision, you'll end up getting, by default, a man-made horizontal vision from others—most likely, from the negative vision vandals in your church.

I've seen the ministry from many different angles. Throughout the years, I've found that the most dynamic and longest-lasting Christian leaders are those who catch their vision vertically from God. And when they start building this vision in innovative ways, people are reached for the glory of God.

All leaders will face negative people who surround them and threaten their leadership—people I call vision vandals. They are usually the power brokers of your congregation. These people leverage their stash of cash or their influence against the leader and his vision. They say things like, "Hey, change the way you preach and change the way you sing. Let's spend our money here instead of there."

If we allow these vision vandals to influence us, we are headed for disaster. When we try to appease these types of people, our vision goes from the vertical to the horizontal. We stop serving God and start serving the vocal minority.

Remember that old axiom, "The squeaky wheel gets the grease"? Every time you grease the wheels of negativity and criticism, you give momentum to vision vandals who want to redirect your vision to the horizontal. And once the vision goes horizontal, you are in serious, serious trouble.

You might say, "But, Ed, people will leave my church. They will take their money with them!" This is true and has happened to me many times. However, if you let these vision vandals dissuade you from following the vertical vision God has given to you, you will begin to serve man instead of God. And as the point person in your organization, you will be held accountable to God for turning aside from the vision He forged in your heart.

Let me share what happened to me as we started Fellowship Church. God had given me, along with a core group of people in the church, an amazing vision to reach people for Christ in a creative and dynamic fashion. A handful of these power brokers were not on board with the vision and made life miserable for the rest of us.

When I think back to that trying time in the life of Fellowship, one particular family comes to mind. This family, in a sense, "owned" the church at the time, or at least they thought they did. They had given us the sound system, the piano, chairs, and other essential items. But when I began to articulate the vision for a radically different kind of church, things turned sour in a hurry. They began to cause dissension in the church, pitting one family against another and one group against another. And ultimately, they ended up turning many people against the leadership and our vision for the church.

I'll never forget "Black Sunday," which occurred when this family hung a black wreath on the door of the rented office building we were meeting in at the time, symbolizing what they thought was the inevitable death of the church. They also took back almost everything they had given us—they even tried to take back a car they had given me to drive. Fortunately, we were able to scrape enough money together to pay them for that.

When push came to shove, we had to let these vision vandals leave our fragile church. These negative people took some key leaders with them and a lot of financial resources. The way we handled them set an important precedent in how we protected God's vision for Fellowship Church: We didn't cave in to these power brokers. And because we have strategically and tenaciously protected that vision, our vertical vision has prevailed for more than fifteen years.

Do the Push-Back

One of the quickest routes to ministry burnout is ignoring this next important leadership principle. Remember that ministry is a marathon not a sprint. To keep your creative juices going and flowing, you cannot ignore this one. Leaders need to *practice the push-back* as their influence and responsibilities grow. Practice the push-back by prioritizing two important assets: your time and your church's ministries.

Know Your Limits

First, you must recognize your relational, pastoral, and administrative limitations. You cannot do it all.

During the first few years of Fellowship, our staff hung out all the time and often ate breakfast together. As our church grew, I had to push back, lessening my time with staff to keep up with the increasing responsibilities on my plate. And as our staff grew, I spent even less time with each individual staff member—far less than I would have liked. That is one of the realities of a large church: to continue reaching the people God has called you to reach, you have to make some necessary (albeit sometimes difficult) subtractions along the way.

Also, you must learn to say no. You cannot be everybody's best friend and carry out your commitments as the leader. Why do you have to say no? Behind every "no" is a bigger "yes." Some leaders say yes to so many good things that they wind up missing strategic opportunities that would have radically transformed their ministries. You have to be the kind of leader that keeps the main thing the main thing. Be considerate to people but allow yourself to say no to some of their requests so you can lead effectively.

Again, the biggest change in my leadership style as my responsibilities have grown has been having to say no more often. I had to say no more in the ninth year than I did in the sixth year. I've had to say no more this year than I did in our fourteenth year. This has been an ongoing battle requiring great discernment to know where and how God is leading. People will have some incredible opportunities for you, but if it doesn't fit in with your weekly commitments and your overall vision from God, you have to do the push-back.

Focus on the Weekend

The second way you have to push back is in prioritizing where your church's human and financial resources need to be focused. Again, keep the main thing the main thing. Starbucks must focus on improving their selection of caffeinated beverages. McDonalds must focus on improving their line of fast food. The local church also has a primary focus, and for that I've adapted a slogan that

James Carville used when he was managing President Clinton's campaigns. He hung an "It's the Economy, Stupid" sign over his desk. The church needs an "It's the Weekend, Stupid" sign.

Like you, your church or organization can do only so many things and still maintain a level of excellence in staying true to its vision. For most churches, the largest point of entry for people is the weekend service. That means the majority of your people will walk through your church doors only an hour or two a week on Saturday or Sunday (depending on when you hold your services). It wouldn't make much sense to divert the majority of your resources to ministries that are only serving a small minority. Those other ministries are important and need to be resourced but must not distract from the main thing. Your weekend services are the gateway to reach your community. And as the impact of the weekend grows, the other ministries will follow.

Sometimes, people come up to me and say, "Ed, God has given me this vision of a new ministry for Fellowship." More often than not, this new ministry idea will take resources away from our core strategy. These ideas may be good or bad, but my advice is to be careful about adding new ministries to your church.

We made this sort of mistake when we first started Fellowship Church, deciding to start a women's ministry just because other churches had one. After a few months, we realized we had taken a key leader away from our primary focus just to conform to what other churches were doing. Obviously, this didn't make much sense. We still have special programs and activities specifically designed for the women in our church, but these events support rather than take away from the weekend focus. For example, we never allow our men's or women's ministries to schedule a retreat that will conflict with our Saturday evening or Sunday morning services.

Be very strategic about how you deploy your financial and human resources. It is a lot easier to add a strategic ministry after careful evaluation than it is to dismantle an existing ministry.

Sometimes, though, you need to do just that. Cancel something. Each of your ministries should be evaluated regularly as to its contribution to the overall mission of the church. If one is not meeting expectations, it must be cancelled in favor of another initiative that will advance the primary weekend focus.

Break Away

The final mark of the creative leader is to *break away before the ministry breaks you.* This reminds me of a story about two lumberjacks. They were working through a forest and were being paid by the tree. The first lumberjack worked through the entire day, never resting once. The second would work for a few hours then take a short break. After six hours, they counted up their work. The first lumberjack was stunned when the second had actually produced more lumber.

"How in the world did you beat me? I saw you resting at least three times and I never stopped once!"

The second lumberjack wryly replied, "While you were busy chopping away, I was sharpening my axe."

Creative leadership can be demanding on leaders and their family. If you don't implement regular intervals for rest, your creative juices will dry out and, ultimately, threaten God's vision for your ministry. As a leader, you must keep your mind, body, and spirit sharp for the tasks ahead. Remember that ministry is a twenty-six-mile marathon, not a 100-meter sprint. The pastor must treat his body as a finely tuned Olympic instrument. Without adequate rest, he will be watching the Olympic final from the stands rather than competing in the race itself.

After several years of creative cramming, I realized I was heading toward burnout and driving my family crazy. These days, I try to take at least four weeks off in the summer. I also take several days off right after Christmas to recharge and I plan several minibreaks during the year to keep my priorities and energy in check. This might be a day to enjoy with Lisa, to fish with my son, or to do something special with one of my daughters.

Getaways with my family are our greatest source of excitement and refreshment together. Not only do I recharge my creative batteries but I also get to enjoy spending uninterrupted time with my wife and kids. The ministry is so demanding that I'd get funky if I didn't build this time of rest into my annual schedule. During the year, I usually spend a couple of weeks strategizing, journaling ideas, praying, and sometimes planning messages. The rest of the time, I'm just relaxing and hanging out and just being Ed—not Pastor Ed, just Ed. It is so important for a public pastor to check out of the rat race for a few weeks and be (you hear me screaming now) a *regular* guy.

When was the last time you were able to just be yourself, to leave the stresses and concerns of ministry behind and be a regular person? To be a regular guy or gal, you have to be with people you trust, people who love you for who you are—I'm talking about family members or very close friends. Getting away does not include mission trips or other ministry trips where you are still expected to be the pastor, the counselor, or inspirational speaker.

Let me also suggest that there are times when you need to take a break from preaching and teaching but are not actually taking time off from the church. You are still there; you're just not speaking. This gives you time for strategic planning with your management team, for a staff retreat, for leadership development, and perhaps for writing and researching upcoming writing projects or sermon series.

Building in regular, strategic breaks benefits not only you and your family but also your organization. The most significant benefit to the church is the building up of other teachers and speakers. Several speakers in our church have been built because I have been absent for a few weeks in the summer and other times throughout the year. As they develop into excellent speakers, the lead teacher is free to spend more time in vision-casting and leadership development.

You'll find that as your church grows and matures, spending quality time on vision-casting and leadership development becomes crucial. If you ignore these elements, your leadership structure will not keep pace with the growth of your church and its expanding opportunities. These days, I speak about forty-three weekends a year, and my goal over the next five years is to go down to about thirty-five weekends a year.

When you schedule these regular times away, you need to give priority to your spouse first, then your children. You need to schedule these times so you don't burn out and your family doesn't become a casualty of workaholism.

I am so passionate about this subject that we monitor our staff's work-to-rest ratios. We are very, very serious about taking a rest day each week. We talk to our staff about spending quality time with spouses and kids. If we don't get that right, we are in big trouble. None of us would be where we are now without our family's support.

It is far too easy to become a workaholic in our culture. Through failures of wonderfully talented leaders, I've discovered that the best message I preach is how I conduct myself as a husband and father with the members of my family. They could care less about the size of my church or the books I write. What they care about is that I'm there for them when they need me.

So schedule blocks of time during your normal week to give to your family, making that time off-limits to your staff and congregation. Show the church where your priorities are by preaching through your lifestyle. At the same time, enjoy the increase in intimacy, communication, and vitality in your marriage and your relationship with your children. Granted, church emergencies happen that take you away from family. The problem is that most people in your church don't know what a real emergency is. Plan times when people cannot get to you. If you are always available, you will simply flame out from all the demands on your time.

Leadership encompasses many important qualities. It requires vision, courage, love, and commitment, along with an efficient use of your God-given abilities. But the leader who is effective, dynamic, and vibrant for the long haul must throw something else into the mix: a constant commitment to creativity. Without this endless commitment, our ability to lead and inspire others will slowly begin to decelerate. And the momentum and excitement we started out with will eventually grind to a halt.

Our challenge again as Christian leaders in the church is to transform a drive-through generation into disciples. Answering this challenge takes all you have and more. It takes your full commitment as a leader to submit to the power of the Holy Spirit. And fueled by the Spirit, it also takes your full commitment to the creative process.

Fortunately, the burden doesn't have to rest exclusively on the leader. Not only do we have the promise of the Holy Spirit, who empowers us for the ministry, but we also have talented teammates who can multiply our effectiveness as Christian leaders. The first step in attracting these kinds of people to our side is to create a culture that teaches and infuses creativity. In the next section we take a look at how to enhance your creative environment, beginning with a chapter specifically focusing on the characteristics of a creative church culture.

Creative Q & A: Section 1

Q: When did you first begin to rely on team creativity? What brought you to the realization that team creativity was the best approach for your ministry?

A: Team creativity has become a huge part of my ministry over the years at Fellowship, continually driving me to higher levels of creativity. I allude to various aspects of it throughout the book and have devoted an entire chapter to the team-planning process. Our team-creativity model came about mostly because of the stress and pressure that I put on myself years ago. For the first few years of my ministry, I tried to do everything on my own—from sermon prep to the worship guide and everything in between—and began to experience some serious health problems as a result. I believe God used that time to drive me to discover this process of team creativity. It was like God was tapping me on the shoulder, saying, "Hey, Ed, share the creativity, man. Share the burden. Pass it out. If you don't, *you're* going to pass out."

Communicators tend to put too much pressure on themselves, particularly when they are first beginning their ministry. And that self-inflicted burden of responsibility ultimately becomes a creative bottleneck since one person is trying to create everything alone. The resulting stress is unusually high and the cumulative pressure can lead to health problems, not to mention the dreaded problem of predictability.

Dr. Howard Hendricks once said, "The higher the predictability, the lower the learning." When your audience knows what's next, they either tune out or waste their time in hearing the same message. They sit there and say, "Here he goes again with another acrostic or the same old alliteration or intro." And when that happens, they shut out the rest of your message. They already know what's coming.

Once you begin to share creativity and bring in ideas from other people, amazing things happen. You'll get ideas you hadn't considered before. You'll begin to use tactics and tools your listeners aren't expecting. You'll be able to keep their attention and they'll learn more than if you tried to do it all on your own. That's the reason and rationale behind team creativity.

Q: How do you keep track of how and *if* creative ministry is working in your church?

A: Jesus said in Luke 19:10, "For the Son of Man came to seek and to save what was lost." How do you measure evangelism? How do you keep track of whether it is working? Through numbers. Evangelism is about numbers. Count the people who once were lost and now are saved. That's how we know if it's working.

We count people, because people matter to God. Some church leaders like to talk a big game when it comes to reaching people. "Yeah, I want to have this seeker-targeted, seeker-sensitive, contemporary church." Well blah, blah, blah. Are you actually doing it? Are you really reaching people? The only way to know is to count them. And in counting them, you've got to look at the five big indicators: attendance, baptism, giving, stories, and involvement.

We look at attendance numbers. We have kept very, very detailed attendance records from the get-go at Fellowship Church. How many people are showing up? Is that number increasing as time goes on? Who is coming into membership? Those are some questions we have to answer to evaluate our ministry.

We look at baptism numbers. How many people are making the faith decision and then going public with it? Who are we baptizing? Four or five years ago we talked to a ministry leader in our church who hadn't been baptizing. And I said, "Listen, you've got hundreds of people plugged into your ministry that need to step over the line and get baptized!" And as this leader began to catch our vision, he began to baptize a huge number of people. So baptism is another way to see if the church's ministry is working.

Giving is another important statistic to monitor. Are they giving—or as we say at Fellowship, *bringing* (Malachi 3:10)? Are people bringing the whole tithe into the storehouse? Are people consistently financially supporting the work of your church? If you're reaching people, if those hell-bound unbelievers are becoming baby Christians and the baby Christians are maturing in their faith, then they're going to bring the tithe. Is your giving going up as the years go by?

How about the number of life-change stories in your church? If what you are doing is working, you will hear story after story after story of people coming to Christ. These accounts will rally your troops and build excitement into your church while showing the effectiveness of your ministry.

Involvement is another area to keep an eye on. Are people volunteering and joining small groups? Do you have new small groups starting up all the time? You've got to count those people to know if you're reaching them. And those numbers should be going up. As people become assimilated into the life of the church, they should be serving as volunteers in at least one ministry.

At our church, we make it a point to measure the results of our mission and our vision. People are the reason we're doing all of this. And to know for sure if it's working, you've got to count them.

Q: As the senior pastor of a large church, how do you spend your time now compared to when you first began your ministry? What have you done to make your time more effective?

A: I wrote earlier about doing the push-back. Over the years, I have had to make some major adjustments to my schedule. During the first year or two, when our staff was small and our congregation was a few hundred people, I could spend a lot of time seeing appointments, having meals with people, and visiting the members of our church—particularly at night. But as our church expanded, I wasn't able to do that as much and still do my senior pastor and lead communicator duties. So I had to stop saying yes to everything. In fact, as our church has grown, there have been a lot more nos for every yes.

Another factor that has affected the way I spend my time is my family. At the beginning of my ministry, my wife and I had one daughter. It was easier in the early years to spend time with people outside of my home and not take away from my family time. But now we have four kids and every one of them needs my attention and affection.

So today, with a larger family and a much larger church, I cannot spend as much time visiting people or meeting with people. I can't spend thirty minutes here or an hour there with every person who would like to spend that time with me. That's just the reality.

It's true with the staff as well. I used to meet regularly with our core staff members. We would have breakfast or lunch together several times during the week. But as our church began to grow, the load on my shoulders began to grow, and I had to learn to do the push-back. Yes, even from the staff.

And as difficult as it is (and don't kid yourself—there is an emotional cost to expanding your ministry), there's no way one person can meet all the demands of a growing church. You've got to be able to do the push-back and hand the ball of ministry into the capable hands of others on your staff. As the church grows larger, you simply cannot continue to spend the same amount of time visiting and meeting with every person who asks you to, because something—your relationship with your family, your message preparation and delivery, your health or something else—has to give.

Our staff and our church are phenomenal when it comes to understanding this reality. They have learned from day one that I'm not going to be available to meet with everyone. Would I like to? Of course! But that's not feasible. I have to focus on my own family first and then continue to make the main thing—the weekend service—the main thing. I can't allow anything to distract me from presenting the gospel in relevant and innovative ways. This is the one ministry priority that I must guard above all others if I'm going to maximize my effectiveness as a Christian leader.

Section 2

Enhancing Your Creative Environment

A Case Study in Creative Leadership

W. L. GORE & ASSOCIATES

IN 1958 AN ENGINEER AT DUPONT by the name of Bill Gore left his well-paying job to begin his own firm. That year, in the basement of his home, Gore established a fledgling corporation known as W. L. Gore & Associates. The "associates" were Bill, his wife, Vieve, and his son, Bob. As the three began their new venture, the plan was simple—to develop and produce useful and cutting-edge products for an ever-changing and growing society.

By the end of the 1960s, Gore's dream had become much more than reality; his products were everywhere. The world's highest performing and most innovative computer systems housed Gore's electrical wiring and cables. Gore's products even found their way to the moon. By 1969, W. L. Gore & Associates was literally launched into an elite group. And the drive and desire for innovation and creative thinking that began the company in 1958 has grown exponentially since the company's first year.

Although the company is privately owned and does not release its financial records, it boasts of an annual revenue growth percentage in the double digits. In 2004, W. L. Gore & Associates Inc. totaled more than $1.3 billion in sales. And for six straight years it has been featured in *Fortune* magazine's "100 Best Companies to Work for in America" list.

If you are still unsure of what company I'm referring to, you are no doubt familiar with some of its products, the most popular of which is Gore-Tex fabric. But Gore's products aren't all that distinguish the company. It is Gore's innovation outside of the realm of scientific research and development that sets the company apart.

Bill Gore has always believed in face-to-face communication among his employees—something that is rare in today's corporate world of e-mail, office memos, and instant messaging. And Bill Gore refuses to allow his people to be boxed in.

W. L. Gore has developed a thriving culture that promotes teamwork and cutting-edge thinking. As a result, the company has experienced product breakthrough after breakthrough, affirming their long-term goal to affirm creativity.

Almost every aspect of W. L. Gore & Associates is outside the box—from its lateral, or "lattice," infrastructure to table-less meeting rooms to the Gore "beach" Olympics held at a recent company convention. It is that kind of environment that has enabled the company to keep its finger on the creative pulse of the world.

I can't help but admire a company that provides such a dynamic environment and welcomes creativity and innovation. By eliminating barriers to creativity, W. L. Gore & Associates encourages its people to think creatively, come up with new solutions to problems, and develop inventive ideas on a regular basis.

As church leaders, we could learn some valuable lessons from such a creative example. If the corporate world can develop an environment that welcomes imaginative and inspired thinking, shouldn't we be able to do the same? After all, God invented creativity and, as the second person of the Trinity, Jesus Christ modeled creativity long before Bill Gore founded his company.

Jesus led the charge in developing creative environments and encouraged His followers to do the same. He never used the same method to communicate. He never stuck with only one style or even sat in one place. He was constantly changing how, when, and where He worked—He taught from boats, hillsides, and houses, using uncommon techniques to teach a foundational message. Jesus never compromised His message but welcomed creativity in the method with which that message was delivered. As creative leaders, we should continually strive to foster the same kind of innovation and creativity in every part of the organizational structure.

CHAPTER 4

Creative Church Culture

A couple of years ago I bought a bright orange turtleneck at the Gap. I really liked that orange turtleneck and wore it all the time, so much so that people began to make fun of it. My son, who was ten years old at the time, asked if he could have a turtleneck just like mine. So my wife took him to the store and bought him a junior bright orange turtleneck.

He brought it home, proudly showed it to me, and said, "Dad, this weekend, let's dress alike, OK? Let's wear our matching orange turtlenecks."

"OK, E. J.," I said. "That will be great!" Lisa laid out his clothes on his bed, and I helped him pick out a pair of pants to match my pants.

The next morning, I put on my orange turtleneck and black pants, and he put on his orange turtleneck and black pants. We headed off to church together, dressed exactly the same. After

It is no longer merely desirable to develop an
organizational culture that embraces new ideas and
establishes the structures necessary to implement
innovation. It is imperative for the survival of a company.
—SPENCER STUART, "TESTING THE LIMITS OF INNOVATION"

church, Lisa and the other three kids had to go run some errands, so I took E. J. to a pizza restaurant for lunch. As Mini Me and I walked into this restaurant together, a thought struck me: *This is the way it is in the Christian life.* And the passage from Galatians 3:26–27 came to mind: "You are all sons of God through faith in Christ Jesus, for all of you who were baptized into Christ have *clothed* yourselves with Christ."

Our essential wardrobe is Jesus Christ. We are to clothe ourselves in His righteousness and character. And part of Christ's character is creativity. Our Father has set out our wardrobe and part of this ensemble is innovation. The question I ask myself regularly is, Am I clothing myself fully in Christ? Or am I keeping His creativity hidden, stuck way back in the closet where no one can see it?

Notice in Galatians that being clothed in Christ is active, not passive. As a follower of Christ, you have "clothed yourselves." Leaders must strategically create the environment or culture that allows the creative character of Christ to flourish in our lives and the lives of our teammates. That's not an easy task because somewhere along life's journey, the creative genius has been choked out of all of us. All of us are innovative and creative, but the values of our educational system and society in general are at odds with creativity. We are taught to trade dreaming for dogma, the artistic for the analytical, and our imaginations for memorization. Tradition is more highly valued than innovation, and logic more sought after than originality.

In this chapter, I want to help you create an environment or culture in your organization that will help ignite the creative spark in you and your staff. You can't just say, "OK, let's all be more creative. Go to work." Creating a creative culture requires intentionality. Creativity flows from order, and you must order your organization in such a way that fosters creative thinking and planning.

Creativity Is More Environmental Than Informational

As we think about creating a creative culture, the first thing we need to understand is that creativity is more environmental than informational. No one has a corner on the creative market. Creativity must flow from who you are and the environment God has placed you in. You might hear about something that we have done at Fellowship Church that you think is very cheesy and would never work in your context. That's OK. You shouldn't do anything that doesn't fit your personality or audience. Maybe my wild idea might set off a spark in your brain to come up with something better, something even more creative that fits who and where you are.

Do you know what a seine is? A seine is a big net with weights on the bottom edge and floats on the top edge. If you seine a six-foot area of the ocean, you will end up with a lot of extra treasures when you drag it from the ocean onto the beach. You'll have little crabs and little fish, maybe even a tire and license plate caught in the seine. There's no telling what else you might find in the ocean. When you use a seine for fishing, you want to keep the good bait fish and discard the waste.

You need to do the same thing with creative ideas. Keep the stuff you like, imitate a creative idea, tweak an idea, or just throw it out. If it doesn't work for you, let it go. A leader catches a lot of ideas and has to process a ton of information. The key is learning how to sift through it to find the useful elements for a particular context. A cowboy illustration or theme might work to support a message in Dallas–Fort Worth, but that same idea might not work very well in Seattle. What works in one environment oftentimes will not work in another. You might be able to use a variation of an idea, and hopefully improve it by contextualizing the idea so it fits better in your setting.

The ability to think creatively and implement those ideas does not come from a textbook. No class will give you all the ideas you need to become a creative genius. Real creativity flows from the inside out and is a very personal endeavor. It is, in a sense, a mirror reflection of who you are and what your surroundings are. A really great creative idea is only great once you own it and demonstrate that you are comfortable with it. The best creative ideas reflect your life, your leadership, your personality, and your passion.

Creativity Transcends Style and Size

It is so tempting to say, "It's easy for that organization to be creative because they have a much bigger staff or budget than I have." But that's an excuse and doesn't even accurately reflect the nature of true creativity.

The smaller church or ministry often has the creative advantage over the larger one, because a smaller ministry or church can make creative decisions on a dime. You don't have a massive corporate church structure or complicated logistics to contend with. You can also use small objects and props for illustrations, and people can connect with them because you are in a more intimate environment.

Sometimes I miss those early days when we were just starting out. It's not that I don't appreciate the resources we have now, but I do miss the excitement and creativity that could be fleshed out in a smaller venue. Size and style don't alter creative potential. Don't buy into that lie; it would please Satan. He wants you say, "I can't do that. I can't be innovative. I can't be creative in this environment. My church is too small, our resources are too limited, and our style is too confining."

Any time you say things like that, you're making a mockery of God's creative genius. In reality, you are denying the fact that you are made in the image of the creative God. Be who you are. Don't look at another church or pastor and get discouraged because you can't do what they're doing. Don't try to be someone you're not. Be the uniquely creative leader God has wired you to be, no matter the size or style of church in which you find yourself.

What Does a Creative Culture Look Like?

You might be wondering what specific elements might help you and your staff in the creative process. Let me direct you to ten key principles that have empowered Fellowship Church to make great strides in creating a creative culture.

1. Draft Impact Players

If you want to develop a great team, you have to pay close attention to the draft. Your organization is only as strong as your impact players. I'm talking about people who can really make things happen. These people have the skill sets, the passion, the drive, and the leadership qualities to help propel your church or ministry to the next level.

Pastors and leaders looking for these people need to do their homework. They need to check all the vital stats on these potential staff members by getting to know them and asking around about them. Don't be afraid to look under every rock when it comes to your staff; in key leadership positions, you cannot be too careful. I address some of the practicalities of hiring staff in chapter 7.

When you do find these impact players, don't soft-sell the job. Tell them it is going to be a long, hard journey. Creative leadership is just that. However, you can also promise them that they will experience an incredible ride marked by creativity and faith. Tell them that you want them to partner with you on this exciting journey.

Also, when these players hit training camp, don't be afraid to throw them in the deep end. Leaders learn best by doing. Allow them to grow by experiencing both successes and failures.

Give them the resources they need and then let them run with the responsibilities you have entrusted to them. Allow them to develop and grow while they try new things. By developing these playmakers with both creative freedom and appropriate account-ability, they will score the touchdowns for you.

2. Develop Double Vision

Whatever your church's or organization's head count is, lead like it is twice its present size. For example, when our church had about 150 people, I led the church like it had 300. Today we have more than 20,000, and I am trying to lead as if it were 40,000. That mind-set is essential for organizational growth.

I have always intuitively led the church with this principle in mind, but I just recently was able to articulate what it has meant in practical terms. In fact, my wife, Lisa, helped me understand how this has played out over the years. We were preparing for a talk we were giving for a group of pastors at our Creative Church Conference, and this idea of developing double vision came up in our discussions.

I asked her how she thought my leadership of the church had changed as the church had grown.

"The main thing you have done differently," she answered, "is to say no to more things. Even when we were very small, you were saying no to a lot of things because you believed we were going to grow."

As we looked back to the very beginnings of the church, she helped me realize that developing double vision means begin-ning now to say no to things that you will not be able to do as the church grows. In other words, if your church has 500 people, prepare for growth now by not doing the things you know you couldn't do if there were 1,000 people attending.

You need to push back and delegate the tasks that can be done by your teammates. The vision-caster needs to be free to plan for the future and do the few things that only he or she can do. Don't show up for everything the church does—every party, barbecue, small-group meeting, and Bible study class. Don't try to have a hand in everything that happens in the church, like stacking the chairs, sweeping the floor, teaching the newcomer's class, or visiting people in the hospital. These are all very important ministries and opportunities, but you can't pretend that you're Superman or Superwoman. You don't wear a cape.

Begin delegating the ministry now so you will be free to do the unique things only you can do. This will, in turn, provide strategic leadership opportunities for your teammates. Show your church as well as your staff that you value your teammates enough to give them these important challenges.

3. Pursue Big Events

Using big events to bolster church growth was a huge key to our growth when we were a young, start-up church. When our church was a year old, about 785 people were attending our services. This was also during the time the first Gulf War was ending. So we decided to do something that really honored our country, our veterans, and the people who fought in the Gulf War. We found a large open area near our church and hosted a July 4 concert to celebrate the ending of the Gulf War. The idea was for people in the community to come out, relax in their lawn chairs, and enjoy some good music.

This event was a high-risk deal for us. Our giving at the time was running maybe $5,000 on a good weekend, and it was going to take $40,000 to host this one event. Looking back on it now, I shudder. But we did it because we believed it would have a huge upside for our young church, and it turned out to be a great success. But you know what? Even if it had rained out, it was worth $40,000 just for leadership development. We developed a ton of new people who came out of the woodwork to volunteer for this event. Our people got off the stands and into the game. They took charge of security, concessions, staging, and even the Porta Pottis.

A local Christian radio station partnered with us in this event, and we brought in several Christian music artists. It took 500 of our people from the church to pull it off. The police estimated that we had more than 20,000 people show up. We were blown away!

Big events are important because (1) people like to be a part of sometime bigger than themselves, (2) they build unity and momentum, and (3) they help develop leaders in your church. People will step up for those big challenges like you wouldn't believe.

Another big event we sponsored years ago was Hoops for Hope. After the Oklahoma City bombing tragedy, we wanted to do something financially for the victims. We held a creative session in one of our staff meetings to plan the event, and someone came up with the idea to play the Dallas Cowboys in basketball and give all the proceeds to the bombing victims' families. Some of the Cowboys were known to be good basketball players, and I had played some college basketball at Florida State. (Well, I pretty much just sat and watched, but at least I wore the uniform and my name was in the program.)

It was a terrific idea and thousands of fans showed up. Troy Aikman was nice enough to play on our church team. The press got wind of it (probably because Troy was playing against his Cowboys) and featured the story in the local news and even ESPN. We raised a lot of money and, forgive the gloating, beat the Cowboys. But it was just another instance of thinking creatively for a big event to draw people to the church.

These events take tremendous team creativity, hard work, and organization to pull off; but they are big winners. You won't believe the benefits of adding a big event like this to your church. It builds momentum, exposes and develops leaders, and brings many new people into your church who otherwise would not have known you existed. The local church should be the most exciting entity out there. What can you do to show your community that your church is the place to be?

4. Go for a Promotion

Don King is truly the king of promotion in the boxing industry. He is unbelievable. Pastors also need to do the Don-King thing (excluding the wild-hair part). You have got to promote. We promote our programs and events at Fellowship in everything we do.

We have done a lot of direct mail over the years, and when we do it, we make sure that it is done creatively and with excellence. Christmas Eve and Easter are the two hit-or-miss times to invite the unchurched since many of them attend only twice a year (I call them the "lily and poinsettia crowd"). So pack some heavy promotion behind those two events (see apps. 1 and 2).

This past Christmas, we held a high-risk event to help promote our satellite campuses that were set to open up in mid-January. Instead of hosting eleven Christmas Eve services at our facility in Grapevine like we have done the past few years, we decided to rent out the American Airlines center in Dallas for two services on Christmas Eve. This state-of-the-art venue can seat 20,000 people. If people didn't show up, you'd probably hear crickets chirping during the service. The venue is also twenty-five miles from our main campus. Despite all these odds, we had a very successful event. We had to send away more than 1,000 people for our first service and were almost full for the second. It was an amazing opportunity for our entire church to be together in this venue. To have 20,000 people worshipping together under one roof was a picture of heaven.

Again, this event built incredible momentum for our church, developed many new leaders, and brought a lot of attention to our new campuses across the Dallas–Fort Worth area.

For the Christmas direct mail piece (see app. 2), we created a Christmas card highlighting the American Airlines Center. We sent out 80,000 of these, focusing the direct-mail blitz to the two areas where we would be opening our new campuses—Uptown (just north of downtown) and Plano (a far north suburb of Dallas). The piece also promoted the grand opening of those new satellites (see app. 3 for PowerPoint and brochure graphics). And guess what happened as a result? We had monstrous crowds Christmas Eve and both satellite campuses had a great opening weekend.

We do a lot of cross-promotion like that. Whether we are promoting the next big event, the new sermon series, the new lineup of Power Source classes (adult Bible studies), the summer youth retreat, Adventure Week for children, or the singles New Year's Eve party, we almost always promote something else at the same time.

An exciting way to promote is through giveaways. To promote our new Saturday night services years ago, we printed up hundreds of T-shirts with "What are you doing Saturday night?" on them. It was a great way to create awareness of this new service. We've also done giveaways to promote capital campaigns. One weekend we launched a campaign in which we put little basketballs imprinted with "Get in the Game" on everyone's car antennas. We promoted a series called "Thread" on the lordship of Christ by giving everyone thread bracelets to wear during the six weeks the series was going on. When someone would ask them what the bracelet was for, it was like an automatic invitation for them to talk about Fellowship Church and share what the message series was all about.

I also like to promote what's coming up with little teasers during the weekend service. Many times in the middle of my messages, after just briefly mentioning a certain topic, I will stop and say something like this: "I don't have time to cover that today, but next weekend I am going to talk about the fact that conflict in marriage is a good thing. You heard me right—let's get ready to rumble! You do not want to miss next week's message." Promote. "Two weekends from now, we are having a baptismal celebration following the last Saturday evening service and the last Sunday morning service. If you have made a life-changing decision to follow Christ and have not yet been baptized, now is the time" (see graphic for baptism form in app. 4). Promote, promote, promote.

5. Put on Your Shades

There was a song in the eighties by Timbuk 3 called "The Future's So Bright I Gotta Wear Shades" that reminds me of how we at Fellowship like to regularly communicate our vision of its bright future. We might preach it, teach it, or do a creative video, but we make sure to highlight what God has called us to do. People forget the vision of your church and mine about every forty-eight hours. As previously mentioned in chapter 3, vision leaks, so you've got to be willing to say it, spray it, wheel it, deal it, preach it, teach it, and sing it.

To repeat our mission statement, we exist to reach up—that is worship, expressing love to God. We exist to reach out—that is evangelism, communicating Christ to others. We also exist to reach in—that is discipleship, developing full-court followers of Jesus Christ. We express that over and over and over and over again. This is our core message in our newcomers membership class. We also remind people of the mission at every volunteer training function.

One time we did a weekend on vision that coincided with a capital campaign called "Build the Vision." To drive home the message that our future is bright, we gave everyone a pair of sunglasses. These aren't expensive things. In fact, we got them extremely cheap because the logo word of the company was misspelled—something that no one would even recognize. They turned out to be almost free. We had everyone put the shades on during the message, and our people have never forgotten this image. Every now and then I'll walk around town and see people with the "Build the Vision" glasses on.

Often when I prepare to do yet another vision message, I'll second-guess myself: *Didn't I just do one of these? Are people getting tired of this? Surely, everyone knows the vision of Fellowship Church by now.* I've done these so often that they seem repetitive to me. But people always approach me after a message or a series on vision and say how happy they were to hear the message. "Now I understand why we do what we do!" they say.

So create a concise, memorable mission statement to promote that vision. Write it down for your staff to memorize and remind your people of it over and over again. You cannot state your vision enough. Put on your shades and talk about the bright future of your church every chance you get.

6. Conduct an IRS Audit

In this case, *IRS* stands for *Internal Response System,* which is what I check on every once in awhile to make sure the staff is responding to the congregation in a timely manner. Here's how my audit works. During every weekend service, I tell the audience to fill out the guest page in the worship guide (see app. 5 for an example) if they have questions about the church, membership, or events. Then I tell them to tear out that page and place it in the offering bag. I promise that someone will get back to them within the week.

It occurred to me that I ought to evaluate how our call-back system was working. So I made up some creative names and checked off different areas—music, athletics, baptism, etc.—as categories that I wanted additional information about. Then I rigged up a phone with a fake answering machine and waited to see how long it would take someone to call. If I wasn't pleased with the response time I received from a certain area, I went to the appropriate staff members and told them they needed to improve in their response efforts.

You need to check up on people sometimes. That's your job as a leader. People often don't do what you expect; they do what you *in*spect. They need to be reminded that they are held accountable for how effectively they carry out their responsibilities. But the same goes for you: Don't just talk about assimilation; do it. Don't just talk about recruiting more people for the music ministry; do it. Make sure you are following up with people just as you expect your staff to.

Another way to encourage staff participation is to report church attendees' prayer requests during weekly staff meetings. Use these times to pray about the needs of the people the staff have spoken with. Show them you are serious about a commitment to follow up with people.

Whether you are talking about personal evangelism or calling prospective members, make sure staff is following through. Don't be fearful of confrontation. If they are repeatedly refusing to carry out their responsibilities, don't be fearful of having to dismiss a staff member. One time, I asked a friend and successful businessman what his biggest weakness was. "I waited too long to fire people," he said. I address this issue in greater detail in chapter 7, but let me just say here that firing someone is not usually our first response to a staff problem. Our first move if someone is not working out in his current position is transitioning him into another position on staff. If that doesn't solve the problem, we do pull the trigger when necessary. Sometimes it is better to let people go to find their niche in another church than to waste your time and theirs in an unfruitful situation.

7. Do a Clean Sweep

It probably should go without saying that the church should be a clean place, but I've not always witnessed that in my travels around the country. The campus of any church, inside and out, should be clutter-free. What is communicated when you have

Scotch tape and thumbtacks all over the walls, broken-down chairs and other furniture littering the classrooms, and boxes sitting in the corner of every office? Is excellence communicated when there are bits of trash all over the campus, stained and smelly carpets, or cracked walls that saw their last coat of paint during the Nixon administration?

What kind of message does that send, particularly to today's unchurched audience? Does that communicate a constant connection with our creative God? We have to do things with excellence. Don't let your church become dirty or sloppy.

I've found it a good practice to ask someone who has just walked into our church to check out our facilities. They see the facility with fresh eyes and will give you the feedback you need. Also, do a walk-through with your staff. We have a rule: when staff members see a bit of trash (paper, cigarette butt, etc.) on the ground, they pick it up. Cleanliness is a team effort. You can't just write that value down; everyone on your team has be committed and involved in executing this value.

We finally hired someone to do the maintenance and cleaning in our facilities. The transformation was incredible. I had no idea how dirty things were before this guy came on board. But the staff is still involved in trash patrol.

Your facility should glorify God. God is a God of excellence and order; your church should be a reflection of that. It should communicate that this is a holy place to meet God. Don't let a junky atmosphere distract people from the message of the gospel.

Even when we were in rented facilities like a local high school or arts center, we did clean sweeps all the time. We had volunteers go through and clean up after the places were supposedly clean. You'll be amazed at what you'll find if you do a walk-through periodically. A commitment to cleanliness will communicate the right messages to people and, I believe, will honor God since you are managing the facility He has given to you.

8. Make Your Signage Paramount

From time to time, my family and I check out another church in the area. On one such occasion, as I was driving up to a church, I didn't see a single sign to direct me to the visitor parking area, much less the congregational parking lot. And there was no sign to show me where to take our four children. We were clueless. I went up to an usher and asked where the children's area was. He answered, "I don't know, man. Sorry."

No signage (and uninformed ushers) is a major turnoff for new people. You are in the hole from the very beginning with seekers or visitors if your signage is subpar.

Make signs to welcome and guide your visitors. And when you make signs, think like someone who has never been to church before—what information would you need from those signs? It doesn't matter if visitors are Christian or non-Christian, the first emotions they have are fear and uncertainty. Even as a pastor, my first response when I go to a different church is fear. The signs help people to relax.

Signs do not have to cost a lot of money. Check out sign companies for inexpensive, yet professional-looking signs. We print a lot of our signs on our own printing equipment at the church. We've been making good-looking signs since our budget was nonexistent. Just remember to be very strategic about your signage to connect with visitors from the get-go.

9. Create a Climate of Healthy, Helpful Criticism

We are constantly tweaking things and as such need an atmosphere of healthy, helpful criticism. Criticism can be hard to take sometimes but is so important. We are communicating the story of God and His love through salvation. We are talking about eternal life and death. God is using our creativity, skills, and gifts to make a lasting difference in people's lives, and we can't afford to do a half-baked job. We want things done to our best ability, knowing that God desires our very best.

We are ruthless on ourselves because of what's at stake. Just like a football team reviews game films, we watch the videos of the services to evaluate how well everything flowed and synched with the message and whether the message was as good as it could have possibly been. One benefit to our four services (two on Saturday night and two on Sunday morning) is that we can evaluate the first service on Saturday night and make improvements to the other three.

We've experienced "off" weekends: even though our attendance was strong, the service itself was not smooth. Maybe the preliminary song did not work well or the drama was a bit cheesy or my talk was filled with too much information and not enough application. Whatever the reason, we missed it. And all of this was uncovered in our critique session after the first Saturday evening service that helped us improve for the next three services.

We also critique our ministries and conferences periodically to ensure that we are riding the crest of the creative wave and not sinking into mediocrity. Every staff meeting is essentially a critique session. We ask what's working and what's not working. If something's not working, we discuss ways to improve it. Sometimes, after the same thing keeps coming up again and again for critique, we realize that we are beating a dead horse and just need to cancel that program or ministry.

We've got to critique things. If you'll take golf lessons and let a pro pick your swing apart, or if you'll hire trainers to criticize and change your weight-lifting routine, you may as well gather some criticism about how and if you're bringing people into salvation. So it only makes sense to create a climate of healthy, helpful criticism in the church.

You will learn that you and your staff need to have thick-enough skin to take criticisms effectively. It is crucial that your staff members understand that everyone is subjected to the same process and that you love them. Without that crucial relational capital, your critique will come across as insulting. Criticism is meant to help your staff grow and benefit the church at the same time. When a multitalented, multifaceted team comes together for evaluation, new ideas emerge to improve ministries, sermons, and a myriad of opportunities to influence the world.

We've even had critique sessions about the baptismal celebrations that follow our weekend worship services. What could we possibly have to evaluate about a baptismal service? Well, we've had some meltdowns that needed to be addressed. Maybe the pastors were taking too long to baptize the candidates, the volunteers were not moving the lines fast enough, or the service didn't start on time. When you potentially have 200 or 300 people getting baptized in one service, any of these things can cause a huge problem.

You might say, "Well, people are only human." Yes, we're obviously going to make mistakes. We're never going to be perfect this side of heaven. However, in a baptismal service, we want the baptizees to have a meaningful encounter with God and their church family and we want the audience to enjoy the celebration of the Christian faith. The baptism service that we critiqued hindered both of these realities, so we thought through our process and improved it for the next time.

10. Develop a Committed Core

When you plant a church or take over any organization, you must have a committed core. You might think that an obvious point, but I'm telling you, this is a huge principle missed in many organizations that ultimately fail. They do not develop a loyal group of people who are willing to go all the way for the sake of the ministry. I deal with this in greater detail in my chapter on staffing, but I'll touch on it briefly here. It is so important to pray like crazy for your core, asking God for the discernment and wisdom to find your core. You've got to have people who are willing to put it on the line for the vision. And then, when you find these people, give the ball of vision to them. They need to own the vision and spread it to other people.

When I go to the doctor, I am under his authority. If I don't want to be under his authority, I am free to go to another doctor. When I go to the dentist, I am under his authority. I can ask questions, but at the end of the day, when my mouth is numbed and propped open, I am under his authority.

How do you develop this core? First, pray for committed people to join your creative journey and expect God to bring them to you. Second, expect your people to trust your leadership. Loyalty is so important, so make sure you have committed teammates surrounding you and supporting you. Finally, choose people you can work with and to whom you can confidently hand the ball of ministry.

When you are discouraged or overwhelmed, these people will hang onto you. You will thank God every day for a committed core that is willing to stand with you no matter the pressures and the obstacles. God has given you these people to share the love of Christ with a hurting world.

We have seen that creativity is an essential part of God's character. The Bible also tells us that we are to clothe ourselves in Christ and imitate the character of God. Creativity is exciting, inspiring, and rewarding in a work environment. The problem is that most of us don't know how to start implementing that creativity at work.

If we want to create a creative culture, we must be the man or woman God has designed us to be. Creative environments flow from the personalities that lead them. If you are a deep thinker, don't shy away from those gifts when you speak for God. Embrace the creative questions that emerge from hours of contemplation and then share the creative answers God gives you with your people. They will eat it up because people need creativity.

Ultimately, creativity is not about gimmicks or copying programs from one organization to another. Effective creative thought occurs in a particular context. Only you, with God's help, can determine what the creative culture will look like in your organization. What works for me may not work for you. We have to be willing to explore new frontiers with the help of our teammates and the inspiration that comes from our creative God.

For the Son of Man came to
seek and to save what was lost.
LUKE 19:10

CHAPTER 5

Creative Worship

If you grew up learning Bible stories on flannel board like I did, you might also remember lacing your fingers and repeating, "Here's the church, here's the steeple; open the doors and see all the people!" Four decades ago, it was that easy for the church. For the most part, the church just had to have a building, put up a steeple, open the doors, and in came the people. They attended in droves.

But since the 1960s, our culture has taken a swan dive from the local church into the cesspools of contemporary culture. Church attendance has dropped and people are effectively ignoring the local church because it is not connecting with their needs. The church is not answering the questions they're asking or meeting them in their family and work culture.

The bridge to that culture and those questions is the weekend worship service. That is the entry point into the church, and if we aren't capturing people there, we aren't going to capture them anywhere. So this chapter addresses the most important aspect of a church—the worship bridge.

The Church exists for nothing else but to draw men into Christ,
to make them little Christs. If they are not doing that, all the
cathedrals, clergy, missions, sermons, even the Bible itself, are
simply a waste of time. God became Man for no other purpose.
C. S. LEWIS, *MERE CHRISTIANITY*

Building the Worship Bridge

As mentioned earlier, senior pastors should have offices adorned with It's the Weekend, Stupid signs.

The worship service is the common port for everyone. You have got to make the worship service your top priority. It was true fifteen years ago when we started Fellowship, and it's true today. When we consider adding or expanding a program or ministry, we have to ask ourselves, What is the main thing? And we remind ourselves of the answer—it's the weekend, stupid. It takes a deep commitment to stay that course and keep the main thing the main thing.

For the church, the main thing is worship. Undoubtedly, worship is the one area of the church that will impact the masses. If the weekend worship isn't working, the church isn't working. When starting a new ministry endeavor, ask yourself, Does this interfere with the weekly worship service?

Inevitably, I'll face a showdown between two great opportunities. Throughout the year, I have the opportunity to speak outside the church at various conferences and events. I am also able to write new books and develop other church resources. But there is one reality that trumps all of that. About forty-three weekends a year, I am scheduled to speak at our four weekend services. And whether I'm speaking at our annual Creative Church Conference or an outside conference or delivering a talk to 350 junior high students in Alabama during the summer, the weekend service at Fellowship must always come first. It demands my highest level of attention.

That's an overwhelming proposition. Though I love speaking at conferences and sharing my experiences through books and other resources, my main priority is leading and teaching the people who attend Fellowship Church each weekend. If anything is going to suffer, it's going to be the activities outside of the worship service. This has to be our main priority as church leaders.

I believe church staff members—the senior pastor especially—should spend about 75 percent of their time on the weekend services, including both the planning and implementation of that pivotal time. We invest a lot of financial and human resources in our worship service, and it's because we consider this time a bridge to those who are outside the Body of Christ with the rest of us who seek biblical answers to life's most profound questions. We want our worship service to attract people and help transform them into mature followers of Christ. Our desire is for people to connect with their Creator and have real take-home value for the questions and problems they face every day. The worship service is equally for seekers and believers. To that end, I have come up with seven core principles that I believe are crucial to build a dynamic W.O.R.S.H.I.P. bridge. (I realize that acrostics are not very "postmodern" or "emergent," but this has worked for me over many years of church leadership conferences, so I think it's worth including in this book. Sometimes the old-time way is still the best way! That's part of the creative equation: knowing when to go back and when to go forward.)

Welcoming

The *W* is for *welcoming.* At Fellowship, we have a triple-team approach to welcoming people into our campus, because (as previously mentioned) the biggest obstacle for most people when they enter a new church is fear. This is especially true for those who have little or no church background. However, it is also true for those who have become disillusioned with other churches. As a team, we work very hard to help make everyone feel welcome, loved, and accepted as soon as their tires touch our property. So we've enlisted parkers, greeters, and hospitality folks to work that welcome.

You may have heard it said that the worship service begins in the parking lot. It's true. Before anyone enters the worship center, they should already have the impression that this church is a welcoming place. When people drive onto our church property, they see our parking areas dotted with orange-vested men and women who are trained to greet the people as they navigate the campus and get out of their cars. Often you'll find that when people come to church, their lives are hanging by a thread. Maybe their marriage or their career is on the verge of disaster. Just one handshake, pat on the back, or "May I help you?" can set the tone for what happens inside these walls and potentially affect what happens outside the walls when that person leaves.

Our second layer of welcome involves greeters. We recruit dozens and dozens of people in our church who have the gift of greeting. These high-energy people clearly love people and love doing what they do. They have that twinkle in their eye and spring in their step. Most of all, they understand the high stakes of welcoming people as they come through the doors of the church. They may give them a map of the facility; point them in the direction of the nursery, preschool, or children's church; or they may show them where the information kiosk is. They may even need to show people where the auditorium is. First-time visitors know nothing about your campus, so you need people on the front lines who are ready and able to answer their questions and allay their fears.

The third welcome entourage is our hospitality team. The hospitality team makes sure the coffee is percolating and the lemonade is in abundant supply. When people come into the church, the hospitality volunteers make sure there's a relaxed atmosphere of fellowship and serve with a smile. The goal is to treat people who come into the church the same way we would treat guests in our houses. We want them to grab a cup of coffee, relax, and make themselves at home.

Obviously, all of these ministries require training. You don't want a parker who doesn't know the difference between the children's building and the main worship center. You don't want a greeter who constantly frowns and says, "I don't know." You don't want an irritable hospitality person with the energy of a slug. Although it doesn't take a Bible scholar to participate in these ministries (that's the great thing about them—even baby Christians can get in the game), the impact of these front-line volunteer positions is critical to the overall success of the weekend.

Here's a crucial insider's tip. Everybody in these people-sensitive ministries pops Altoids to avert any bad breath that might inadvertently knock someone over. We also train our volunteers how to dress appropriately, how to meet new people, and what to say when they greet. You cannot assume anything. You must tell people what you expect. We even show pictures of what clothing is appropriate and what is not—like a fashion show. Given our current cultural climate, people must be given concrete examples of what is expected of them. We emphasize over and over again that hospitality is one of the most important ministries of our worship service. If people don't have a great experience entering your worship center, they probably won't have a great experience inside it either.

Another important ministry related to welcoming involves the ushers. Parkers, greeters, and hospitality workers welcome people prior to their entering the worship center. Then as people come into the auditorium, the ushers provide another wave of welcome. Nothing is revolutionary about having ushers, but making sure your ushers are friendly, helpful, and well organized is another matter entirely. Are they really doing what you expect and need from them? Our ushers are very busy handing out the worship guides, sincerely greeting people as the come through the doors, and quickly and efficiently seating them throughout our worship center.

Sometimes our volunteers have to run interference with parents who want to bring their preschoolers into our worship services. We do not allow children under five in the worship service. Our philosophy is that our worship service is an adult service intended for an adult audience, while our children should enjoy age-appropriate teaching in their own excellent facility. Our "family-friendly greeters" have been trained to redirect the parents with young children to our family-friendly service located in an adjacent classroom in our facility. Should these parents not want to take their young children to our excellent nursery or preschool ministries, we have a special service for these young families so they can enjoy a live video feed from the main auditorium, while eliminating distractions for our adults worshipping in the auditorium. (We also have pastors on site for this service to administer communion and for general announcements.) As you can imagine, these greeters need to be well trained and understand our commitment to our worship philosophy. A great usher ministry takes a lot of organization and a team commitment to pull off with excellence.

We have other elements that contribute to our welcoming atmosphere. When people walk in before the service, they see slides showing information about the church and its upcoming activities and hear some upbeat music. Again, we are trying to create an environment that helps to drive out that emotion of fear. We're thinking about what people are dealing with, especially a lot of families who've driven in their minivans here and dropped their screaming kids off. The parents grab a cup of coffee, sit down, and get acclimated to the worship environment, seeing if any of the upcoming events on screen might appeal to them.

What if you don't have big screens or are in a rental unit like a high school or office complex? We did this when we only had one tiny screen. We were advertising our women's retreat, our youth beach retreat, our Power Source Bible classes, and our children's Adventure Week in the summer. We painstakingly went over all of these slides, ensuring that every word was spelled properly and the information was correct. People remember these slides; they are the first impressions inside our sanctuary. So we think carefully about how we word things because we are trying to connect our people with what Fellowship Church is all about.

We also show a slide before the service asking people to turn off their cell phones and beepers. I can't stand it when a cell phone goes off in the middle of my sermon. Several times, people have actually answered their phones while I was in the middle of my message. For really extreme cases like these rude dudes, you may need to make a verbal announcement at the beginning of the service as well. Say it nicely and respectfully, but don't be afraid to do it. People need to know that this time is sacred and needs to be as free as possible from outside distractions.

Another aspect of welcoming that we're very serious about—and this takes a lot of hard work—is our CPR ministry. *CPR* stands for *Call, Promote,* and *Recruit.* CPR keeps the church alive and vibrant. When people attend your church and fill out any information on any aspect of your ministry, make sure you have teams of people to call them and do so quickly—within forty-eight hours after they've visited your church. I've already mentioned the IRS audit, and this is precisely what that audit is for.

Maybe the people who request information are members who've asked to work in the preschool area or the greeting ministry. Or maybe they're visitors who have made a decision for Christ and want more information about what that means. Whatever the situation, we follow up quickly. We're always promoting over the phone, telling them what's going on, how they can serve, and what's going to happen next.

Also, we're constantly recruiting. We may have a good volunteer base, but we are always saying, "Well, let's double the base and then triple the base." I deal with recruiting in more detail later in this chapter.

Organized

O is for *organized*. As I've already stated, creativity emerges from order. Organization is fundamental to the creative process. Because we have found that thematic services are an excellent way to reinforce the central message each week, our worship staff has to demonstrate tremendous dedication and teamwork to pull those off week after week. If you have ever tried thematic services, you know that they are wonderful for the audience as far as clarity and focus but very difficult on your staff.

Every worship team participant—all staff members who are responsible for the speaking, music, drama, videos, lighting, sound, and stage design—has to be on the same page, working together on the dominant theme each weekend.

Just recently, to aid in this team approach, we have moved the offices of all the key people involved in the weekend planning closer to one another. Specifically, the key people in the worship team have all moved their offices in close proximity to mine. My office was already near various staff on the creative team who help me craft the weekend message, but moving the worship and arts team over to the same area will make the weekend planning process more effective and efficient.

Obviously, the speaker has to prepare effectively to deliver a compelling biblical message each week (more is said about this in the next chapter, on communication). The worship or music staff must exercise teamwork and discipline to coordinate the message with the worship service. They chart responsibilities, think through the dramas, find and cast the appropriate people, organize the proper singers for the Praise Team, and coordinate the service with the technical staff for the sound, lighting, video, and timing issues.

All of these elements require weeks of planning and an inexhaustible amount of creative thought. I have already talked about being consistently inconsistent, and because we value growth and creativity, we change our songs, sets, and worship flow regularly. We try to change this out for every message series (which usually lasts anywhere from four to six weeks). This may mean that we vacillate between rock and choral music from one series to the next. I want people to come to church saying, "What are they going to do next? What's behind the curtain this week?" Obviously, this standard is very demanding for the various people involved in planning the weekend services. It may mean that we have to scrap the original plan at the last minute if I, the leader, feel led to change the direction of the service. That's just the name of the game in a creative church.

So far we have covered the welcoming and organization aspects of the creative church. The next part of the worship bridge is perhaps the most crucial in answering the "so what?" question in the church today.

Relevant

R stands for *relevancy*. That's the "so what?" question. What difference does all of this make in people's lives? As leaders, and especially as pastors, we're always asking the "so what?" question. That's the most important question we can ask. When we're planning worship, the creative team and I will say, "So what? Great, the drama is provoking; it's funny. But does it make the cut?" Just because it's thought-provoking doesn't mean it advances our central message. Maybe the video is funny, but is it necessary to make a lasting difference in their lives?

A lot of times, my illustrations will go through the same filter. I'll ask my team, "What do you think of the illustration?" And they'll say, "Ed, it's hilarious, but so what? What does that have to do with the take-home message?" We've got to put a high value on the take-home thing.

"So what? Where does this take me?" Our job as pastors is to take people on a journey of faith, and that journey needs to go to the irrevocable truth of the gospel of Jesus Christ.

"What do you want me to do because of what you've said?" Relevancy is huge. If you're into the search for the Holy Grail, relevancy is the Holy Grail of the worship experience.

We'll address this more later, but I'll say it here as well: Be willing to cut the creative fat when something doesn't work in the worship service. I don't care how much time you've put into an element—a drama, a song, an illustration, a video, or a point in your sermon—if it doesn't serve the intended purpose, cut it out. We typically review our worship service at the end of the first of four weekend services. Take the spiritual scalpel and make a strategic surgical incision. More often than not, we'll have to cut a drama or a video if it doesn't pass the "so what?" test. If you can't answer that question satisfactorily for any given element in your service, don't use it.

Look at the example of Jesus as it pertains to relevancy. As mentioned in chapter 1, 72 percent of all of His words were words of relevancy and words of application—the "so what?" principle. If your services are not answering the "so what?" question for your people, you need to think about what you're doing and why you're doing it. Don't ever forget, R stands for relevant.

Sensitive

S stands for being *sensitive*. When guests come over to your house or mine, we're sensitive to their needs. We're thinking about who they are and what their particular needs and desires are. When we go through the exhaustive process of planning, we think about the individuals we expect to have as guests— individuals in our church who have marital problems, are going through a financial setback, are seeking the ultimate mate, and so on. We have those pictures in our brains. Sometimes we even write down their names as we plan what we're going to say during the worship service. That's all about being sensitive. In fact, as I prepare for all my messages, I have an old college friend in mind who doesn't know the Lord personally. I try to prepare a message that would meet him where he is and answer the questions that he may be asking. I realize that he probably isn't going to attend the service, but I prepare, nonetheless, as if he were coming.

As for worship style, we should be sensitive to all forms of public expression. Some people like to stand up and sing from the bottom of their hearts. Others are more contemplative and may want to sit and reflect on the words being sung. Some folks may be hurting so deeply that they just need to immerse themselves in a Christian community and enjoy the fellowship around them. Seekers may be totally clueless about the rules of church. They definitely can't be expected to know old hymns or new praise songs. To be sensitive, you need to put yourself in the shoes of your audience—a valuable lesson I learned with my friend Scott back at Florida State.

When we use drama, we really think about the audience. We used a drama one time about blended families and wanted to make sure that it was really sensitive to the struggles, joys, and pains that they go through. Tears are not the indicator of a successful drama, but I think the drama was very effective because of the emotional impact it had on those who were experiencing problems similar to the ones we portrayed. I believe we were sensitive to their needs and addressed some real issues in this drama.

We try to make those dramas very real. If we can't, we don't use them. You must be very sensitive to how drama is used in our entertainment-driven culture. Dramas, if and when they are used, must be exceptional. The contemporary church audience can spot a cheesy drama a mile away. If it isn't real, if it doesn't drill to the heart of the audience, and if it doesn't accentuate the main point of the message, don't use it. I don't care how many hours went into its preparation and rehearsal. Cut it!

Also, be prepared to sweat the details. You don't need to become paranoid because "paranoia will destroy ya." But it will help you and your people to constantly and consistently sweat the details. Remember, God is in the details. He is intimately acquainted and deeply concerned about the nitty-gritty details of the worship service as well as the nitty-gritty details of life. So seek Him as you get welcoming, organized, relevant, and sensitive in your worship planning and you're well on your way to building the worship bridge.

Hour

The worship hour should be just that: an hour. That's the *H*. We like to jokingly call it Preparation H, because we prepare for an hour. Now, sometimes our services go a little bit longer than an hour, sometimes less than an hour. But we are very deliberate in timing every part of our service to fit into the context of the entire service lasting no longer than an hour. We initially got into the hour timeslot because, being in a rented facility, we had to execute all of our weekend services in a certain amount of time or be charged more money. The excellent discovery resulting from being forced to adopt this model was that the one-hour worship service is optimal. And I would challenge you to plan your services the same way.

When someone is hurting or uncomfortable, ninety minutes can seem like an eternity. We work hard to make our services succinct and short. We would rather people think, *It's over already?* than *When is this thing gonna end?* I believe if you can't communicate what you're trying to say in an hour, you'll never be able to do it no matter how much time you have.

I think about the story in Acts 20 of the apostle Paul preaching past midnight. Some kid named Eutychus was sitting on the windowsill of the house Paul was preaching in and fell asleep during Paul's message. I think Paul was a little long-winded, but you can draw your own conclusions.

No doubt, the one-hour worship adds pressure to how we execute every area of the service. For instance, we have to put strict time constraints on drama—it has to be fewer than five minutes long. In fact, we've done very powerful dramas in just a couple of minutes. Many people think dramas need a good seven to ten minutes, but I totally and wholeheartedly disagree. I realize that, especially for serious dramas, it's harder to do five minutes. But I think it's the time amount you need to shoot for. You can make them short and to the point. You've got to realize that, by and large, we have an A.D.D audience. And like it or not, you have to pander to the attention span of your audience. A seven- to ten-minute drama will lose most of your audience after the first four or five minutes.

We also try to make sure that our video clips are not too long. A video clip should not go beyond three minutes. We've made several mistakes in that area. We've had video clips go four or five minutes and beyond, to the point that you can hear the audience shifting or snoring. People don't come to church to watch video clips; they come to hear a word from God. Any video you use must accentuate that message.

I also put a parameter on myself as far as preaching. We've all been to churches where the preacher goes on and on and on. After about thirty minutes, I'm looking for the usher to bring me a pillow and a blankie. So I really try to keep the message in the range of twenty-five to thirty minutes, because I believe if you can't communicate the main point of your message in less than thirty minutes, you probably can't communicate it at all.

Inspirational

The next letter in the W.O.R.S.H.I.P. bridge is the letter *I* for *inspirational.* We want our worship services to be motivational and inspiring. Several years ago, we came up with a slogan for our worship service: "Innertainment for the heart." We were frequently accused of being too entertaining, so we adapted this slogan from the definition of *entertainment*— "capturing and holding the attention of someone for an extended period of time." And we decided at Fellowship that that's exactly what the church is called to do. We should provide "innertainment for the heart" by capturing and holding people's attention with the power of creativity.

Someone asked me recently, "Do you receive any criticism for using the word 'innertainment'?" Now and then we'll face opposition because of this slogan. However, as the local church, I think that we need to capture and hold the attention of someone for an extended period of time. That's the only way to communicate the life-changing message of Christ in a meaningful, relevant way. Obviously, God is the One who convicts people and drives home the message, but we also have a role in capturing the attention of our people so that they can connect with God.

When I think about creating an inspirational worship environment, the different moods of the service come to mind. Our teams work at varying the highs and lows throughout each service. Sometimes we'll start off with a high note—with an upbeat tempo and a very celebratory feeling. Other times, we'll start off with a low note and a more contemplative mood. We may open the service with a statement like, "Thank you for being here. Let's worship God." And then we spend fifteen to twenty minutes in nothing but back-to-back worship songs. Or we may begin with a serious drama or a humorous video opener. We're constantly changing.

Hopefully, through changing moods and innovative methods of worship, our people will be inspired to live a Christian life of excitement and vitality. The good news is just that—good news. It should create an attitude of adventure as we live out the reality of it day after day. We have the hope of the world and we need to give that hope out in a way that inspires others to worship a living and dynamic God.

Everything we do is done with the goal of life change, from our FC Sports activities to our E2 assimilation classes; from the Mix senior high ministry to our adult Power Source Bible study classes. And, as I've said repeatedly, the worship service is the greatest opportunity we have to effect change in the greatest number of lives. Worship is all about life change—doing something that will change people's lives for the better as they encounter God in new and different ways.

Maybe someone has come to one of our services to investigate the claims of Christ, and one defining moment captures their heart and secures their eternity forever. We pray and work diligently for these critical moments. Sometimes a divine moment will occur in the middle of a drama. Other times, a video testimony might break down the final barriers of unbelief. Maybe a U2 song will connect the seeker with the truths of the upcoming message. Life change happens by loving people enough to help them connect with the Savior in a real and personal way. And we do that as we inspire them through creative worship experiences.

Promotion

Before we address the final part of the worship bridge, let's review. So far, if we're going to build a worship bridge that connects people to God, our services must be welcoming, organized, relevant, sensitive, an hour long, and inspirational. *P* stands for *promotional.*

The worship service is the ideal time to promote events to your entire church. However, exercise caution here. I'm talking about strategic promotion. Don't use the worship hour to promote every activity and program in your ministry. You promote the things that influence and affect the most people.

Let me make another suggestion. Do not interrupt your worship service to take care of these announcements. A lot of churches do that, and they break the mood and the work of the spirit of God. If you're going to relay the announcements, do them before or after the service. But only hit the most important things—we agree to do one out of every ten "important" announcements. And I approve those personally. I take that announcement card every weekend and cut it down to the bare minimum. Do not let someone or some group henpeck you and influence you to give a certain announcement. You only give the announcements that matter most to the most number of people. Typically, we use the end of the service to give those three or four quick announcements that I've determined need to be made during that time.

We'll also create videos to promote big events that are coming up, especially related to our children and student ministries. We've done videos to promote our student beach or mountain retreats, our Adventure Weeks (or vacation Bible school in the traditional church lingo), and our children's camps. In addition, we run video promos on our women's retreats, major singles events (like New Year's Eve), and upcoming series.

When I talk about promotional videos, I'm not suggesting that you shoot an epic. These videos should be no more than a couple of minutes long, straight to the point, with a biting and edgy feel. And the purpose is to compel people to attend, so keep it upbeat, positive, and, yes, entertaining. We use these videos to say, *Here is what we're about at Fellowship Church. And here is what's coming up in the summer. You and your family do not want to miss out on these incredible events!*

After showing a promo video, I've even gone so far as to say something like this, "If your kids are not signed up yet for children's camp or beach retreat or Adventure Week or the Elevation high school retreat, I have to ask, 'What are you smoking?' You will not find a better time for your kids this summer than right here at Fellowship Church, and you need to make sure that they are a part of it."

What are these videos saying? They're saying to parents, "Hey, young people matter. Children matter. Students matter. This church is concerned about changing the course of our culture." And they come. They come in droves when they see that Fellowship cares about kids. We concentrate our promotion on children and students, because not only does a church rise and fall on the effectiveness and growth of its ministry to the younger generation, but the spiritual climate of our culture rises and falls on that as well.

One of the perennial challenges of the church is how to get the lily and poinsettia crowd to come more than twice a year. One of the things we decided to do is start a big series on Easter Sunday. Most churches do a stand-alone Easter message. We rarely do that. Easter is usually the start of a new series that we've promoted heavily ahead of time. And then we make sure the Easter service gets them talking and wanting to come back for the entire series. It might be a series on marriage, friendship, lust, priorities, or any number of topics relevant to their everyday life. We tie the Easter message of the death, burial, and resurrection into the first installment in the series and leave them wanting more, so they'll come back the next week and the next.

The remaining weeks in the series are also critical, especially the second week, when we show unchurched attendees what a non-holiday weekend is like at Fellowship. They need to know that we strive for excellence every weekend of the year and not just at Christmas and Easter. How you handle the weeks after holidays will determine the number of unchurched people who get plugged into the life of the church. Since we've begun to focus on those post-Easter weeks, our numbers following Easter have been incredible.

On Christmas, we usually do not begin a new series, because we know many people are gone for a week or two after Christmas. We may end a series on Christmas weekend, but we've not found it to be a good time to start one. We do, however, promote the new January series during that time. In fact, our Christmas mailer that promotes the Christmas services always promotes the upcoming series for the new year as well. And we promote the New Year series heavily in the Christmas services as well. We show a creative video promo, announce it from the stage, and print a big ad in the worship guide. Again, the series after Christmas must be something that reaches people where they are. This last year we did a series about getting the priorities God has given us to sync up with our daily commitments. We've done a New Year series on health, decision-making, and any number of other practical topics.

Promotion is not a bad word. It gets people in the right place at the right time, so their lives and destinies can be changed forever.

The preceding seven W.O.R.S.H.I.P. principles have been born and implemented as God has allowed Fellowship Church to help reach the Dallas–Forth Worth area. The church is once again at a critical stage in North America. If we church leaders can't provide the bridge to our communities, thousands of seekers will lose out on the amazing blessings of the Bride of Christ. I encourage you to go through these seven principles with your staff and leadership team and evaluate the creative culture of your church against this W.O.R.S.H.I.P. paradigm.

*He did not say anything
to them without using
a parable.*

MARK 4:34

CHAPTER 6

Creative Communication

God, please use my voice box to communicate the words You want me to say today. Use me to creatively connect the life-changing message of Jesus Christ to every heart and every life here. And it's in His name that I pray, amen."

I pray a prayer like that every weekend. Whether I whisper it privately in the green room before I speak or publicly in corporate prayer, I never, ever forget that I am speaking for God.

What an awesome privilege it is to speak on behalf of God! Take a moment to reflect upon that amazing responsibility. Teachers and preachers in the local church are called to pass on the timeless truths of Scripture to the people God has entrusted to our care. It doesn't matter if you are a children's pastor, a youth pastor, or a senior pastor, we all share in this high honor. I told a group of senior pastors recently that 75 percent of their weekly schedule should revolve around the preparation and delivery of their weekend message. The other stuff is important, but nothing is as important as preaching

*If I am to speak ten minutes, I need a week for
preparation; if fifteen minutes, three days; if half an
hour, two days; if an hour, I am ready now.*

WOODROW WILSON

and teaching God's truth to the hundreds and thousands who sit at our feet week in and week out.

Because preaching is such a high honor and responsibility, I have committed most of my ministry to improving in this art and science and would like to share some methods from my own teaching ministry that hopefully can help you in yours. Some of the best insights I've gleaned have come from other creative speakers, whether through interacting with them at our annual creative church conference or through learning from some close friends in the ministry. You can learn what to do and what not to do by studying others.

Notice I said to *study* others, not copy them. The most important principle for effective communication is to let you be you. Don't imitate another speaker. You can learn some tips and techniques from others but be the unique person God has made you to be. Just be yourself and improve on the personality and skills that God has given you. Ineffective speakers are counterfeit communicators who seem to transform from their usual demeanor into a foreign, phony version of themselves when they hit the stage. Remember that we are called to preach with our words and also with the lifestyle we lead. There has to be a connection between who we are every day and who we are on stage—a theme that runs throughout this discussion on the four principles to add creativity and vitality to your teaching ministry.

Think Big

Whenever you speak, especially as a Christian communicator, you must address two fundamental questions: (1) What does the listener need to know and (2) what does the listener need to do? In other words, before you speak, ask, What am I going to say and how should the listener apply it? It's the old "so what?" principle. That's thinking big.

The "so what?" principle is all about application. As previously mentioned, 72 percent of Christ's words were words of application. If our preaching is not patterned on the greatest and most creative Communicator, something is wrong. Most of us struggle to communicate; we include too much content and too little application. When people leave the auditorium or sanctuary, they should not be saying, "So what?" or "Big deal!" They should be saying, "Wow, I get it! I need to make some changes in my life."

You are not teaching a seminary class with a focus on imparting information from a syllabus. The goal of preaching is life change. Preaching is an incredible challenge that requires sensitivity to the Bible and sensitivity to our culture. The Bible is already relevant. But you have to ensure that your message highlights and underscores that relevancy. Fill your message with points of application that are organized and communicated with the greatest potential impact possible, so that your congregation will be compelled to conform to the powerful truths found in Scripture.

To help prepare such messages, I use something called a *mind* or *message map*. I have given a couple of examples in the appendixes (see apps. 6 and 7). If you are visually oriented like I am, I would encourage you to try it. I first learned about mind mapping from author Michael Gelb's *Mind Mapping: How to Liberate Your Natural Genius*. I have modified Gelb's method over the years, but I still develop what I call a mind map, which is the entire sermon on one legal size sheet of paper, front and back, in clockwise order starting at the top (you'll have a better idea of what this looks like by referencing the appendix).

I used to painstakingly handwrite, color-code, and illustrate my mind maps. But now we use a computer to develop them. I still do quite a bit of color-coding and add handwritten notes to aid in memorization; however, the format has changed quite a bit from my earlier versions (you'll also find a handwritten version in the appendix). About four years ago, someone on my staff developed a template in Microsoft Word to create this document electronically. I have heard that there is also mind-mapping software out there if you're interested in that. We have also made my mind maps for various message series available on CreativePastors.com when a "pastor's kit" is purchased.

The idea behind the mind map is that organizing your outline or word-for-word manuscript in a clockwise rotation aids in memory retention. Because of the way the mind stores and associates words and images, the map helps you quickly identify the big idea and major transitional phrases, illustrations, and sub points that flow from that big idea. The mind map has served as a very helpful visual cue to remind me of what the talk is all about, to aid in memorization (though I memorize only major elements and key phrases that I need to remember word for word), and to keep everything connected to that one big idea.

Sweat the Small Stuff

Often, the most important and powerful ingredients of an effective talk are tacked on at the very end of your preparation time, and the overall message suffers as a result. Those ingredients—titles, terms, intros and conclusions, transitions, and illustrations—deserve more time and energy.

Sweat Your Titles

Titles should be tantalizing and build interest for your message before you speak one word. It's just like fishing: if you want to catch a big bass, you have got to have a lure that turns the bass's head.

It's easy to come up with seminary-friendly titles like, "Sanctification and Social Ethics," or "Unrealized Eschatology in a Postmodern World." You may love these titles, but they are not very audience-friendly. To most people in your church, it sounds like you are from another planet. It is vitally important that everyone in your audience can connect with your title.

What does an effective title look like? You'll have to make that determination based on your communication style and your particular audience. Here are a few series titles that have worked well at Fellowship. I believe these titles have helped to bridge the gap between the ancient complexities of the Bible and the contemporary world of our audience.

- God Online (worship)
- Know Fear (fear)
- The Ulti-Mate (dating/spouse selection)
- Sinetics (sin/temptation)
- Parent Map (parenting)
- Got Stress? (stress/anxiety)
- Tri-God (the Trinity)
- You Got Game? (church vision/ministry involvement)
- The Perfect Storm (navigating the crises of life)
- Everything You Need to Know about Life Is in Your Fishbowl (relationships)
- Just Lust (lust/sexual temptation and addiction)

I'm not saying these titles are the best out there or that you need to compare your titles to ours. I've seen many churches and pastors come up with better stuff than this. And you can too, if you take time to sweat the titles.

The speakers at our church exhaust themselves trying to come up with titles that both creatively and accurately describe the main point of the message. It takes a lot of work to take a complex subject and make it concise as well as compelling. Anyone can spout theological jargon, but the road from a complex subject to a simple title is filled with obstacles. And those obstacles must be navigated successfully if you are going to improve as a communicator. The greatest communicators know how to take the complexities of the Bible and make them simple.

Define Complex Terms

Making the complex simple goes way beyond the creation of the title. If you are going to really connect with today's audience, you must take time to define complex terms in your message in easy-to-grasp language. Not simplistic, but simple; there is a difference. Being simplistic is condescending to your audience and communicating in a way that is naïve and disconnected from real life. Simple is respecting your audience enough to explain in easy-to-understand terms exactly what it is they *need to know* and *need to do*. It is loving them enough to make sure they get it.

You don't need to talk to them like children, but you do need to think long and hard about how your language and terminology is connecting with the real world of the listener. That may mean finding other, more contemporary, ways to communicate heavy theological terms. And if you need to use those theological terms, explain and define them. Many seminarians don't fully understand what sanctification or salvation means, so how can the average church audience (especially those from an unchurched background) be expected to grasp terms like that?

Remember: if you cannot explain something in a simple way, you don't really understand it. It's easy for us to talk over people's heads by using theological jargon or by speaking "Christianese," but then we're not explaining ideas in simple terms that meet people where they are. On the other hand, when we communicate biblical principles in clear, relevant language, powerful communication occurs.

Concentrate on Bookends

The bookends are the introduction and conclusion. The introduction, in my opinion, is the most important aspect of the message. In the first ninety seconds of your talk, people are attentive and curious, but you must give them a compelling reason to continue the journey with you for the next twenty-five to thirty minutes.

One Sunday after the service, my wife and I flew to Tulsa and then drove about three hours to a place in Missouri. As we drove to Missouri, we paid close attention to the road signs. We need road signs in strange cities because they tell us how to get where we are going. I have heard too many messages that feature an attractive speaking voice, funny stories, and dramatic illustrations but lack clear direction. The listener is stranded out the middle of unknown territory without any road signs.

The introduction is the first crucial step in providing that much-needed direction to your listeners, who are wondering, *Where is this speaker going to take me?* You have just a few minutes to impart that the destination is worth the ride. If they find the first leg of the journey unappealing or irrelevant, you have lost them for the duration.

That doesn't mean that you have to give your entire outline during the introduction. It's OK to keep them wondering what's coming next or to build tension in the sermon. In fact, I recommend a lot of tension. You just need to give them enough direction to get them to the next sign. Every road sign leads to the next and gives hints as to the final destination. Effective communicators reveal the final destination at the end, building a case from the beginning as to why listeners should pay attention. You've got to give them a reason to listen, even if it is just to relieve the tension that you've built along the way. A good introduction can hook the audience and allow you to reel them in little by little until you have reached the final conclusion.

Everything you say in the introduction must be purposeful and related to your big idea. Don't walk behind your Plexiglas pulpit or lectern, turn, and say, "Thank you, choir. That reminds me of a joke. You know Roy Clark one time said . . ." if Roy Clark doesn't have anything to do with your big idea. Everything you communicate from the moment you stand up must contribute to the big idea.

With that in mind, I submit that pastors should never speak until it is time for the message. You might say, "Well, Ed, my church has fifty people." Others might respond, "You don't understand, Ed, I am the best guy to do it." I still believe the speaker should not utter a word until the message is at hand. Instead of stretching yourself too thin and taking away from the impact of your message, try an alternative. Train others for those roles that require leadership from the stage—for pastoral prayers, for Scripture reading, for the welcome, for announcements, for leading music, and for anything else that takes place during the weekend service.

If you are trying to do all of that and still give a powerful, relevant, creative message, you are not only setting yourself up for burnout but also taking away from the impact of the message. Give the ball of ministry to others and you'll develop competent stage leaders and ensure that the impact of those first few crucial words of your introduction will not be muted.

Let me also suggest that you use a variety of approaches in your introductions. I know how easy and safe it is to come out week after week and use the same format for your messages. You tell a funny story, introduce the big idea, transition to your three main points and conclude with a summary and restatement of the big idea. That's not a bad approach, but it's also very predictable. If you're going to keep your audience guessing, if you're going to keep the connectivity high, you must keep the predictability low.

I'd like to offer a play-by-play description of a recent series I did, not to say that my ideas are the benchmark but to illustrate the randomness and variety that can be achieved in introductory remarks throughout a series of talks. A recent six-week series on the lordship of Christ was called "Thread: Reconnecting the Disconnected Fabric of Our Lives" (the same one we handed out thread bracelets for). For the first weekend, which was Easter, we introduced the message with a video of a tailor making a special suit coat for me to wear on Easter. I came out wearing that coat (which is a departure from my normally casual attire) and talked about the fact that our culture is into fashion—a reality that is especially true in the Dallas area.

Then, as I was talking about our passion for fashion, I took off my jacket, grabbed a pair of scissors, and began to cut up the suit coat. The audience had no idea why I was doing that. Later, I revealed the reason—our lives are torn and fragmented and we need God's tailor-made coat, Jesus Christ, to make us whole again.

The next week I came out and asked the question, Where are you? and tied that into God's question to Adam and Eve when they first sinned. This led to the fact that we all hide from Christ from time to time and hide Him from others.

The third week I talked about our affinity for mirrors in the introduction; we all love to look in the mirror. That reflected the truth that we are to be mirror images of God, because that is why He created us in the first place.

The fourth week in the series was my personal favorite. I began the sermon sitting on the bandstand, singing the classic pop song by Gemini, "Feelings, whoa-oh-oh, feelings . . ." After I sang the song, I didn't explain why I sang it. People didn't know whether to laugh or to take me seriously, as if I were really singing a special number. After the song, I just stood up, as if this performance was perfectly normal, and started reading the story about Jesus' encounter with a prostitute in John 4. My brother calls her the "whore in John 4" (the word *whore* is used at least seventy-five times in the Bible, so no letters or e-mails, please). Anyway, I went from singing "Feelings" to Jesus talking to a prostitute about worshiping God in "spirit and in truth."

What's that got to do with feelings? Well, I brought the talk around to the misconceptions that many have about worship. We cannot focus on the spirit to the exclusion of the truth (that's overemotionalism). And, conversely, when we focus only on the truth and ignore the spirit, we step over the line into legalism. Spirit and truth are interconnected and interdependent.

The fifth week, in a message on the names of God, I began by describing a common scenario where you see someone you recognize at a party, but can't remember their name. And to your horror, they come over to you as you are chatting with a group of friends. "You have two choices during the awkward moment when this person is expecting to be introduced to your friends," I told the audience. "One, hope they take the initiative and introduce themselves first, or two, tell them the truth—you are an idiot and can't remember their name."

This led to the idea that God introduces Himself to us in the Bible with various names that describe His relationship with us. I won't go into each name here, but the names of God correspond with a way in which He provides for us, protects us, saves us, and leads us. Later in the message I said, "You may be able to introduce God—sure, you know what His name is—but can He introduce you? Does He know you as a friend?"

Finally, in the concluding session of this series, I did something I've never done before. I came out on stage totally drenched. I had just been dunked backstage and came out drying my sopping wet hair with a beach towel. Water was dripping on stage as I began to recount several events in the New Testament. I told of John 1:29 where John the Baptist sees Jesus in the distance and shouts, "Look, the Lamb of God, who takes away the sin of the world!" I talked about the day of Pentecost when three thousand people became believers. I mentioned Philip's encounter with an Ethiopian eunuch and how this man came to faith. And then I talked about Peter and Cornelius in Acts 10 and the spreading of the gospel to the Gentiles.

I ran through all of this very quickly in the introduction, and then I said: "What do these things have in common: Starbucks coffee, a jet ski, a catfish, a lily pad, a rose, and a Christian? The answer is, for each of them to realize their full potential, you have to 'just add water.'"

And then I went back to each of these biblical stories and added the fact that Jesus was baptized by John the Baptist, 3,000 were baptized at Pentecost, the Ethiopian eunuch was baptized, and the Gentile believers were baptized. That led to a message on the significance and symbolism of baptism in the life of every Christ follower.

Something else we've found very effective is to occasionally give something to each person in the audience as an illustration prior to or during the introduction. I did a series several years ago called "Juicy Fruit," on the fruit of the Spirit, in which we gave a piece of Juicy Fruit gum to every person in the audience. Then I said, "One, two, three, take out the gum and chew. Feel that burst of Juicy Fruit flavor? Doesn't this taste good? But you know what? I have timed it. In three minutes the flavor will dissipate and begin to taste like Styrofoam."

Later, I compared food that loses its flavor to the Spirit's fruit, "The flavor of the food we are talking about from the Bible does not dissipate. It keeps getting juicer and juicer and juicer. Every time you put gum in your mouth, think about producing the fruit, the character qualities, mentioned in Galatians."

Those are just some of the ways that can create variety in introducing your message each week. Variety is essential to keep your audience guessing and your creative juices going.

The other bookend, of course, is the conclusion. When people leave the auditorium, I want them to have a final thought to take home—a thought that pulls together everything I've talked about in the message from the introduction on. In effect, the conclusion is what the entire talk would be if you delivered it in two minutes or fewer (which is what the length of concluding remarks should be). As one of my former seminary professors said, "Land the plane already!" Anything longer and you'll start preaching the whole thing over again.

Don't underestimate the importance of your conclusion. I believe one of the reasons why the Beatles songs are still so popular is because every one of them has a definite conclusion. You never have to wonder when the song is over, unlike many songs these days that just kind of fade out. I learned this principle while studying musical theory at Florida State University and have never forgotten it. Too many preachers' messages just fade out instead of concluding powerfully.

Highlight and Memorize Transitions

A third ingredient that is often overlooked in the preaching process is the effective use of transitions. Consider highlighting and memorizing transitions, because these pivotal segues are critical to retain the interest of your audience and clarity of your message. Not only do they smooth out the flow of your talk, but they also provide important verbal clues in your mind as you move from one major point to another. Be sure you critique yourself rigorously on these transitions. If you are going to memorize anything word for word, transitions are the best way to invest this time.

Transitional statements are some of the most important, yet most neglected elements in speaking. Without them, you are lost in a jumble of disjointed facts, illustrations, and points—and so is your audience. These transitional statements (indicated on my mind map with the initials *T.S.*) bring unity, cohesion, and integrity to your talk. Especially important are transitions from your introduction to the body of your talk as well as from any major illustration to its corresponding application. If you don't transition well, your listeners are spending so much time trying to figure out what one part of your talk has to do with another that they miss half of your message. Transitions help your listener stay cued into the organization of your message.

Don't ever assume the connective fiber of your talk is obvious or understood. It may be understood in your own mind, but transitional statements help the audience understand the direction in which you want them to go.

Personal and Biblical Illustrations Are Best

While most speakers know the importance of timely illustrations, few consistently offer personal and biblical illustrations, which is unfortunate. Why? Because personal and biblical illustrations are always the best way to give an abstract truth a concrete home in everyday life.

I have nothing against illustrations and anecdotes from books, but I have not found those as effective as using stories from my own life or those of biblical characters. I love to hear speakers talk about their lives, so why would I expect my audience to be any different?

When we allow the audience into our lives to discover that we aren't perfect, we connect more deeply and identify more significantly with them. An important warning here is to emphasize our weaknesses more than our strengths when we use personal illustrations. In other words, don't make yourself the hero of all your stories. Talk about your bad days as well as your good, showing how you have submitted to God in circumstances and have been blessed because of it. In other words, whether you're talking about good times or bad, God is always the hero of the story. His strength, not ours, is the catalyst for change.

As far as biblical illustrations go, you know as well as I do that the Bible is rich with stories that perfectly communicate the love, mercy, and grace of God. God could have had the biblical authors pen a heavy doctrinal dissertation on His historical interaction with humankind, but He didn't. He had them write the stories of their lives and God's faithfulness in spite of their failures. God knew that we would connect in a deeper way with stories, so He used them to communicate His great love for us. We should follow His lead when we teach and preach.

One of my favorite biblical illustrations to contemporize is the David and Goliath story. In one message I said that if a modern-day sports announcer from ESPN had been on the scene when David fought Goliath, it might have sounded like this: "Welcome to the Valley of Elah arena for this afternoon's World Heavyweight Biblical Championship. In this corner, fighting out of the Hebrew camp, standing five feet three and weighing 138 pounds, he is a shepherd, a poet, a musician . . . the Hebrew hillbilly, David! His opponent from Gath stands over nine feet tall, weighs 438 pounds, and has an undefeated record of seventy-two victories—all by decapitation. He is the heavyweight champion of the world: Goliath! Let's get ready to rumble! Sports fans, it is going to be a short bout because Goliath has a four-foot advantage."

I do this to entertain the audience for a few minutes but also to, as Tony Evans says, take the listener and put him in the sandals of the biblical characters.

In another message, I talked about the time when Samson torched the foxes' tails and they burned up the grain fields of a Philistine homemaker. I told people to put themselves in the sandals of the Philistine homemaker. Let's say she is doing her dishes when she looks out her window and sees 300 foxes with their tails on fire, burning up her field. Suddenly, they can relate to that.

Use the creativity God has given you to bring those legendary stories of the Bible to your contemporary audience. And then stand back and watch God work in the hearts and lives of your people as they identify in personal ways with great men and women of faith.

So sweat the small stuff. Obviously, your main points are important and you've got to have the meat of your message down pat. But don't neglect these crucial ingredients that bring the whole meal together in the best presentation possible: the titles, terms, introduction and conclusion, transitions, and personal and biblical illustrations.

Know Your Audience

Other pastors often ask me if Fellowship is "one of those seeker-sensitive churches." The short answer is yes and no. Here's the long answer. I do not buy into a *seeker-targeted* approach in the popular meaning of that term. Our weekend services are not designed for the unchurched seeker or the veteran saint. They are designed with everyone in mind.

I am seeker-sensitive or seeker-targeted in that I believe everyone is a seeker. We all want answers to the complexities of life. And when you proclaim the Word of God in comprehensible language with contemporary illustrations and applications, the truth will feed everyone. You can plan services each and every week that simultaneously serve the seeker and build the believer. Any given service may be weighted in one direction or another, but they should all have meaning for everyone in your church.

Speak to the Chairs

Something that helps keep me balanced in the way I plan and deliver messages is remembering to *speak to the chairs*. I envision a table with four chairs. I am sitting in the head chair and in the three other chairs are a hell-bound seeker, a baby Christian, and a mature believer. As God has built Fellowship over the years, and as I have observed the growth of other church bodies, I have become convinced that any growing, vibrant local church is going to comprise one-third hell-bound seekers, one-third baby Christians, and one-third mature Christians.

When all three of these groups are equally represented, tremendous vitality will result. The mature Christians can train up the baby Christians. Both the mature and baby Christians can evangelize the seekers. You might remember my friend Scott from the story in the first chapter. My experience with him helped me realize that the local church cannot be exclusively reserved for the already-convinced crowd. We should always be sensitive to the person who does not know Christ, while at the same time, think about the veteran Christians in the audience and those who may be new in their faith.

Speaking to the chairs is a great visual reminder as I prepare for any new series of talks. When I study, I target specific groups in our church and mentally assign a specific person to that chair. For instance, when I speak about single parenting, I set up a chair in my mind and visualize a single parent that I know in our congregation. I might also set up chairs for high school and college students when I'm doing a series on dating. I have chairs for the married couple, the elderly, and always the chairs of spiritual development for the pre-Christian, the baby Christian, and the seasoned believer.

Certain series lean more decidedly toward some of these groups. When we planned a series on worship, I set up chairs for baby Christians, struggling Christians, and mature Christians. We still had seekers attend who, although they could not fully understand it since they were outside the family of God, caught a glimpse of what it means to worship God in spirit and truth. Other series may feature sermons that are more targeted toward the seeker crowd. Just remember to let your preaching target specific people filling the mental chairs in your audience.

Serve a Balanced Diet

If you're going to reach everyone, not only should you speak to the chairs, you must also *serve a balanced diet*. When it comes to planning your weekly speaking calendar, you must think strategically through your messages and maintain a varied menu. Just like parents need to plan ahead to ensure that their children are receiving their proper nutrients, pastors and teachers need to consider the spiritual and emotional needs of their audience and plan accordingly.

Some series will be lighter in nature and geared toward a specific contemporary issue of the day. Other series might be more intense, theological talks on the doctrine of worship or the Trinity. I am very fond of series and messages on biblical characters, but I don't do those every time I speak—more like one series a year. I also typically do one series on dating and spouse selection every year, because it is the second most important decision we ever make. Parents also eat these messages up since they are responsible for training their children in dating and spouse selection. And speaking of parenting, I try to do a parenting series at least once every other year. The same is true with teaching on marriage.

Regular evaluation is necessary to ensure that you are serving a balanced diet. Make sure that you are including expository messages, character studies, relational series, topical studies on other contemporary issues, as well as casting the vision for your church regularly. I try to do a series on church vision at least once a year, even if it's just a two- to three-week series. Are you serving a balanced diet? Evaluate yourself regularly to make sure your people are being fed a healthy diet from the pulpit.

Deliver the Goods

Obviously, we cannot talk about creative communication without thinking about the speaker's delivery style. Many pastors and teachers excel in preparation and study but fall short when it comes time to delivering the goods each week. As pastors, we are pros at the academic level, aren't we? It's no doubt a habit we picked up in seminary and that follows us into our preaching and teaching ministry. But we have to transfer that knowledge to a contemporary audience that did not attend seminary. We are tasked to communicate what we know in the most effective, compelling, and creative way possible.

Let's focus on a few suggestions to help your effectiveness as a speaker.

Go Noteless as Much as Possible

To recall the structure of your talk, keep a message outline with you to glance at very briefly (see app. 8) but don't get to a place where you are forced to read your sermon. When I say to go noteless as much as possible, I mean that you should know your talk so well that you need your notes only as a fallback. In other words, if the dog ate your notes, would you be able to go through with your talk?

On the notes I paperclip to the pages of my Bible, I have only my main points, a couple of key words to describe my illustrations, and the text of the Scripture I'll be using. Occasionally, I will also include the exact wording of a phrase, a quote, a statistic, or a definition I want to use. That's it. And most of the time, I just use my notes when I'm reading Scripture or an exact quote.

The communicative process is easily broken when you break eye contact to read something from your outline. If you glance down quickly, that is fine. Too many of these breaks, though, will disconnect your audience from what God has given you and what you have worked so tirelessly to prepare.

An advantage of reading your points is that you can use the exact word choices you planned on. But you can do that without glancing down at your notes. Most churches today have teleprompters or monitors that can be used to display your main points and Scripture text. Your media guys should know the order of your talk and have the notes loaded in so that the next point or Scripture verse comes up on the monitor before you say it. I would not put the entire text of your sermon on those prompters, but it is helpful, again as a fallback, to have the points and Scripture (along with any detailed quotes, definitions, stats) available on stage monitors for your eyes only. It limits the distraction of watching the pastor look down at his notes.

I used to have my main points of application displayed on the side screens for the audience to see, but I don't always do that now. Sometimes I do and sometimes I don't—I like to keep the audience guessing. Sometimes the talk will have carefully worded points of application that I want to display for the audience, and sometimes the talk is more free-flowing, so the only thing I display on the side screens is the Scripture I use.

Do Something Unexpected

I hope by now we've sufficiently addressed the need to change things up regularly in the church. We've called it being "consistently inconsistent," but whatever title you give it, doing the unexpected is critically important when it comes to communication. As a speaker, I ask, *What are the people expecting?* and then try to do the exact opposite—something out in left field, something totally unexpected.

One example is when we began a sermon by opening our stage curtain to reveal a military tank (a British Scorpion, to be precise) that covered our entire stage. The talk was on spiritual warfare and my message began inside the tank via live video. People still talk about that years later.

During a recent series on stewardship and tithing, I delivered part of my message from New York City's Times Square. I gave part of the message live on stage, then transitioned into the prerecorded video from New York, then eventually switched back to the live delivery. This takes some advanced planning and careful coordination as you transition from live to video, but it was extremely effective. What better place to talk about materialism, greed, and money management than from the heart of Times Square?

At times, I'll go through an entire series without using one video or visual. Other times, every week of the series will have one. Sometimes I will start a message with a controversial statement; other times, with a passage from Scripture. Sometimes I begin with prayer, and other times I will start with a story about something that happened the past week. I think you get the picture.

Another great way to introduce variety is by interviewing people in your church about real struggles and successes and then showing those videos during the weekend service. We do interviews with people to constantly remind our church of the life change that is happening week in and week out. We've even done an entire series just on these stories called "FC: True Stories." Those real-life stories keep the purpose and vision of the church white hot in people's minds.

Seeing these interviews is like a breath of fresh air for your audience as well as for the person responsible for speaking every week. Hearing how real people are impacted for eternity keeps you going as a speaker and keeps your people motivated to serve. It's one thing to tell a secondhand story about someone's life being changed; it's quite another to see it in Technicolor from the person's own mouth.

One of the biggest hang-ups I see in communicators is that we are wired for routine. If we aren't careful, we will box ourselves in and become too predictable. When this happens, we stifle our creativity and limit our communicative potential. I realized a few years ago that I was using too many acrostics. Several people on staff, during our critique sessions, said I might want to cut back a little on them. People started calling Fellowship "the church of acrostics." That was true. Variation is key because (again) the higher the predictability, the lower the communication. So throw in a change-up. It's not easy, but it is essential.

Touch Their Senses

We have been given five senses, so a good sermon should touch more than the sense of hearing. The most effective communicators combine other senses for a richer, more meaningful experience for the audience. You can use artwork, sculpture, aquariums, music, or lighting to help create the proper mood and setting for what you're trying to communicate. Or you can hand out items like Juicy Fruit gum, Life Savers candy, thread bracelets, or a book to drive home a point. We've used all of those visuals to do just that.

You can even create different aromas to bring people into the context of your message. For one sermon called "Parental Popcorn," we brought in popcorn machines so that the smell of buttered popcorn would hit people as soon as they entered the lobby. During a series entitled "Espresso Yourself," we had a scratch-and-sniff worship guide that smelled like espresso (at least, it was supposed to).

I hope these examples show you that it is possible to bring our senses of hearing, sight, touch, taste, and smell into the mix. It's not just about the big three—video, drama, and music. The options are limitless. The more senses you awaken in the audience, the more effective the delivery. And the more effective the delivery, the more potential you have to move people toward life change for the glory of God.

Preaching is a tremendous responsibility and an honor given to very few Christian leaders. We must cherish this God-given task and use the best we have to share the truth about Jesus Christ. In this chapter we have looked at thinking big, sweating the small stuff, knowing the audience, and delivering the goods as ways to enhance your creative communication style. Remember to study other speakers you admire but commit to finding your own voice.

Having already said that I tend to use too many acrostics, please allow me to close with an acrostic that helps me know if I am ready to deliver the goods each week. I often wonder if I'm ready to preach. Spend some time asking and honestly answering the same question: Are you ready to P.R.E.A.C.H.?

P.R.E.A.C.H.

P is for *prepared*. Have I put time into sermon preparation? Even when our church had 200 people, I put at least 70 percent of my time in message preparation. Have you committed enough time to get ready for your responsibility? People desperately need the truth of God served in a compelling fashion.

R is for *relevant*. Make what is complex simple. Ask the questions the audience is asking and bring up questions the audience is not asking.

E is for *encouraging*. When you talk about a difficult subject— say, Samson pushing down the pillars, destroying the Philistines, and ending his own life—offer the hope of God there. Include encouragement for the audience in the midst of a biblical tragedy.

A is for *application*. What does your audience need to know, say, and do in this situation. Answer the "so what?" question. Give them the take-home.

C is for *concise*. The test here is to boil down the goal of your talk into one phrase or short sentence. Can you do that? If not, you might not know enough about the destination of your talk or your reason for preaching it. Remember, the best communicators make the most difficult truths simple and concise.

H is for *honest*. Am I showing some vulnerability? Am I touching people's hearts? You don't need to air all of your dirty laundry or be the hero of all your stories. Show them that you are a flawed sinner like they are and win their respect.

If you occasionally begin to feel overwhelmed, as I do, by the waves crashing on your head week after week, I pray this chapter on creative communication will help you get your head above water to be the kind of preacher and teacher God wants you to be.

Creative Q & A: Section 2

Q: You talked about being "consistently inconsistent" in ministry. What are some practical things that I can do to in my own church to apply this principle without having to make major adjustments or changes right off the bat?

A: When I talk about being consistently inconsistent, I'm simply saying that you need to get people out of the normal routine they are used to.

Some very simple things can introduce variety to produce growth in your church and can be implemented today. For example, change the songs used by the praise team or choir. Choose a few songs that not everyone sitting in the seats knows by heart. And change what time during the service they sing. Maybe change the time you take communion. Or change your attire a little bit—try a sweater instead of a tie! You can even change the bulletin and use it as an outreach tool—include invitations to future services for people to hand out to their neighbors or friends (see app. 9).

You won't believe what will happen when you start to make some minor adjustments to the way you do church. I'm not talking about radical stuff. Small tweaks will take you to giant peaks.

When people come to your church, they should be literally sitting on the edge of their seats, saying, "Wow, what in the world are they going to do next? Man, this is incredible!" Again, I'm not talking about style or flair; I'm talking about the innate value of creativity that God has given you to change the way people look at church.

When something is biblical, whether it is your weekend service or your relationship with your family, it will be creative. And with creativity, you always have change. But change is not all about chaos; it's about confusion. So change your routine from time to time and keep the people on their toes. They will look expectantly and excitedly to what's coming up the next week, and the next, and the next.

People in our church are always expecting us to change something. We have changed so much over the years—locations, our name, the style of worship, the look of the bulletin—that they are always looking for the next change. And we are going to continue to make changes. Our church will not look or act as it does today five years from now. We will still be teaching the Bible in an uncompromising fashion, but I can guarantee we will be different. Our message won't change, but our method will. It's what God wants us to do to effectively and actively reach people.

Q: How do you develop series and message ideas? Is there a set format or process that you follow every time you develop a message?

A: When it comes to developing material for series and messages, there's no limit to where ideas can come from. For inspiration I've used everything from feeding my dogs to family vacations and from bug zappers to fishing lures. I just keep my eye open for anything that could lead in the direction of a message and let God show me what I can use.

Using everyday events in your life is a key element of effective communication. For example, one time I found a snake in my garage and had one of our video guys come out so I could capture it on film and use it later as a sermon illustration. A pastor friend of mine joked about that: "If I had found the snake," he said, "it would have been a nuisance. For Ed, it was a sermon illustration."

I also keep up with current events, trends, fashion, music, and television shows to know what's going on in the world, so that I can reach the people inside (and outside) our church. But I'm not the only one who comes up with ideas. As I mentioned earlier in the book, I also rely heavily on staff members and other people in my life. Some of our greatest series and messages have come from the ideas of other people.

After we develop some ideas for a message, I take some time on my own to develop the idea. Typically, I spend at least twenty to twenty-five hours a week on message preparation—that includes time on my own and with the creative team. I have found that I need that quality time each week if I'm going to deliver the best message that I can. I spent that much time preparing ten years ago, and I spend that much time preparing today.

On Mondays, I study for about half the day on my own. I have an extensive library but usually open only the Bible during that time. I also use that time to brainstorm, writing down everything that comes to mind on whatever topic I'll be speaking on. The other half of the day is for appointments and a critique of the past weekend.

Tuesday morning I study for two to three hours then meet with the department heads for three to four hours. Tuesday midafternoon I bring our creative team together to work through the upcoming weekend message. This team consists of anywhere from four to six key staff members, depending on who I feel will be able to contribute most effectively.

Wednesday, I typically work all day on the message. I will study by myself in the morning and dictate a rough draft of the message. My assistant types that out, and then I spend the bulk of the afternoon with the creative team, crafting the final draft of the message. This is when I put everything into mind-map form. The message is typically done by Wednesday evening.

Thursday, I see various appointments and take care of regular church business. If we are doing a video or radio broadcast at the time, I might help record, edit, or critique it.

Friday is my day off. That time is reserved for my wife and kids. Then, on a normal Saturday, I get to the church at about one or two o'clock and work on fine-tuning the message until service time. I go back and forth with our media department, discussing slides and graphics and changing a point or tweaking a video.

I go over the message one final time with them, so they know exactly what I'm doing and when. And by the time the service rolls around, everyone is on the same page.

I mentioned earlier the mind-map format that I use. I've been using these to prepare for my messages for about ten years now and think that the benefits of mind mapping are huge. It helps me see the message on one sheet of paper, illustrating how every word is connected to the main idea. And it greatly improves the retention of my message. It's much easier to preach when I can tell my message like a story rather than a lecture.

Once I have gained the confidence that comes from having the material down cold, I am free to work on my delivery style rather than worrying about the details of the content. As you can see in the appendix, I used to write every word of my message on a legal sheet of paper with the big idea in the middle. I started at the top and moved clockwise. I used colors and symbols to memorize the message. It served me very well.

Now that I am doing the messages on the computer, the text is cut and pasted onto a mind-map template in the same clockwise orientation. I still use different colors of text to indicate transitional statements, illustrations, and major application points. And all of the Scripture is put in bold print. All of that is formatted on the computer and printed on a color printer. I then go back through as I'm memorizing it with highlighting pens and mark through each of those sections again to reinforce them in my mind. I pay special attention to those application points. For a message to be effective, you must have a lot of real-life application.

By using the mind map, I can more easily memorize the message because of the colors, the style, and the format. It's what I use as my final manuscript, so to speak, as I go over it on Saturday afternoon. And then I'm ready to deliver that message twice on Saturday and twice on Sunday.

Q: How do you develop, select, and use illustrations in your messages?

A: As I mentioned in this previous chapter, the best illustrations come from the Bible and your own life. Develop those illustrations. Funnel them through the creative seine of your own personality, style, background, and humor and make them a part of your teaching ministry.

A pastor friend of mine once told me that he writes everything down—every thought, every story, and every situation that may possibly have any relevance in the future. He takes notes on all of it. Sometimes he comes home and empties out pockets full of scrap paper with random notes and thoughts he jotted down throughout the day. Then he types them all out and stores them away in his computer in what he calls "buckets." He told me that he may have two years of illustrations or stories built up in each bucket before he decides to use any of them. But he doesn't throw anything out until it comes time to use it. And as he is developing his message, if an illustration doesn't fit the message, he will throw it out. But the key thing for him is to keep anything that may have a potential use in a message.

I like to think that a good illustration is like a good song. You can play it more than once. A bad illustration, on the other hand, should never be played at all. I have done illustrations the right way and I have done illustrations the wrong way. And I have learned several valuable lessons—especially when they crash and burn.

One of the biggest lessons I've discovered is to use an illustration only when it adds to the message. If they aren't doing that and they seem to be on a different train of thought, it doesn't matter how cute or funny or catchy they are—they aren't going to have any lasting significance. Don't use something just because it grabs the listeners' attention for ten or fifteen seconds. Make sure that it has a relevant point.

I heard Tony Evans say years ago, "If a visual does not stand on its own, don't use it." That doesn't mean that the illustration should stand apart from the message; it simply means you cannot force an illustration. Don't just say, "This music stand represents life, and its three legs represents the Trinity," and think it will connect with the audience. Sometimes that works if the illustration is pretty obvious. But if it is not easily understood and it doesn't support the big idea, get rid of it.

Also, find the right placement of those illustrations. They have to fit where they will have the most impact. I once did a message on the gap between our priorities and our commitments. I had a great illustration about a time that my son and I got stuck in my truck. As our creative team looked at the story, we dissected the story and tried putting it in two or three different spots throughout the talk before we found the place that it would have the most impact. We tried it at the end of the message, but that left something missing in the middle. We put it in the middle, but the introduction seemed flat. So finally, after going over it again and again, we decided that the best place for the illustration was in the introduction. It set up the body of the message and allowed me to circle back to it in the conclusion. Had we not gone through that much work on placing that one story, something would have been missing in the message. So make sure you find the right placement for your illustrations.

For illustrations to be great, they not only have to be placed properly, they have got to sound natural and easy. And that comes through the use of transitions. Here is where I have messed up before, thinking I have the perfect illustration and then getting lazy about building a transition to and from it. *Surely I can just do it on the spot,* I think. But when I finally get up to speak, the setup is pathetic, and my transition is sad. And then the illustration loses its momentum and power. You have to come into and get out of the visual with ease.

In one message, we used a Ferrari on stage to illustrate how many people look at dating. And because I have made so many dumb mistakes using visuals in the past, I decided to work for probably an hour and a half driving the Ferrari on and off the stage—just so the transition would go smoothly. Then, when I actually spoke from the back seat of the Ferrari, God gave me even more points and things I could say about the car.

Had I not worked hard on the transition and actually worked with the car, I would have lost the power and momentum that the car brought on stage. So whenever you use a video or visual, don't just say, "This music stand is great," or "Surely they understand what the bucket represents," and then think you're done. Yes, the people may get the point you are trying to communicate, but to take that illustration from a seven to a ten, think about the introduction and the transitions.

One final thing to avoid: the Wayne Newton principle. Wayne is cool, but the guy is overly accessorized—too much gold, too many chains, and too many sequins. Sometimes our messages can have too many gimmicks, and the message gets drowned out by the accessories. Don't allow that to happen. Sometimes the most creative idea is the simplest and most basic. Don't try to out-gimmick yourself with illustrations and stories and videos and props. Instead, develop your talk and only use something that supports it, not something that eclipses it.

Section 3

Positioning Your Creative Players

A Case Study in Creative Leadership

MIRACLE ON ICE

IN 1980, THE UNITED STATES WAS EMERGING from a decade of difficulty and turmoil, reeling from the images of Vietnam and full of distrust because of the Watergate scandal. These were also the days of double-digit inflation and a full-blown energy crisis. The Soviet Union invaded Afghanistan, re-igniting the cold war. And to top it off, a group of American students were taken hostage in Iran by a group of radical militants.

So as the Lake Placid Olympics kicked off in the winter of 1980, the country had little reason to be excited, much less hopeful. The grandest stage of the winter Olympics—hockey—had long been dominated by the Soviet Union. So when a group of relatively unknown college hockey players were joined together to form the United States national hockey team, no one gave them much of a chance to do anything significant—much less cheer a disheartened America.

But not only did that hockey team restore the country's morale by defeating the Goliath-like Soviet Union and winning the gold medal, it gave America hope—hope for the future. Still today, people say that the greatest moment in American national sports was the game known as "the miracle on ice."

What made that moment in America's history so special was not the sport that was being played or the stage the sport was played on. What made that moment so inspiring was the realization that when the right people are brought together under the right leader, anything is possible.

America had almost completely lost its sense of honor before that 1980 national hockey team skated out onto the ice. But when that same team came off the ice as victors, a sense of dignity and self-assurance was restored to the nation. People again believed that anything was possible.

There were no superstars among that group of young and unknown hockey players. But they accomplished something no one thought was possible because of one very important factor— they had a leader who convinced them that they could do it. They had a coach who fiercely believed in their ability to accomplish their dream *together* no matter what the rest of the world thought. That hockey team had a leader who drove them harder and pushed them further than they had ever been pushed before. And in response, they bonded together as a team to achieve the impossible.

If the "miracle on ice" had the power to bring people together in such an incredible way and achieve such an amazing feat, shouldn't the miracle of Christ have the same impact on the church? God has woven creativity into the very fabric of every single person. Creative leaders simply recognize that potential in everyone around them, assemble a team to unleash that potential, and with that team, accomplish amazing feats.

Though one may be overpowered,
two can defend themselves. A cord of
three strands is not quickly broken.
ECCLESIASTES 4:12

CHAPTER 7

Creative Staffing

Throughout my fifteen years at Fellowship, I've seen many staff members come and go. Many of them have matured and grown into incredible leaders. At the same time, I've seen many others never really reach their full potential. Obviously, in that amount of time we've made our share of mistakes in staffing. However, it is critical that as we grow as leaders, we minimize those kinds of mistakes. Your staff can either be your church's greatest asset or its greatest liability, depending on how you, as the point person, hire, train, and manage them. That's what this chapter is about—helping you make the most of your church's greatest resource.

We have very few staff members for a church with close to 20,000 in weekend attendance on four campuses. Because of that, each staff member has a critical role to play; there is no room for wasted time or potential. With so much responsibility in the hands of the staff, we must make great, not just good, staffing decisions.

So over the next few pages I want to deal with the question, How can I build a creative staff? We all know that recruiting

> *You can design and create, and build the*
> *most wonderful place in the world. But it*
> *takes people to make the dream a reality.*
> WALT DISNEY

and empowering a trusted team is essential to effective ministry. Whether you currently need a new hire or not, knowing how to recruit the right people for the right tasks is crucial. It is far better to be prepared for the challenges of staffing than to learn these principles by trial and error.

The Staff-Led Church

Before we get into the nuts and bolts of finding, hiring, training, and leading a staff, I want to spend a little time making a case for the staff-led church—*staff-led* meaning that the people who are gifted and called to lead in the church are the ones exercising leadership. We at Fellowship have no elders and no deacons, per se—each leader is responsible for the decisions made in his or her department. Think about it: no one knows the church like the staff, so they should be the ones calling the shots.

Please pray about and consider the creative power and potential behind the staff-led church. Fellowship Church would not be the church it is today if we had not adopted this model. Many of the most creative, dynamic, and cutting-edge churches today are that way because their staff members have the flexibility to make ministry decisions when they need to make them.

Most likely, you did not grow up in a staff-led church and have probably never been exposed to this model as a viable alternative for church government. But over the next few pages, I hope you'll consider this alternative, as it will allow you to stay faithful to God's Word and to the vision that God has put on your heart.

How Is It Unique?

Most of our models for church government mimic our federal government rather than the Word of God. We have been taught that the church should be a democracy where the majority rules. But if you page through the New Testament, you won't find a church that allows everyone to vote and then rules democratically. Democratic government was a social invention to govern people in a modern society; it is not a biblical model for church government.

If anything, the church has been designed as a theocracy: a God-run organization in which He uses gifted leaders to carry forth His grand vision. God did not hesitate to put power into the hands of His Old Testament prophets. Did Moses have to wait for a 51-percent majority before pulling out of Egypt? If he did, they'd still be there! Did Solomon submit his temple plans to a building committee? Did Elijah have a little committee of Israelites following him around Mount Carmel, looking over his shoulder and insisting that he explain why he was dousing the altar with so much water? Did Paul ever sit through a five-hour evening meeting with the Corinthian believers to vote on the color of the facility's carpet?

Throughout Scripture, God hands the ball off to the leaders He has chosen. Specifically, He empowers leaders who are entrusted with a vision. He appoints individual leaders to lead His people. He does not appoint groups to lead the leader. Yet, when we start dealing with God's prophets of today (those men and women who are tasked with leading His church), for some reason, we feel that we have to regulate and supervise them to death.

The problem stems from a temptation to read the Bible through our eyes, rather than through the Author's eyes. For instance, as I mentioned earlier, we think that the democratic style of government we've adopted in America has worked great, so it should work in the local church. But if we look at biblical governing examples, we see that during the time of Peter and Paul, deacons were appointed by the elders to serve the local church, particularly widows and orphans. By appointing deacons, the elders could focus on their mandate of leading the church and teaching the Word of God. And the elders were not elected by the people; they were appointed, through the prompting of the Spirit, by the apostles or those directed by the apostles (see Titus 1:5).

The examples we find of elders in Scripture (Acts 20:28–31; 1 Tim. 3:2–7; Titus 1:6–9; 1 Pet. 5:1–4, etc.) are what most would call "pastors" today. The term *pastor* is actually not found in Scripture. *Pastor* is a Latin word that means "shepherd," coming out of the frequent use of the term *shepherd* in the Bible to describe a minister of the gospel. Those who were called by Christ to the full-time ministry of the gospel appointed elders to assist them in that task, and those elders were in effect the staff of the New Testament church.

Christian pastors today are in the line of the apostolic ministry of Christ. Jesus Christ is still appointing and calling key leaders into the ministry of the gospel. And as key leaders are led to a particular church to work out the vision God has given them, they must be free to lead the church and appoint other leaders to assist them.

Obviously, there are other educated opinions on how the church should be run, but I believe Jesus and the apostles wisely kept issues of running the church to a minimum in Scripture, so we would be free to use our creative and God-given leadership to reach a culture that changes daily. If you want to use an elder system of government, you have that choice. If you want to use deacons, you have the freedom to do so. When I read the passages on church government, I see an emphasis on plurality of leaders, the need for godly character, and the ability to defend the doctrines of the faith. And above all, to recognize that Jesus Christ is the ultimate authority for the universal church.

I strongly believe, however, that the most effective form of church government for today's church is the staff-led model.

Don't get me wrong. The apostles were certainly accountable to one another (see Paul's rebuke of Peter in Gal. 2). But nowhere were the apostles held accountable to a group of people who didn't understand their unique calling from God. To me, the staff-led model is the best model as it allows the gifted, called leaders the freedom to lead God's people with the guardrails built in for plurality and accountability.

What about Accountability?

We believe in accountability. We believe that the plurality of elders was designed for accountability. Each of the staff is accountable to one of the pastors on our executive team, and that group is accountable to me. I, in turn, am accountable to our board of trustees. This is a board of lay leaders (appointed by the staff) that works with me and our chief financial officer to oversee the business side of running the church. The trustees keep us accountable financially, as all outgoing checks must be signed by one of them. They also keep us accountable legally, making sure we are in compliance with all applicable local, state, and federal regulations.

Notice I used the word *appointed* to describe how this board is chosen. The appointment of leaders in the church is a biblical pattern in the New Testament. Again, I don't see any democratic elections in the early church. You must appoint people who will help and support you as the leader of the church and uphold the vision God has given you. Our board is deeply committed to the vision of Fellowship Church and deeply committed to me personally and professionally. Without commitment and without love, there is the potential for abuse. One of the key reasons for the success of our model is that we have committed lay leaders who love the church and love their pastor.

This body of lay leaders should have limited power as set forth in your bylaws. Again, for our church, their leadership is focused on financial and legal issues. Too many boards are given free rein in how the ministries of the church are run, causing the staff to spend too much time battling these lay leaders instead of doing the real work of the ministry—reaching people.

The primary responsibilities of the board of trustees are to provide general oversight in the financial area and to provide counsel and guidance to me in legal, fund-raising, and major expansion issues (such as a building program). They have the power to fire

me (if such a drastic measure became necessary), but they do not
have direct control over the rest of the staff. That's my job. Here's
the real key of the staff-led church. The trustees leave the daily
ministry decisions of the church in the capable hands of the staff
and then step in to assist me as needed. They realize that the vision
for Fellowship Church was birthed by God in me. The vision did
not originate with our board. For this reason, they allow me and
my teammates (who also own the vision) to accomplish the vision
through our leadership. This accountability is based on affinity and
trust. I have worked alongside these committed men for years. We
definitely work together as a team, enjoying the ride along the way.

That, after all, is what accountability is all about: relationship.
Accountability is not an adversarial assignment but born out of
a desire for another person's best interest. You cannot be truly
accountable to someone, at least in the biblical sense, if that person does not love you and want the best for you. So be sure you are
accountable to the right people for the right reasons.

Most of the time, if people you don't know tell you you need
more accountability, they are saying that because they want to
control you. Don't get sucked into a divisive power play that can
eventually destroy your ministry and your church. Take the ball of
vision that God gave you, give that ball to your staff, and let them
run with it. And then make sure you have the proper accountability mechanism in place to deal with major issues as they arise.

Why Does It Work?

We won't know if something is going to work in any organization, much less the church, unless we try it. Putting leadership
decisions in the hands of the staff gives us the ability to try new
things based on what we know is best for any given ministry area.
We also need to quickly stop something when it's obvious that
it doesn't work. In a staff-led church, you can jump off a dead
horse, rather than sit on its corpse while a committee argues over

whether it has completely expired and takes its temperature. It is vital to be able to make quick, on-the-dime decisions in our ever-changing society. The key element of the staff-led model is that the leaders have the freedom to make those quick decisions.

For example, a couple of years ago I did a message on discipline from a child's point of view. It was about God's chain of command and the responsibility of the children to line up under the authority given their parents by God. The arts team came up with a brilliant, hilarious drama about two parents who were on trial for forcing their child to clean his room and do his homework. The drama segued into Pink Floyd's "Brick in the Wall." This is obviously not a typical song for a weekend service, but it fit well into the context of this drama. The arts team knew that kind of creativity would make a great transition into my message but didn't come up with the idea until the Monday before the service. There's no way it could have been approved in time for rehearsal and planning if they had had to convince a committee that it was a good idea.

This freedom is also essential to any Web-based ministry. The World Wide Web is a fast-paced environment, and there is no time to wait when decisions need to be made. Our technology pastor has said that in a committee environment he would have to pass at least three decisions by them each day regarding cost, content, and structure. But if he spent so much time making a case for what he wanted to do, he would never get anything done.

How Is It Set Up?

People repeatedly ask us how Fellowship Church is set up. I answer, "We are set up for success." Success in any organization can only be achieved when leaders are allowed to lead. The key word is *freedom:* being able to shift quickly when necessary. Set your church up for success, set it up for vision, and set it up for leadership. That's why Fellowship Church is a staff-led church. Too many churches are set up for failure because they have not put leadership decisions in the hands of the staff who are gifted and trained to lead in ministry.

What if your dentist could not make a decision unless ten of his patients voted on everything he did? Your dentist would leave his practice because that's a formula for frustration; it's ridiculous. The only way a dentist can do his job is if he has the control to carry out his responsibilities in meeting your dental-care needs. Yes, there are medical and dental review boards to deal with unethical issues or accusations of malpractice, but for the most part, medical professionals make and carry out decisions based on their expertise and training.

Pastors are often given all of the responsibility (the buck stops with the pastor) without any of the control. In these cases, deacon boards want control without responsibility. The elders want control without responsibility. They want to control you, but your rear's going to be on the line if something messes up. If you are a staff leader in the church, that's not what you want. You are right to want both control and responsibility. And if you are a lay leader, please hear me out: Let your leader(s) lead. Structure your church in such a way that leaders can flesh out the vision God has given them.

I realize that most churches are not set up this way. And that's one of the reasons why we've started this network of churches called Fellowship Connection. It's to help other churches get set up for success. Check out our Web site at creativepastors.com where we have made the bylaws of Fellowship available to you, so you can set up your own church as a staff-led organization. I'm going to shamelessly promote this because I believe in this resource so much. Log onto the Web site and get the "Corporate Governance Synopsis: Church Bylaws Kit" we have available. It's worth its weight in gold to every church leader who is ready to lead a church that is up for success.

Before we leave this section, let me encourage those who are trying to make this change to the staff-led model of ministry.

I realize this change is not going to be easy. It may take awhile to get people behind you to make the necessary changes to your corporate governance documents. People don't like giving up control and will do everything in their power to fight you. You may have to wait out the opposition until a more supportive group comes around to help effect this change. Pray for God to bring people like that into your church.

I also believe it's helpful to bring in some legal counsel (an objective third party) to sit down with your leadership structure and talk through a positive strategy for making this happen. The Brewer Law Group (Brewer, Anthony, and Middlebrook), located in Irving, Texas, is one of the premier law firms representing churches and nonprofits in the country. And they did an incredible job of helping us form our bylaws. Whether you contact them or another firm, get the help you need.

Keep moving in this direction whatever it takes; the stakes are simply too high to give up. We don't have time to waste in the quagmire of church politics and committees. Life is short, the fields are ripe, and church leaders need the ability to leverage their God-given vision for the local church.

Having set the stage for a staff-led church, let's turn our attention to how to build this great staff of leaders. To help you build a creative staff and position your players for maximum effectiveness, learn what to look for in potential staff, how to hire them, how to lead them and, finally, how to fire them.

What to Look For

Hire for the Heart, Not the Head

This value is often counterintuitive to many corporate leaders who tend to value the intellect more than anything else. But great church leaders must seek teammates whose hearts are bigger than their heads. I don't mean that they wear their emotions on their sleeves or that they lack the requisite background and education for whatever position they will fill.

When I talk about heart, I'm referring to what I call the *TLC* principle of hiring creative staff. They should first be *teachable*, meaning they should have an openness and readiness to learn. Their attitude should be "How can I learn from you?" not "You need to learn from me." People who think they know it all are a big turnoff and a huge red flag for me. I have been burned too many times by hiring for knowledge or academic prowess rather than a passionate heart for people and tenacious work ethic. If you are evaluating someone who hasn't demonstrated a consistent attitude of humility, show him the door. If this person hasn't willfully submitted to leadership, he just isn't teachable and will become a cancer in your church.

Also, we want someone who is *loyal.* Loyalty is the highest value that I prize here on our staff, especially from those in upper levels of leadership. How do you know if people are loyal? Look back at their life and relationships. Do they have a good track record of long-term relationships? Do they speak negatively about their present or former employer? If they do, head for the hills. Don't even think about letting them have a position on your staff, because if someone is going to trash their former employer, whether in the corporate marketplace or the church arena, they will trash you too.

These potential hires will undergo some severe tests of loyalty during their time with us. They will have to carry out decisions that they may not fully agree with but will have to own as part of the team. They may not fully understand why a decision is made, but if it comes from the leadership of the church, they must carry it out with a positive attitude. You don't want staff members who say, "Well, here is what we are going to do. I didn't come up with it and I don't agree with it, but we have to do it whether we like it or not." That's disloyalty. You want staff who, when the decision comes down, put their personal opinions aside and wholeheartedly support the team.

Disloyalty is not just what a staff person does or says; it's also what he or she doesn't say. When someone begins to throw darts at the church or its leadership, disloyal staffers don't say a word. They just sit there and silently allow the gossip and slander to fly. Loyal people are tenacious defenders of the church and its vision to creatively reach people and are flexible enough to move where they are most needed in the church.

Finally, we want someone who is *committed* to the overall vision of the church. The last thing you want to do is waste time and resources on someone who's not on board with what you're trying to do. If people can't submit to you as the leader, they will not contribute to the overall vision for the church. If their commitment quotient is lacking in your particular organization, perhaps there is another ministry where they can contribute in a more positive way.

Teachable, loyal, and committed teammates are a breath of fresh air. Head knowledge is a great asset, but a heart that is devoted to God and devoted to your specific vision for the local church is to be prized above all.

Focus on Plus-Side People

When I review our staffing needs, I look for "plus-side people" to add to our team. In other words, I hire quality people who will make a significant impact on the strategic ministry vision. I look for great leaders who are able and willing to leverage their gifts and experience to enhance my God-given vision.

Be sure to put more people and emphasis on the plus-side staff as opposed to the administrative staff. Please don't misunderstand me: I'm not against support staff; they are critical to the day-to-day operations of the church. But their numbers can spiral out of control and Pac-Man your organization if they are disproportionate to your major players.

Support staff are essential and positive when used appropriately, but, first and foremost, let me challenge you to target leaders who will add long-term value to your vision with the talents, abilities, and resources they have been given. These kinds of people have a unique giftedness for leadership, are intrinsically driven, and have a track record of improving the environment around them.

Don't Get Sidetracked by Superstars

When I say someone is a major player, I mean simply that he or she is a great team player. We don't have a bunch of superstars on our staff, but we do have people who are teachable, loyal, and committed. None of them have a Ph.D. in creativity, but when you find people who share your vision and are freed up to lead in their respective areas, the creative ideas will go and flow.

As we have grown as a church and built our creative staff, we have been strategic about finding the right people to do the right job and letting them do their thing. In the creative church, we should have tremendous freedom to pursue the dreams God has given us in our own ministries. But for that to happen, we must find great team players who care more about the overall success of the church than their own status or success. Superstars can score a lot of points for their *own* glory, but they usually don't do a very good job of helping you build a creative team for *God's* glory.

Avoid Cruise-Control People

Another way to impede ministry momentum is to empower uninspired people who are on cruise control. You don't want to have to continually light a fire under your key leaders. They should have already demonstrated initiative and a passion to advance the mission of your church. If you find yourself with a cruise-control person on your staff, don't waste your time in trying to change him. Cut and run. Work with workers and leave the slackers in your dust. I know that sounds harsh, but we don't have time to play games with lazy staff members.

I want people we have to rein in. We actually have had to ask some of our staff to back off from working too hard. I was speaking to a member of our media team awhile back and said, "You need to take some time off, man." This guy was up at the church at all hours of the day and night. While we don't want to encourage workaholics, we do want to hire people who have that healthy drive, that determination to get things done. If you find someone working too much, you need to determine if he just doesn't know how to maintain balance in life or if he needs some more staff in his area. That's all part of strategic staffing.

It's great to talk about creativity and innovation, but behind all of it are people with a humongous work ethic. One of the reasons many churches do not grow is because the staff is not willing to do what it takes for growth to occur. Your staff and mine need to understand the grueling process of bringing creative ideas from conception to implementation. When a creative idea floats down the pipe, it doesn't have an Armani suit on; it's wearing some overalls with a tool belt attached to the hip. You need staff who realize the tremendous work that goes into the creative endeavor.

Develop a Clone-Free Environment

As you consider the personalities, giftedness, and skill sets of potential staff, resist the temptation to hire clones of yourself. It's only natural to seek people who have been educated as you have, grown up in similar situations to yours, and look and act like you. That is a great recipe for getting an entire staff of you. But if you really want to reach all kinds of people, you have to be strategic about filling up your staff with all kinds of people—people who reflect the diversity of your church.

For example, I don't thrive in the hospital room as a pastoral counselor. A good friend who helped start Fellowship now handles most of our pastoral care. He thrives around hurting and sick people. God has wired him to minister to these people, and I thank God for this valued staff member and friend. Obviously, when our church was smaller, I wore all the hats. However, I very quickly began to hand off the ball of ministry first to volunteers and then to the staff as they were brought on board. As we have gotten bigger, I have tried to capitalize on my gifts and hire staff for my weaknesses.

Do your best to seek out a wide range of people who are uniquely gifted in their own right and contribute something different to the leadership table. If you look to hire clones of yourself, you will end up with a one-dimensional organization that will grind to a halt. Truly gifted top leaders will strategically add teammates who are more skilled in certain areas and are wired differently than the leaders are. This will be a dynamic staff with the synergy to propel your church or organization to levels you never dreamed possible.

Keep Your Staff Lean

The final principle in looking for new staff is one I learned through necessity. Keep your staff on the lean side. Because Fellowship Church was a church plant, I was forced to be the one-man band for quite some time in its early days. I was the church's preacher, secretary, visitation pastor, administrator, and janitor—all in one. I had some incredible and loyal volunteers to help me, but I was the only staff member, responsible for everything in the church.

As God began to add numerical and financial growth to our vision, we had the ability to add staff to relieve some of these pressures. When this happened, I began implementing these same principles that I am now sharing with you. I looked within our little church plant before I looked in neighboring seminaries or other churches. All of these gifted and loyal leaders sacrificed much as volunteers for Fellowship Church, but the point is that I didn't rush out and hire staff just because we could afford to.

What I've learned through these lean times is the same principle that we practice today when reviewing the efficiency of our staff. Avoid the temptation to just fill holes without due diligence. We have about one-third to one-half the staff of other churches of comparable size and budget as ours. And this is intentional. Every time you're considering whether to hire a new staff member, ask yourself if a lay person could function in that role. If you hire people on your staff before asking this question, you are sending the wrong message to your congregation.

Our job as the staff is not to do all the work of the ministry; it is to lead and equip the church to work with us in reaching people (Eph. 4:12). Aren't all believers supposed to be in the ministry? If we believe it, we better practice it as we survey the needs of our church or organization.

Now that you know what I look for in a staff member, let's jump into the actual hiring process and some of the difficult issues involved in that.

How to Hire Them

Ask any realtor what the three most important elements in real estate are, and you'll hear "location, location, location." Ask any hiring manager in corporate America what the three most important elements in hiring staff are, and you'll hear "interview, interview, interview." It's through the interview process that you find staff who are teachable, loyal, and committed. The hiring practices in this section are basic to every company in America and should be no less familiar to the hiring church leader. Especially in the church, we cannot neglect due diligence in bringing the right people on board.

Check Their References

When you have a résumé in front of you, take the necessary time to check the references. I don't care if it's a volunteer you have watched develop in your church for seven years—check the references. I have gotten burned in a major way a couple of times by not doing this. Pathological people who prey on the church are out there, and they are instruments of the Evil One. I am astounded at how many church leaders I talk with who say, "This person was on my staff and I thought he was incredible. But I found out that he was embezzling money/abusing someone/habitually lying."

I had lunch one evening with a couple of senior pastors, and as we began to share some staff war stories, I couldn't believe some of the unfortunate events brought about by disloyal and downright dishonest staff members. So check references. If that potential hire can't provide you with the names of three people who can say something positive about them, move on to the next candidate.

"Ed, this guy is my brother." Check his references.

"You don't understand. I know this girl. I went to school with her." Check her references.

Do Background Checks

Contracting with a company to do background checks will cost you some money, but it's well worth it. And it may end up saving you a lot of money in the long run. Contract with a good, reputable agency that can conduct local, state, and federal background checks for all your job applicants. And don't hesitate to conduct a credit review of the applicant. This can give you additional information about how responsible he is. If people don't keep their personal life in order, chances are they won't be able to keep their professional life in order either.

Again, you can find information on this topic on CreativePastors. com in the section on bylaws and legal issues. We also make our personnel policy manual available to you.

Consider the Spouse

I'll make this next point short but sweet. Please don't skip the importance of the spouse in the hiring equation. If you are in a position to hire someone for the ministry, let me give you an insider's tip—one that I learned the hard way. Take this potential staff member and his spouse out to dinner with you and your spouse. I have noticed that my wife Lisa can pick up a lot of things that I miss. I'm talking about emotional issues and relational issues, along with a sense of the couple's readiness to enter into the unique pressures of ministry in your church environment.

I don't think you should include the spouses in the entire interview process, but you should intentionally make a point to meet them and get a feel for how they will fit into the overall picture.

Hire from Within

People who are already involved in your organization on a volunteer basis are the first place to start when looking for potential staff. They have already demonstrated an attitude of loyalty to your leadership and are committed to the vision of the church. Not only can you observe their track record firsthand, but you can also observe their passion for your local church. So before you go to a seminary or another church, look first within your own church.

I sincerely believe that, for the most part, God equips your church with the staff and leadership to do what He wants to do. It's our job and our mandate to have the discernment to call them forth. When you are thinking about staff positions, think about the track record of service in the church on a volunteer basis. The good thing about looking within your church is that the volunteers' track records are obvious. You don't have to rely on second-hand references to know how they've been involved in the life of the church. You can see how they've performed and know they are already on board with your vision.

I began hiring from within right off the bat. Owen Goff was fifty-two-years-old when I tapped him on the shoulder and asked him to join our staff. He owned his own insurance company at the time, but because of his faithfulness as a volunteer and his heart for people, we brought him on board. He has served in various positions, but most recently he has led our pastoral care ministry.

Doris Scoggins, another church member we brought on our staff in the early days, was also recruited from the corporate world. She has served as our finance manager, in our newcomer's ministry, in hospitality, baptism, and many other areas.

Preston Mitchell, who now serves as our executive pastor, was in management at a utilities company when I asked him to join our staff. Again, he had demonstrated his faithfulness during those first difficult days and months of our church, so I knew he would make a top-notch staff member. And he has proven me right.

I could go on and on about people we have hired from within, because almost 90 percent of our staff came from within our church. That's a staggering number compared to most churches today. Granted, with about 20,000 attendees, we have a broad base to choose from. But that is still way beyond the norm for most churches. Before you go on some nationwide search for a particular staff member, I would challenge you to ask God if He has someone from within your own ranks who would fit the bill.

Feel Good about Them

Obvious though it may sound, you should like the people you bring on staff to work side by side with you. If you don't feel good about them, if you don't light up when they walk in the room, don't hire them. I'm not saying we shouldn't love them in the Lord, but let's be honest: we don't always like everyone we work with. We have hired people here at Fellowship whom I loved as brothers or sisters in Christ, but when I saw them coming, I ran the other way.

This is especially true when hiring people to work in your department. You don't want to be around someone day after day whom you don't connect with. If it's a chore to be around someone because your personalities don't click, then it's not a good work environment for either of you. In a culture that values teamwork, we cannot afford to bring people on the team who don't gel with the current roster of players. I'll deal more with teamwork in the next chapter, but suffice it to say that you must have an affinity for people on your team if you want to achieve your collective creative potential.

How to Lead Them

You've looked in all the right places for your staff. You've done your due diligence in the hiring process. So now what? You have to lead them. Getting them on board is one thing; leading them is quite another. Let's tackle ways to keep your team focused and committed to expanding your creative vision.

Just like in the business world, it is expensive and time-consuming to train new people. For churches, however, our mission is much more critical. We're not worried about dollars and shareholders. We are trying to reach people in all walks of life with a message of eternal importance. Obviously, eliminating costly and painful turnover is minimized when you hire from within. If you have found skillful candidates from your own backyard, you won't have to spend as much time orienting them to the vision and mission of your organization. But any way you slice it, human-resource development costs time and money. So it only makes sense to do all we can to keep our staff happy and healthy as members of our team.

Two key expressions really communicate the value of the staff in any organization: *human resources* and *teammates.* Remember that your skilled workforce—your human resources—is your greatest asset. They are not just badge numbers; they are the people integral to creatively carrying out the vision for the church. As Michael Eisner says about the Disney employees, "My inventory goes home every night."

And they are not working in isolation. They are, in fact, teammates who are fighting for the same goals and working synergistically to accomplish greater levels of ministry for God's greater pleasure.

Don't Lock Your Teammates into One Position

One of the best ways to free up your staff to greater fulfillment is to create a culture of organizational freedom. Don't be afraid to change up your team. I can't tell you how many key leaders have been shifted around to new areas. If staff members are struggling, take some time to diagnose the problem. Are they simply in the wrong place? Is the issue a bad fit or a poor work ethic?

If you create an organization that allows for mobilization, you will encourage your staff to stay loyal to the vision of the church. Even if staffers are not in the perfect position, they know that they will not be hung out to dry. You have shown them that there is a real possibility of giving them a new start with another opportunity in your organization.

Another advantage to moving your staff around periodically is that it stimulates growth. It not only keeps your church or organization dynamic, but it fosters important personal growth for your staff members. Change produces conflict and conflict produces growth. If you have the same people filling the same roles year after year, it will negatively impact your ability to realize positive change. Since the world around us is changing so fast, we need to be mobile enough to turn on a dime when necessary to meet the changing needs of our culture head-on.

Pay Now or Pay Later

The traditional mantra in the church for pastoral positions has been, "Lord, you keep him humble and we'll keep him poor." Fortunately, that is changing. Church leadership is starting to wise up to the notion that being in ministry doesn't mean you have to be destitute. When you think about it, there aren't many professions that are as demanding as full-time ministry. And, of those other demanding enterprises, how many deal with matters of eternal destiny? How many know the 24/7 tension of trying to serve spiritual seekers and disciple Christ followers week after week? The last thing that you want to do is burden your key staff with financial hardships. If my staff is struggling to make their mortgage payment or put food on the table, something is wrong.

You and your church simply cannot afford to have your staff distracted by this financial burden. You also cannot afford to lose them by not valuing their contributions. A great way to keep your teammates happy and healthy is to ensure that they are being compensated fairly. Obviously, this means different things for different churches in different cities. You need to gauge your compensation with the standard of living in your own area. You also need to do a fair market analysis of both corporate and nonprofit compensation. It takes only a little investigation and discernment to know what fair compensation for each staff member should look like in your part of the world.

Another side benefit to paying your staff well is that you are putting money in the hands of the most generous people in your church. While we can't count on every Jack and Jill who enters our doors to tithe, we should expect it from our staff. A culture of stewardship in the church begins first with the point leader, second with the staff, and third with the members and regular attendees. So make sure you are paying the people who participate on the front lines of this stewardship culture.

Advance with Retreats

Staff retreats are an important part of team building, but they are often difficult to pull off. Still, you have got to build in a strategic time when your key leadership staff can plan to be away for an intense time of creativity and communion.

You cannot put a price on the planning and team building that comes out of a staff retreat. It doesn't matter if you are going to a nearby lake and pitching tents or going away to a beautiful resort; it's worth it. You won't remember the destinations, but you will remember the events that happen there. And you will reap the rewards of some focused time away from your normal environment. You can escape for a few days to strategize, pray, and vision-cast with your management team. You also need to spend time in recreation and building relationships. I cherish the times that our staff has had together on these retreats. We laugh our heads off.

I realize that many church staffs don't look forward to these annual retreats and instead fear them like a boot camp because the meetings last for ten hours each day and you have to get a hall pass just to use the bathroom.

Obviously, our retreats are intense, but we don't neglect the fun. We work hard and then play hard. You and your staff spend most of the year in the pressure cooker of intense ministry. Why not invest a few days together where you can cut loose, get away, and do some serious vision-casting? I promise, the dividends will be huge.

Include the Family

Whether you are planning staff retreats or simply a staff party, it is vital to weave the family into the culture of your church or organization. When you are intentional with family members, you are sending the right message about priorities to everyone who is watching. Most important, you are improving relationships among your team and ensuring that families are included in the big picture of what the church is and where it is going.

By intentionally including the family, you will avoid some of the horror stories of burn out, divorce, and rebellious kids in ministry. If spouses or kids are having to compete against the church for your staff member's time, you aren't placing the same value that God places on the family. Rather than being an instrument of blessing for the family, some churches have earned a reputation of tearing the family apart. This cannot be. We must not only talk the talk but be willing to walk the walk when it comes to our priorities and commitments in the family arena. I dive deeper into family issues in chapter 9.

Expect Excellence

The expectation of excellence goes back to the core values of your organization. We are by-products of our real values, not our idealistic values. For instance, if one of your stated ministry values is excellence, but there are no systems for evaluation and no expectations in place from your top leaders, excellence will not happen. From the very beginning, God has impressed upon me the need for ministry excellence. We're not talking about perfection, but we have a can-do attitude around Fellowship. Just like any company that expects to thrive in the global economy, the church must exude an atmosphere of excellence.

How many times have you covered your eyes (or ears) in shame or embarrassment during a church service because it was evident that the songs, transitions, prayer, and message were thrown together at the last minute? What kind of message does that send to your unsaved audience? How do you think Christ feels about a church that only provides the bare minimum—when He wants His bride to be magnetic, to draw all people to Him?

The church should lead the way in creativity and excellence. We are not performing for one another but attempting to honor our creative Creator. Excellence in our worship services will motivate our congregation to bring their friends. When a church is excellent in what it does, it will attract people to hear the message of Christ.

The church needs excellence as part of its core values. It is essential that your staff is committed to each one of your core ministry values and that they strive to implement those in their specific areas of ministry. It is also essential that your top leaders are reminded of these values in staff meetings and retreats. When you model excellence as a leader, you will set the tone for your entire staff.

Evaluate Regularly

As I previously mentioned (in the IRS audit bit), people don't do what you expect; they do what you inspect. It is a sad but true reality in any organization, church or otherwise. Therefore, it is critical that systems are in place for a regular review of your expectations for employees and the results they achieve. It sounds funny talking about results in the context of the local church, but the Book of Acts talks a lot about how evaluating numbers was a critical system necessary to quantify life change in the first-century church. Look, for example, at the record in Acts 2 of 3,000 responding to the gospel and being baptized.

I'm not saying that you need to micromanage your employees or that you should not trust them to do their job. However, it is your job to make sure that they are doing what you expect them to do. And that happens by inspecting their work. That doesn't mean you bug them every hour on the hour. It doesn't even mean you have to have daily meetings with them. What it does mean, however, is that you have a management system in place to regularly and strategically evaluate the productivity and effectiveness of your staff.

How to Fire Them

I don't like having to include this section, but it is a necessary element of leadership. Having to fire staff is inevitable. No matter where you go as a leader, you cannot hide from this unfortunate reality of ministry. And while you can never really make the termination of an employee pleasant, you can minimize the unpleasantness.

Deal with Difficulties Rapidly

As you consider the best way to deal with staff problems, I would encourage you to *deal with difficulties rapidly*. What do you do when staff members aren't pulling their weight? Do you just hammer them and yell at them? Or do you confront them in love? Obviously, the biblical thing to do is to let love be your guide. But whatever you do, don't delay the confrontation. You must deal with the issue quickly.

As mentioned in chapter 4, if a staffing problem emerges, the first thing we say at Fellowship is not, "You're fired." Our first response is to move the person to another area. That is why we believe organizational mobility is so important. First, we consider whether this person is in the right position and in the right area for his or her experience and skill set. Now, if the situation involves unethical behavior, that is a whole other issue. But if we have struggling staff members in positions that are simply not working for them, we move them to other positions.

If that still doesn't work, we always take the higher ground. If they are truly not gifted for our church, we will help them do something else that suits them. Maybe they want to go to another church or into a corporate environment. We will help them do that. If they are struggling with immorality or substance abuse, we will make sure they have access to the help they need.

Now, for staff members who are lazy or disloyal, you need to be firm with them. They need to hear you say, "It's over." Do not allow these problem people to hang around. Their negativity will only damage your staff and your church as a whole.

Use Discretion

Sometimes being a good leader is not saying anything. Sometimes it is better to let a staff member go and not explain to your people why you had to do it. That is tough to do. Your people will wonder what happened, but you know it is the wisest and most prudent course of action to keep the details to yourself. You can't reveal everything because many churchgoers won't know or understand the context in which you had to make the decision to let a particular person go. They simply have to trust that you made the right decision.

Several years ago we had to release someone because of several reports of his inappropriate behavior toward the opposite sex. It didn't involve an affair, but there were unwanted advances toward the opposite sex. We felt it was in the best interest of this staff member and of the church as a whole to not divulge the details of this person's release. While we did let this person go, we also helped him find the appropriate counseling to work through this issue.

Releasing people from employment is never easy, and our leadership team and I will not complicate the situation by giving out information that is unnecessary and confidential in nature.

You must also consider the legal ramifications of divulging sensitive information upon the termination of an employee. I would encourage you to consult legal counsel, perhaps even have them present, whenever you are firing someone in a particularly difficult situation—for reasons of gross incompetence, sexual misconduct, harassment, criminal activity, substance abuse, or any number of other sensitive issues. Protect the church and protect yourself by including your church lawyers in the process when appropriate.

Use Your Leadership Team

Another important element to keep in mind when it comes to firing is to use your staff and board. Whether you're hiring or firing, consult with these trusted teammates before you make a decision. Maybe they will catch something you missed or help you see things in a different light. Use the counselors around you for protection in a situation of staff termination. Better yet, ask them to help you eliminate potentially negative staff before they are ever hired.

Even after you've exhausted all the proper channels, you cannot eliminate all hiring errors. I assure you, I have made several stupid mistakes in hiring over the years. One that stands out in my mind is when we hired a young believer to work part-time on our staff. He also happened to be a model, so I told him that when he modeled, he would have to make sure he was doing things that honored God. He assured me that he would use discretion and his modeling job would not cause problems with his job at the church.

Well, one Friday he called to tell me that he had done a photo shoot that might have been a little out of line. It was an advertisement for men's underwear. But again, he told me that he didn't think it would be a problem, because it was highly unlikely that anyone from our church would see the ad. Well, the following Sunday morning his underwear ad appeared in the *Dallas Morning News*—the most widely circulated newspaper in the area. Needless to say, that was his last weekend with us.

People are going to leave your staff, whether by their own volition or yours, so it's important to build a team that can go on even if you lose one talented staff member. One of our former staff members was a creative genius but was led to another city and another ministry. Though this was hard at the time, it has turned out to be the best for both of us. They inherited a phenomenal leader and we benefited from new creativity that has emerged from staff members that he mentored. The people left behind have taken it to the next level because of the team dynamic. It's been a win-win.

When people leave, just think of it as a blessing to another church and a blessing to your church, because God always fills the void. A commitment to the team concept will help you minimize losses and learn how to adapt quickly when change happens.

Surrounding yourself with a team of committed and talented people can make all the difference. A great staff will make the good times greater and the hard times easier to manage. They can enhance your abilities in every area and fill in for your weaknesses. While a competent and committed team will lead you to greater heights, a team of incompetent and disloyal people will poison your entire church culture. Hiring the right people for the right positions will transform your entire ministry. You will accomplish things that only God has dreamed for you. Hiring the wrong people will create a multitude of problems that will rob you of your resources and keep you from achieving your God-given vision.

It takes vision and strong leadership to keep your staff motivated and committed to the same goals. Ask God to bring you the right people for the right positions at the right time, so that they might complement your strengths and help you explore new creative territory for His greater glory.

As iron sharpens iron,
so one man sharpens another.
PROVERBS 27:17

CHAPTER 8

Team Creativity

In the world of professional sports and in the era of free agency, a dynasty has emerged in the NFL. The New England Patriots, regardless of what their lackluster roster might suggest, have dominated, winning three of the last four Super Bowls (2002, 2004, 2005). They are not the first team to meet that kind of success on the playing field, but the surprising thing about their accomplishments is the amazing lack of superstars on their championship teams. Instead of a string of highly touted free agents, the current slate of players exemplifies a team commitment to one another and to an unselfish style of play.

The same commitment was seen in the 2004 NBA Finals. The talent-laden Los Angeles Lakers, featuring the two most prolific basketball superstars in the world, were overmatched by another team that was better because they played as a cohesive unit rather than five individuals. The Detroit Pistons truly represented the word *team*. And if the world of sports has taught us anything, it is that championships are won by great teams. Even Michael Jordan

When all think alike,
then no one is thinking.
WALTER LIPPMANN

needed Scottie Pippen and a host of other supporting teammates to reach the pinnacle of his sport.

Not surprisingly, the church also desperately needs a team commitment to achieve success. Up to this point, I have alluded to the dynamic of the team environment for unleashing creativity in the leadership of your church. However, this chapter on team creativity takes the discussion into greater detail on the dynamics of team creativity in the process of planning a weekend message. For me one of the greatest benefits of team creativity is that my speaking abilities are enhanced and more focused when I am with my creative team. However, there are many other benefits that I want you to see in the context of creative leadership.

I believe in the power of team creativity so much that this entire chapter is devoted to sharing what I've learned about the dynamics of team planning. It also will address how a creative idea goes from conception to implementation. First, though, I want to give you a little history to explain how and when I began using the team approach, particularly in preparation for the weekend.

A Turning Point

I have already stated that the senior pastor should devote at least 70 percent of his weekly schedule toward the preparation of his sermon. For most pastors who do this work alone, that is a bunch of time spent in solitude surrounded by books. This process is lonely and draining, as the pressure of shouldering the communication load continues to build week after week. Every weekend is like another wave crashing against the shoreline of your body, mind, and soul. Preparing and delivering that weekly message takes its toll on both the speaker and his family. My tendency, along with that of many other lead communicators, is to put too much pressure on myself.

From year to year, I have seen the creative juices in my own speaking ministry ebb and flow. Ideas and insights would flow for awhile, but then I would begin to feel a certain staleness and predictability rising out of my routines. I could feel the audience thinking, *Oh great! Here comes another acrostic from Ed.*

What was wrong? Was my passion for creativity waning? On the contrary, my passion was as strong as ever. The reason I hit these creative downtimes is because I was trying to do it all by myself. And I finally began to realize that, by going it alone, I was becoming the sole bottleneck in the creative process.

Not only were my creativity and connection with the audience suffering, but my health worsened as well. As I found my body giving in to the mounting pressure of going it alone in this ongoing process, God taught me an important lesson. He allowed me to experience stress and health issues to drive me to the need for team creativity.

I remember riding in my truck and praying to God one day. I was frustrated and exhausted but began to hear God speak to me in my spirit. He was saying, "Hey, Ed, share the creative load. Share the burden. Pass it out. If you don't, *you're* going to pass out."

That was the birthplace of team creativity in my speaking ministry. I began to recognize and use the creative geniuses around me. I started bringing other staff members into the message-preparation process and continue to do so to this day.

No matter how creative you are, you will run out of steam and ideas fast if you try to do everything yourself. I've studied other communicators and discovered that the truly effective speakers have longevity in their ministries. One of the best ways to ensure longevity is by enlisting a creative team to help shoulder the joys and trials of ministry. You might say, "That's not for me. I am the man or I'm the woman; I can do it by myself. I'm strong enough. I'm autonomous enough. I'm big enough. I'm bad enough. I can create by myself." Sure, you might be able to do it for awhile, but I'll tell you straight up that someday you will hit the wall.

I've run one marathon in my life, and everyone told me before I ran, "Ed, you're going to hit the wall." I didn't believe them. I thought, *I'm not going to hit the wall. I've played college basketball; I've worked out for months getting ready.* But sure enough, after twenty miles—bam! I hit the wall. My body gave out. My toes were begging me to quit. My knees were rebelling against me. My stomach was churning. I wanted to stop. I wanted to quit. But even though every part of my body was telling me to throw in the towel, I persevered to the finish line. Do you know why? I kept going because I was surrounded by people cheering me on. I knew I was not alone.

You will hit a similar wall in ministry if you try to take everything on yourself. But if you want to stay in the race, all you have to do is look around you. You are already surrounded by creative and innovative people. The key is to enlist and empower them. Let them join you in the creative journey. Don't allow yourself to be the bottleneck of your team's creative potential.

My hope is that, by sharing my own struggles with you, I can help free you the way God has freed me through the creative team process. No matter how passionate you are about creativity or even your vision, you can't be the lone ranger. The local church is built for community, and that community is modeled to your people first and foremost in the way you and your staff work together as a team.

The Benefits of Team Creativity

If you're almost convinced that creative-team planning is the way to go, I hope this next section will help you cross the finish line. In it, we're going to highlight some of the benefits of unleashing a team of creative geniuses.

It Helps You Become You

I've been saying throughout this book that we're created in the image of our creative Creator. We're all exquisite pieces of art. We're all unique. We're all innovative. Creative-team planning helps you as a leader and communicator realize this truth at a greater and deeper level. You will begin to discern how your creative software differs from everyone else on your team. And you will begin to value the unique contributions that everyone brings to the creative table. In other words, it will teach you how to be the best you that you can be.

One time I heard Bill Hybels say, "God is tired of your cold-hearted servility." (Yes, servility is actually a word.) I had to replay the tape two or three times to even understand what he was saying. I then said to myself, *Wow, that's an awesome statement. I'm going to use that in a message.*

So the next Sunday I stood up in front of my church audience and said, "God is tired of your cold-hearted servility."

And the response I got from the crowd was what I imagined cold-hearted servility would feel like. What was the problem? The statement just wasn't me. Only Bill can say something like that with great impact and power. I'm not Bill. And Bill's not me. Bill needs to be Bill. Ed needs to be Ed.

I had dinner not long ago with a prominent pastor in the Dallas area you might have heard of. I don't like to drop names, but his initials are Bishop T. D. Jakes. *Time Magazine* did a cover story calling him America's best preacher or something like that. Obviously, they didn't attend Fellowship before running the article! Seriously, though, Bishop Jakes *is* one of the best communicators I've ever heard. In fact I have a video library of Bishop Jakes, including some of his old sermons. They're kind of like fine wine; they get better with age (so I'm told).

Jakes has one classic talk on the prodigal son called "Stay in the House." It's an unbelievable message on the temptations that led the prodigal son astray. He uses the phrase "stay in the house" over and over again as the tension builds and escalates to a fevered pitch. Then, masterfully, he slows the roller coaster down before sending it out of the chutes again. There is no way I could do that talk for my audience at Fellowship. I've tried to impersonate Jakes doing this talk, but that's as far as I can get. Bishop T. D. Jakes is the only one who could really do that talk. Jakes is Jakes and I am me.

I was in Atlanta a couple summers ago and heard John Maxwell talk about what was then his upcoming book, *Today Matters*. He told a story, as only he can, about being picked as the captain of the high school basketball team because of his attitude. Again, I can try to impersonate John, but I can't speak like him. He's a one-of-a-kind master storyteller.

I'm not Bill. I'm not T. D. I'm not John. I'm Ed. And you've got to be you. You can learn a lot from other creative communicators but please don't copy their style if it doesn't fit with who you are wired up to be. I believe the creative team model will help and encourage you in that regard. It will help you be the best you that you can be.

It Brings a Fresh Flow of Ideas

Surrounding yourself with creative geniuses will propel you to higher levels of innovation and competency in your speaking and leadership abilities. Having a creative team keeps new ideas coming all the time and helps you drop overused ones—for me, this has meant getting beyond my love of acrostics and alliteration every weekend. I have even, in recent message series, moved away from tightly scripted points to a more informal structure. Though a tighter organizational framework is still my default, my creative team has brought freshness and variation to the way I tackle my speaking assignments. As a leader, my teammates help me make more informed decisions and give me new ideas and insights into different ways to communicate the same truth.

Let's face it, if we are Bible-believing and Bible-teaching churches, we are all communicating the same Truth. But the variety and creativity comes in how we package it for the listener. If you do not have trusted people to give you vitality in this area, you will fall into whatever default position you are most comfortable with. And that's not good for you, your staff, or your church.

It Alleviates Your Stress

Good, solid teammates can help you bear the weekend waves that crash up against you week after week. I thank God for showing me the value of the team approach all those years ago. Like many other leaders in church-planting situations, I was trying to do too much by myself. Not only did I run myself ragged, but I also put a tremendous amount of pressure on my marriage and family. When God showed me the possibility of team ministry, it was a breath of fresh air for all the Young family.

The pressures facing pastors today are well documented. Record numbers are either leaving the ministry because of burnout or are disqualified from ministry after succumbing to sin. Team ministry doesn't solve all these problems, but it sure makes the ministry more enjoyable and helps to minimize some of the emotional, spiritual, and relational risks that result from being a lone ranger. There is nothing worse than that lonely feeling that comes from shouldering a responsibility alone. Similarly, there is nothing greater than the excitement and refreshment that comes from sharing the journey.

Team planning does not take the pressure off of delivering messages every week, but it does remove some of the preparation pressure. You are still ultimately responsible for the outcome, but the outlines, ideas, slants, and angles will be off the charts when you use a creative team.

It Multiplies Your Talent Base

The people involved in my creative team change all the time. We always try to vary the roster of players in the creative-planning meetings. We have two or three constant participants in these meetings, but the other three or four revolve in and out. When you allow more people to participate in the creative process, creativity can come from highly unusual sources.

For example, the wife of one of my key teammates, Preston Mitchell, broke a creative stalemate among our team when she came up with the title and direction for an entire series. We were sitting around banging our heads against the wall trying to come up with a creative idea for a series when Preston's wife, Dedo, walked into the office. She came in, saw that we were having some problems, looked at the aquarium against the wall, and said, "Why don't you do something on fish. Ed, you love fishing and fish. Maybe compare life with a fishbowl or something like that."

Wow! Are you kidding me? Preston and I looked at each other and said, "That's it!" The series was called "Everything You Need to Know About Life Is in Your Fishbowl." It turned out to be one of my favorites. If I hadn't been committed to the team approach, I never would have received this very creative idea.

It is vitally important to continue to bring new ideas and new life to your creative table. Learn the lessons that Hollywood has learned. Most sitcoms and dramatic programs on television have a revolving talent base for their writers. Some of these have gone as far as to mandate that their creative writers leave the show after a few years. A team that challenges each member's creativity can eventually raise up many others who are able to unleash their creative potential and join in on the process. Allow your ministry to really thrive by enlisting and empowering your creative people to multiply your talent base.

It Mentors Future Speakers and Leaders

When you have team creativity going on, you're training people to communicate without their even knowing it. One woman on our staff started as a receptionist and then became my assistant for several years. Now she heads up our Leadership Uncensored program (a monthly leadership series on CD offered to church leaders) as a part of Fellowship Connection.

She had been a regular part of our creative team for years. One week I decided to take some time off and approached Laura about speaking: "Laura, I want you to speak a couple of weekends from now."

I loved her response. She said, "OK. I can do it, Ed. You won't be disappointed." And I wasn't. She walked up before about 18,000 people over the five different services we had at the time and delivered a slam-dunk talk.

Training future leaders has been a gradual and almost imperceptible benefit to the team-ministry model. It has been a natural mentoring program for us, particularly in training up other speakers. If I perceive that people who have been involved in those team meetings have potential as speakers, I'll ask them to speak when they're ready for that. God wants to use their abilities and experiences as well as yours and mine. A great way to train the future leaders of tomorrow is by sharing the responsibility today.

At Fellowship, we typically throw emerging leaders into the pool and say, "Swim, baby, swim." We don't throw them into the deep end right away, but we also don't necessarily give them a lot of formalized training. We believe the best way to learn is by doing it.

If we see people with the gift of communication, we will bring them in to our creative-planning meetings to observe the process firsthand. They will learn the importance of the introduction and conclusion (bookends), as well as how to integrate visuals and some methods to improve their storytelling. After they have spent some time with us (from several months to several years), we'll say, "Here you go. You're up next. You have next weekend's four services. Bam! Go for it." Just like that, they begin to preach and teach. And whether they realize it or not, they are usually ready to go.

It Expands Your Knowledge of Your Audience

As I've said, the makeup of the creative team changes. And as different people rotate in and out, they tell me about what's going on in the lives of believers and seekers in the church. This gives me faces and names of people with particular needs that I need to have in mind as I speak, providing a greater breadth of knowledge related to what real people are dealing with and a greater sense of urgency as I communicate.

As your church grows, you cannot possibly know everything that's going on in the lives of all your people. But as you are forced to do the push-back that we addressed earlier, you must find a way to stay connected with the real needs of real people. Using the relational base of your creative team can help in that regard.

As we leave this section, remember that team creativity is not the easy way out of hard work. The work ethic cannot change if you want to advance the kingdom of God. What does change is how you work. Instead of serving as the creative bottleneck, top leaders are given the freedom to vision-cast and prepare to meet the challenges of a changing culture. At Fellowship Church, we still work hard. However, now we work more strategically, more intentionally and more creatively.

The Anatomy of a Creative Idea

We've learned a lot of important lessons in our commitment to team ministry—most of them the hard way. When we started integrating key people into our creative planning, there was very little information on the team approach to ministry. As a result, we had some definite growing pains before getting to the place where the process was firing on all cylinders.

Don't get me wrong; we have not arrived yet. We have much to learn as creative leadership requires a constant commitment to growth. But here are some of the proven principles we have learned along the way.

Think Conceptually and Specifically

Creativity is made up of both broad concepts and specific details. And while theory and abstract concepts are useful as a launching pad, you must move beyond the abstract to more specific concepts so the rubber can meet the road.

Some leaders think it is sufficient to deal in general concepts in a creative meeting. But if you don't move beyond these general concepts into something concrete, you will have wasted a lot of time for your key people.

As our own planning process has matured, I've learned that teams are prolific when they're specific. Move toward specificity for the majority of your meeting time. Once the ball is rolling, pare down to the doable details. In our own creative meetings before a weekend message, our team will formulate detailed wording for the introduction, specific transitional phrases, illustrations, main points, and even concluding remarks.

The abstract part of that process is where I study by myself prior to our team meeting. For each talk, I spend some time doing a mind dump and formulate a rough draft based on my research and notes. By the time the meeting is called, I have a rough structure in place that is eventually sharpened and molded with the help of my creative team—another example of moving from the conceptual to the specific.

Be Consistently Inconsistent

One of my favorite restaurants in Dallas is the Green Room. The first time Lisa and I went to this restaurant, the waiter said, "You ought to try the 'Feed Me' dinner."

We took his suggestion and found out what "Feed Me" actually meant: you get to eat whatever the chef feels like preparing. He's back in the kitchen literally letting the creative juices flow, and you have no idea what's coming.

The church should serve creative dishes just like the "Feed Me" dinner. People should always wonder what's coming next. As our creative teams are preparing the weekend meal, people should expect the unexpected. This approach to ministry serves up a constant flow of new ideas and changing paradigms.

Being consistently inconsistent appeals to a culture that expects change. One of the reasons the church has been accused of being irrelevant or stagnant is because it has not embraced change but sat in neutral. One of the mantras of Fellowship Church is, The only thing that is constant is change. It's also been said that the *FC* in our logo doesn't stand for *Fellowship Church* but *Frequent Change.*

Vary the people you include in your creative meetings. Vary the time you meet and, occasionally, the place where you convene. The important principle is to keep change constant. The easiest way to accomplish this is to identify and empower crucial teammates. When you have identified these players, don't be afraid to tinker with the elements to continue to foster new growth and innovation.

It is paramount that you change environments every so often. Our favorite place to meet is a den we created that provides a comfortable, laid-back atmosphere with couches and overstuffed chairs. It is stocked with refreshments and, of course, coffee. Over the years, I've found that God uses caffeine (espresso in particular) as inspiration in the creative process. Even though the den is our preferred place to meet, we'll sometimes sit around a large table or pull up chairs around the desk in my study or drive to a local coffee shop for part of the meeting. And for long-term creative planning (when we go through our menu of sermon series for the year), we'll go on a retreat for a couple of days. The point is, even if you have a common or favorite place to meet, change it up from time to time for variety's sake. And wherever you are, make sure it's an environment where creativity can flow.

Create a Constant-Critique Mentality

The team approach has also forced me to critique my messages before and after I give them. As previously mentioned, before I preach, we assemble our team together to go over my introduction, main points, illustrations, and conclusion. Before I even enter this meeting, I have done my homework and have enough research to pull the talk together. However, during these meetings, I have to be willing to change my ideas according to the feedback of my trusted teammates.

Obviously, this is easier said than done. After spending hours in prayer and research, it is often difficult to abandon a specific direction. Basically, you need to check your ego at the door. Since even pastors are not immune from the pitfall of pride, this is a great spiritual exercise in humility. We are not afraid to say what is on our minds in these meetings. I have learned that when your team wisely reworks an angle of your message, it is best to listen to them. And if they tell you that they're having trouble following your train of thought, imagine how difficult it will be for your audience. Sometimes a crazy idea will turn out to be a brilliant idea. When there is a lively atmosphere with lots of give and take, the possibilities are endless. I've learned over and over that it's wise to consult with a plurality of leadership before I ever speak a word.

We also have a team critique after our messages. As previously mentioned, I like to have a critique meeting with our management staff after the first service Saturday evening. We'll assemble our worship staff along with our management team and watch the video of the service. We'll evaluate the flow, the length, and the overall impact of the service. Again, everybody has to check their egos at the door. If the drama doesn't advance the message, it is cut. If the music is too long or inappropriate to the sermon, it is changed on the fly. If my message doesn't make sense, the team offers ways to enhance the clarity of the talk. A culture of constant critiquing can be difficult for your pride, but it ensures that you and your leaders are being stretched to greater heights for greater impact.

Come Prepared

Participants must come to the meetings armed and dangerous—a principle that has become even more necessary as our creative team has grown. There is great freedom in the creative process, but that freedom emerges from order and preparation. In the past, we have dropped the ball here, calling a creative meeting without defining a specific agenda or having done enough advance research. When we assembled, the meeting was a bust because we hadn't done the necessary prep work to make the meeting profitable.

But when we launched a sermon series called "Character Tour," I'd given my teammates a heads-up about our need to meet for ideas for our next series. During the intervening days between the alert and the meeting, my creative team brainstormed on their own before we convened as a group. Once we were together, we had a wealth of good ideas and numerous directions to explore.

Have a Good Time

A good indicator of whether your team is working well together is the fun factor. If you don't have a good time, then something is wrong. You may have gotten the impression that these meetings are all work and no play, but nothing could be further from the truth. Though they must be strategic and structured, the process itself should add joy to your ministry. You should laugh and joke around. In short, it should be a lot of fun.

We don't hear often enough that church work should be fun. I would venture to say that the reason ministry has become a drag for many pastors is because they are trying to do it all by themselves. No doubt, there are some hard times that require perseverance. On the whole, though, ministry is supposed to be a privilege. As the apostle Paul reminded us, our work in the Lord should be marked by joy. By and large, our team has a great time together. And that is extremely gratifying for me as the leader.

Choose the Right Players

A huge part of making the planning process enjoyable is choosing the right teammates for the job. We've already spent an entire chapter on the importance of selecting the right staff for your organization, so I won't belabor that point. But choosing the key players for your creative team is even more critical. When it comes to adding team members, you should keep the following questions in mind: Are you glad when this person enters the room? Can you see yourself being challenged by her? Will this person fit into your team culture? And, of course, do you like him? Answering these questions will go a long way toward helping you select the right people for the right roles on your team.

An Example of Team Creativity

You may wonder how you can ensure that your meetings are spent on specifics rather than on abstract or general concepts. Let me walk you through an example from the "Character Tour" series I mentioned earlier, in which I prepared a sermon on discipline.

For my preparation, I spent ten hours by myself in various settings—at my office, at Starbucks, at home—doing a "mind dump." During this phase of the process, I took my journal and wrote out thoughts and concepts related to discipline. I didn't eliminate or restrict any thought, even though it may have been off in left field. Whatever came to my mind, I wrote down. For this talk, I came up with several synonyms or examples of discipline, like endurance, marathon, and hitting the wall. As I began compiling these seemingly random thoughts, I added stories and illustrations into a rough structure.

After I had done this, I looked back at other talks I had done in the past that may have related to discipline or a similar theme. This is an important point for speakers who have been in the game for awhile. Don't be shy about looking at research or other material from previous talks you've given. A great message is like a great song. It has to be heard more than once.

A pastor friend of mine always reminds me of the sad reality that people forget what preachers say after only a few weeks. So as I was studying for this talk, I remembered that I did a series eleven years prior called "That's the Way the Character Crumbles." Because I was speaking to less than a thousand people at the time, this would be new material for more than 95 percent of the audience, and the other 5 percent would have long since forgotten it. I discovered that I had some really good research and information that I was able to rework into a fresh format.

Not too long ago, I reworked a few older sermons into a new series called "Ignite." I took these talks and tweaked them by taking a fresh angle on the main ideas and contemporizing the illustrations. After the messages, people were coming up to me and saying, "Wow, Ed! That was a great message! I've never heard that before. That was so deep." These people had been attending Fellowship for ten years. Never underestimate the value of updating or reworking prior research to give your creativity a facelift. A fresh angle on just one point from a prior sermon might spark an entire new series.

Back to the "Character Tour" series: my team and I were playing with about thirty different titles before we landed on this selection. Since I'm a frustrated artist, we were also playing with the idea of having me draw a new caricature of a biblical character each week of the series for an introductory video. However, after I drew Daniel for the first installment, I realized it would be too time-consuming and that I couldn't produce the kind of high-quality art every week to really make this idea fly.

Another idea that we came up with was for me to begin to draw a sketch during the first installment and then continue to work on the sketch each week until it was complete at the conclusion of the series. I had done something similar in the past for an Easter message. Several years ago, I painted a portrait of Jesus on stage while I was talking and integrated the message with the art. Our people are reminded of that particular message as they see the portrait I painted displayed in our church bookstore.

However, rather than duplicating this creative idea for "Character Tour," we went in another direction. We had a professional artist do a sketch of a biblical character (or what would be understood as a biblical character within this context), and we videotaped him while he sketched. Our video department did what they do best and edited that down to create a short promo to show before each sermon. We also used the sketch for the cover of the worship guide (see app. 11).

Our team came up with all of the specific character traits we would cover each week and which biblical characters best personified those qualities. We decided the individual character traits would serve as the titles of each message (discipline, endurance, courage, and so on), and then we came up with a definition for each one. We also developed our own creative definition of the term *character*, which I thought was worth the whole series. We still use that definition to this day every time I talk about the meaning of character. And then, after the series was over, we printed bookmarks with all of these definitions for people to put in their Bibles. Here's what the bookmark had on it:

> *Character Is an Outward Reflection of an Inward Connection.*
> *Discipline—Doing What You Ought to Do So You Can Do What You Want to Do*
> *Endurance—Stampeding through the Stopping Points of Life*
> *Courage—The God-Given Ability to Stand*
> *Vision—Seeing the Apparent through the Transparent*
> *Creativity—Riding on the Rugged Edge of Innovation*
> *Love—A Supernatural Commitment Lived Out through the Grip of God's Grace*
> *Organization—A Decision Followed by a Process*

This turned out to be one of the most powerful and memorable series we've ever done. And I'm not bragging on myself; I'm bragging on my team and the entire process. I could never have come up with what we did as a group during this series. And that has been true for many, many other series over the past few years.

What's holding you back? Are you ready to take the plunge into team creativity? Do it for yourself. Do it for your church. Do it for your family.

Mapping the Creative Planning Process

The example below is a summary of the way we plan our messages every week at Fellowship. This is only a guideline, not a set-in-stone order of events for planning. Depending on the topic and nature of the sermon, we may not go through each of these four steps every week. But we always go through some version of this process in creating the final sermon.

I am not suggesting that you adopt this exact order for planning in your church context. You need to evaluate the best way for your team to plan based on your personality as the lead speaker and your unique style. You also need to consider whether you are a visual learner or an auditory learner and whether you like to prepare from a linear outline or from the full text of your message.

You also need to consider the particular dynamics of your team, focusing on their strengths and weaknesses. How can the people around you best help you carry the load every week? Maybe you don't need help throughout the entire process but in one or more areas of research, brainstorming, transcribing notes, writing the working document, or editing the final draft. Or you may just need some people to sit and listen to you talk through your message for two or three hours each week. I'm more of a visual and auditory learner, so I'm learning the sermon all week as I talk through it with the people on my team. They know when I need their input and when I just need them to be sounding boards for my ideas.

Whatever you need to do to help lighten the load and better use the people around you, do it. Make this change to creative-team planning and, I promise, it will change the landscape of your ministry and your life. Don't wait until you hit the wall; start allowing the people around you to encourage and help you along the way toward better, more meaningful, more creative leadership. In communicating God's Word, lives are impacted for eternity by what you say and how you say it, so make sure each message is the very best it can be. Your creative team is an integral part of making that happen.

Fellowship Church
Message Preparation Process

1. Pre-Meeting Process
   a. Time: Varies
   b. Participants: Me, my research staff, and my assistant
   c. Objectives
      - Research (me and research staff)
        > Bible study aids—electronic reference software, commentaries, language tools, study Bibles, etc.
        > Current books on the topic—both Christian and secular
        > Internet search for related articles or statistics
        > Magazines/periodicals
        > Past messages in personal archives
        > Messages by other speakers/pastors (Rick Warren, Bill Hybels, Tony Evans, etc.)
      - Creation of research document (me and pastor assistant)
        > I take notes from all research and dictate initial ideas onto audiotape.
        > My assistant transcribes the ideas to create a research document for the creative-team meeting.
        > Document is put in mind-map form, so that the entire text of the sermon is on one legal-size page, front and back.
   d. Result: Main sermon idea and research document created.

2. Creative-Team Meeting
   a. Time: Varies
   b. Participants: Creative team, usually four to six people, including two or three regulars with the rest determined by the message need (if message is on singles, invite singles pastor and a single staff member)
   c. Environment: Comfy living space with snacks and drinks offered. White board and poster-size notepads hang throughout room for note-taking during brainstorming.
   d. Objectives:
      • Prepare participants (if possible) by handing out mind map prior to meeting to help them generate ideas.
      • Hammer out introduction.
        > Use research document to generate ideas.
        > Bounce ideas and get ideas from creative team.
        > Write best ideas down on white board or note pads to be fine-tuned until intro is word-for-word.
        > Work on transitional statement between intro and body of sermon, making sure intro isn't just gimmicky, but really works with sermon.
        > Make changes on mind-map document.
      • Begin to develop body of sermon (based on mind map).
        > Develop points using creative wording and a consistent theme.
        > Start with main sermon topic and, using biblical research as a reference point, work on creating relevant application points.
        > Brainstorm ideas under each point and take notes.

> Choose best ideas and make changes to mind map.
- Work on transitional statements between points (introduction and transitions are most important aspects to any message).
  > Get ideas on illustrations that will enhance points. (Don't force an illustration. If it doesn't fit easily and stand on its own, don't use it.)
  > Make changes to mind map.
- Develop concluding remarks.
  > Pull introduction and points together into the final take-away message.
  > Make changes to mind map.
  e. Result: Rough draft of sermon

3. Follow-up Creative-Team Meeting (CTM)
   a. Time: Varies, takes place the day following original CTM
   b. Participants: Two or three of the regulars
   c. Objectives:
      - Fine-tune content.
        > Tweak introduction and work on verbiage.
        > Hone wording of transitions and points.
        > Check consistency of entire message and trim or add content for timing.
        > Rework concluding remarks as needed for maximum impact.
      - Prepare final mind map and message notes (see appendix—I use the mind map as a study tool and take the notes with me on stage).
        > Try to finish by Wednesday afternoon or Thursday morning.

> Revisit message Saturday afternoon to see it with fresh eyes and make the appropriate changes prior to speaking on Saturday evening.

    d. Result: Final draft of sermon

4. Weekend Study, Preparation, and Critique
   a. Time: Saturday afternoon
   b. Participants: Me and media director (to get PowerPoint presentation of verses and main points done)
   c. Objectives:
      - Study and pray through sermon.
      - Fine-tune verbiage, illustrations, transitions, flow, and conclusion.
      - Cut material as needed (sometimes, I have to cut quite a bit at to get it down to a twenty-five-to-thirty-minute message, but I'd rather start out with too much than not have enough material).

5. Message Critique
   a. Time: Quickly after the first message on Saturday night
   b. Participants: Several of the creative team members including some of the worship team
   c. Objectives:
      - Critique music, message, and drama.
      - Make sure each element in the service ties into the message—if something doesn't, it is changed or discarded.
      - Watch a video of the first-service message and provide any last-minute feedback before I speak at the second Saturday night service.

> \> The final sermon usually comes together after
> the first service on Saturday, but because I
> speak four times, I may continue to fine-tune
> the sermon throughout the weekend. I then
> pick the best of these to be transcribed and
> reproduced in the audio/video package of the
> series.

d. Result: Final sermon

Creative Q & A: Section 3

Q: What are some of the potential problems with the staff-led church model?

A: Although I am partial to a staff-led church model, I also recognize the potential dangers with this model. The greatest pitfall would be the temptation for staff members to abuse power since there's no committee overseeing their actions. The church is run by people, so there is always that potential for corruption. Human beings are, after all, fallible.

However, the safeguard to this is making sure you and your staff are called to their profession by God. The people calling the shots in a staff-led church should be people with a clear vision of where God wants them to go and what He wants them to do.

Certainly, we see example after example of leaders who have corrupted their power and used their position to glorify themselves rather than God. I doubt that such a so-called Christian leader will get very far in ministry. Anyone who tries to maintain control for his own power and purposes will eventually fall, and fall hard! The only way any of us can hope to maintain a creative and leading edge is by the grace and power of Jesus Christ.

I'm not saying that a staff-led model should not have any accountability built in. We must all be accountable for our actions. As previously mentioned, Fellowship's staff is accountable to me, and I am accountable to the board of trustees. The board oversees every major business decision and signs off on every check that leaves the church. There is no way anyone could embezzle money or steal from the church without our board knowing about it. There is no way I could be involved in a major moral failure without the board finding out.

The greatest safeguard, however, is not the accountability of a lay leadership board (although that is necessary) but our accountability to Christ. And the greatest benefit is that leaders, who are responsible for and called to the work of the ministry, are free to lead in the day-to-day work of the church.

Another potential problem in a staff-led church is neglecting to hand off the ball of ministry to volunteers and lay leaders in the church. Just because the church is ultimately led by the staff does not mean that we do all of the work of the ministry. We are still called to equip the saints for the work of the church.

While you and your staff are in charge of safeguarding the vision of your church, you must also be very intentional about recruiting and training volunteers in every area of ministry. Don't let the laity in your church think, *Oh, the church is led by the staff, so they don't need us.* Nothing could be further from the truth. The staff cannot and should not do all the work.

I've said that Fellowship tries to keep its staff numbers on the lean side. One reason we do that is to get the church people involved in ministry—whether in the nursery, children's church, high school ministry, singles ministry, greeting, hospitality, baptism, parking, ushering, or you name it. We could not do what we do without the thousands of volunteers who sign up and show up every weekend. And your church wouldn't be where it is today, either, if it weren't for your volunteers.

Q: What are some specific things to keep in mind when firing a staff member?

A: When it comes to the duty of firing someone, there are several key elements to remember. Remember, as Donald Trump is fond of saying, that "it isn't personal; it's business." Leave the situation at the church and don't take that stress home with you. You are in a leadership position for the long haul; letting stress eat you up will put you out of the game early. That's not to say that you don't care about the people you let go, but it's important to do what you have to do and then move on.

As a leader, you have got to remember that your focus is fulfilling God's mission for your church or organization. Leadership is not a popularity contest. When you fire someone, people may think you are mean or unfair. That's just the way it is. But as a leader, you have to be willing to keep the big picture in mind and focus on the greater good, the greater cause, the greater vision that God has for your church.

I know there's a difficult tension when it comes to firing someone. For one thing, you have compassion for that person. You know they have a family to take care of and bills to pay. On the other hand, if they aren't working out, you don't want to continue paying them for a job they aren't doing. So there's a real tension in deciding what to do. Do you give someone chance after chance after chance? Or do you just say, "Well, you aren't cutting it. You're out of here!" Where is the middle ground on this issue?

If someone isn't working out in a particular area but has a heart for your ministry, a love for the church, and a life that displays loyalty and hard work, try moving that person to another department first. It may be that God has put them in your church, while you have put them in the wrong area. Give them the chance to soar somewhere else within your church. If they still aren't working out after a move, it may be that they aren't cut out to be part of your staff.

Something else to remember about firing someone is not to put the decision off. If someone isn't working out, they probably will never work out. Don't prolong the inevitable. Let them go sooner rather than later. Every time I have waited to release someone, I have regretted it. Trust me; it's better for them and better for you to release these people.

Most of the time, when someone is in a position that they need to be released from, they are miserable. They're usually not doing the job because they're not really happy in the position. By keeping them in place, I'm prolonging their misery. Almost every time I've released those people, it's amazing to see how much better off they are in the long run. Most of the time, those people have gone on to do a bigger, better, and more enjoyable job somewhere else.

God is working in the life of your church and the direction that you are going. But He doesn't stop there. He also has a plan for the person's life that you have to release. And too many times we're keeping that person from experiencing God's hand in their life by not letting them go. So don't prolong the situation. Trust that you are doing the right thing and let them go.

Something else to keep in mind is that you never fire someone and then allow them to continue working on campus for two, three, four, or five more weeks until you find a replacement. That's crazy! If you let someone go but allow them to stick around, they're going to spread negativity and pessimism throughout the staff during that time. That's when back-biting, gossip, and slander will snake their way into your staff. If you want to give that person six or eight weeks of severance pay, release them immediately and pay them. But don't let that person come back and spread negativity throughout your staff.

Something else that is vital to remember in firing someone is having a witness present at the time. Never release someone on your own. Have another staff member in the office with you. For example, we have a human resource director on staff who is always present when we release someone. In some particularly difficult cases, you may want a third or even fourth party present to make sure that you have several witnesses to attest to the fact that everything was done in accordance with both established labor laws and your organization's personnel policies. It's a sad reality, but people will often sue the church after being fired. So it is better to cover all your bases than to leave room for error.

It's also important to document everything prior to releasing someone. Make a paper trail of all that has led up to this decision and the reasoning behind your actions. This protects you and your organization in the event of a lawsuit, and the person being released will know, while he may not like your decision, that you had good cause to release him.

Anytime you release someone, you need to have a plan. The Evil One has a plan to mess up the church. And the way he does that is by attacking it from the inside in, coming after the staff. So when you have to let someone go, remember that the Evil One wants to use that as an avenue for attack. This is where the trust issue comes directly into play.

Often, you can't and shouldn't relay all of the details to the entire staff. Firing should not be a public event. So your staff needs to trust your decision. If your staff trusts you, then you don't have to give all the details as to why you let someone go. If someone on your staff is questioning your decision, that may be a red flag that they don't trust your leadership.

The congregation must also trust your leadership, believing that you had good reason to make that decision. You will probably be attacked when you fire someone. People in the congregation notice pretty quickly when a staff member is missing, especially if you have a smaller church. But as the leader, you need to let the congregation know that you are the one making the decisions, and they need to trust that you are making the right ones. If someone doesn't trust your leadership, that's OK. They may need to find someplace else where they are more comfortable with the leadership and can trust the decisions being made.

Q: God has called me to lead a church, but I am the only staff member. How can I take on such a huge responsibility and still successfully fulfill the vision God has given to me?

A: When we first began Fellowship Church, I was the only staff member. Coming from a staff of more than 300 people at my previous church, I knew it was going to be a difficult task. Like every small-church pastor, I was now solely responsible for everything from the pulpit to the preschool.

I thought and prayed long and hard about the abilities and gifts that God had blessed me with and came to a very obvious conclusion: I wasn't going to do it all alone. I couldn't. If I tried, then I would fail miserably at doing the very thing God had called me to do. So I got together with some of the key members of our little church and said, "You know what? You guys and gals are going to be the staff of Fellowship. I know that we can't pay you right now, but we're going to treat you like staff. I need some help doing this thing, and you guys are going to help." So I appointed these lay people to be my ad hoc staff.

I didn't realize it at the time, but I was doing much more than just filling a few empty slots with some qualified people. I was beginning to implement a principle that has been a huge help in our church over the years—delegation.

When it came to message preparation, I still took that responsibility on all by myself. And I talked about how that affected me earlier in the book. But as far as the other aspects of the church, I learned early on to delegate to those around me.

Leading a church, no matter what its size, is an enormous responsibility that can easily wipe anyone out. I had to do something from the get-go to avoid that dangerous pitfall and, thankfully, a good friend advised me. "Ed," he said, "you need to lead your church as if it's double its current size." There was no way I could fly solo when our church doubled, so I needed to prepare for that growth right then.

So I began to delegate early on, giving leadership responsibilities to the natural leaders in our church. I let the people around me help in areas where they had the greater gift. I've already mentioned that I'm not a very good counselor, so I began to delegate the counseling responsibilities. Every time I handed the ball of ministry to someone else, I was teaching leadership and showing them what our church would look like in the future. I knew God had great things in store for us and wanted others to share that vision. But I also recognized that those great things would never come to pass if I tried to do it all by myself.

Here's where I believe many church leaders mess up. Leaders will start these churches and do everything for the first two or three years—moving chairs, setting up tables, etc. They think, *I've got to do all I can to help, because I'm supposed to be a servant. I've got to be in the trenches, because I want to show the people that I can work too.*

But then the church begins to grow. And five years down the road those leaders are wiped out.

The best way to save your energy for the long haul is to delegate. Find leaders around you, hand them the ball, and let them lead. Remember, you are training for a marathon, not a sprint. We must use discernment regarding the activities we get involved with, given our unique giftedness as leaders. Do those few things that only you can do.

Leaders are often control freaks. We're freaky about vision, innovation, and passion—we've got to be freaky about that stuff because it's what drives us. But we should never do what we can delegate to others. There are certain things that only I can do. Those things I shouldn't delegate. But the things that I know others are gifted at are things that I should delegate. If I don't, then I'm trying to work outside of my giftedness.

God has called me to teach. He's called me to preach. He's called me to write. He hasn't called me to head up the missions ministry or the small-group ministry. So we have put others, who have the appropriate gifts, in charge of those areas. At first, those were volunteers; now we have staff leading those areas.

Obviously, if you have a very small church, you may be required to do more of the work in several different areas with the help of volunteers. But don't wait for your church to double in size before learning the principle of delegation. Begin now to delegate to the gifted people around you. Let them share the burdens and joys of ministry. Don't try to do it all yourself, because that is a guaranteed formula for frustration. Operate in the area of giftedness that God's given you and then delegate, delegate, delegate.

Q: How do I find the right people to bring on my creative team?

A: I have noticed a few things about creative people that help them stand out. They have an insatiable desire to learn. They always look for growth. They don't stagnate. They don't stop. They are always developing, always moving, and always searching.

As a leader, the greatest and fastest way to find those people is to look around and take note of those people who want to grow and learn. Find those people who are always looking for new things to do and new ways to do them. I'm not talking about the people who can't commit to anything. I'm talking about people who are willing to ask tough questions and search for tough answers. Those are the kind of people you need to surround yourself with—those are your creative people.

Creative people are also the ones who aren't afraid to work— grit-under-their fingernails, down-in-the-ditches work. Most people don't want to pay the price for creativity because it requires sacrifice on their part. But it is worth it. And when you find people who are willing to sweat a little, you've found some creative people.

Creative people make their creativity look easy because of their tireless work ethic. The easier something appears, the harder they have worked at doing it. The process of creativity is difficult as it involves making something complex understandable. It would be easy to take a complex book like the Bible and keep it complex. But if you find those people who have a knack for making the difficult understandable, then you've found some very creative people.

You are surrounded by creative people. Every single person you know is creative. They are sitting around you. They are in your family. They live next door to you. They are in the doctor's office and on the bus. Every person you make eye contact with is creative.

So what you need to do as a creative leader is discover those who are willing to work at developing their own creativity. You need to find those people who aren't afraid to sacrifice a little and use their creativity to leverage great things for God's kingdom. And once you find those people, you will maximize your own creativity in great ways.

Don't convince yourself that you have all the answers when it comes to creativity. None of us does. But we can each learn and grow when we surround ourselves with people who continually want to grow.

Section 4

Overcoming Creative Obstacles

A Case Study in Creative Leadership

CHRISTOPHER COLUMBUS

IN OCTOBER 1492, somewhere between the familiar world behind him and the world that lay ahead, Christopher Columbus found himself in a virtual standstill. The wind that had faithfully carried his three ships so far suddenly ceased to propel them any farther. They were 2,000 miles to the west of Spain—twice as far as anyone had sailed in history.

The fleet of ninety men began to wonder if they would ever see home again. Fear and uncertainty ravaged the crews. Did they have enough provisions to last the trip? What if they had to turn around? They knew they had enough food to last only half that distance. Most of the men had given up on ever finding land, much less discovering a new route to China. They urged Columbus to turn back.

Columbus knew that their request was not unreasonable. After all, they had left their families and friends a world away— all in hopes of discovering a new way to a land none of them had ever seen before. Columbus also knew that turning back would mean surrendering to defeat and certain death. He asked the crew for three more days. He knew they were tired, hungry, and scared. He knew their emotions were running high and their enthusiasm for adventure was running low. But he also knew that he couldn't give up—not yet.

The next day, the wind picked up and a new wave of panic ambushed the fleet. The wind was driving the ships westward at a speed of ten miles an hour. If they did finally decide to turn back, making it back to Spain would be nearly impossible. Now that they had missed their chance to turn back, the crew began to doubt the leadership of their captain.

Columbus knew he had to act quickly, so he called his fleet together. He could have pointed out the fact that if they did turn back to Spain and actually made it back home, they would all surely face the hangman's noose for mutiny. But instead, he simply asked them to wait two more days.

Two days later, amid the rolling swells and crashing waves, the crew found a flower floating in the sea. Then a tree limb drifted nearby. Again, fear enveloped the crew. If land was this close, and they were traveling this fast, surely they would be dashed against the shoreline in the middle of the night. The crew began to whisper mutiny, blaming Columbus for their misfortune.

But two hours after midnight on October 12, 1492, a cannon fired a single shot, signaling the sight of land. Columbus victoriously called out, "Land!" And within hours, ninety men were standing on the white shoreline—not one man was lost.

Creativity is not an overnight plane trip; it is a long, hard, and often grueling course that is navigated in the trenches. And much like Columbus, creative leaders must have the foresight to see past the impending perils and to ride out the waves of the creative seas if they hope to successfully reach the shoreline. Serious obstacles and opposition will present themselves. But if Columbus, a bounty hunter and sailor, had the drive and determination to break through the obstacles on the Atlantic Ocean to reach a new land in the name of Spain, shouldn't we be more than willing to do the same and more to reach new people in the name of Christ?

Columbus did not lose anyone in his crew during those three treacherous days at sea. Yet we are surrounded by thousands and thousands of lost souls each and every day. We must work just as hard as Columbus, be just as focused on the goal, and be willing to stay the course to reach out and save those souls from drowning.

Consider it pure joy,
my brothers, whenever you
face trials of many kinds.
JAMES 1:2

CHAPTER 9

Creative Cramps

We were in the midst of a capital campaign, and our technical team had prepared a video to help promote the building program during our weekend service. It was a great video—the camera angles, movement, and music were highly innovative and visually spectacular. But there was one glaring exception. The narration was a bit of a downer: "Are you tired of over-crowded children's and preschool rooms? Sick of waiting in lines to drop off your kids or park? Give to the Fellowship Church Building Fund . . ."

The narration went on and on like that. Visually and artistically the video was right on target. In terms of creativity, it was one of our best. But there was a significant problem that needed to be addressed. The person in charge of this project was new to our staff and didn't understand that *people give to vision, not need*—something I discovered a long time ago. Even though the video was visually appealing, it didn't support the positive message we were

Success is the ability to go from failure to
failure without losing your enthusiasm.
SIR WINSTON CHURCHILL

trying to promote. Just forty-five minutes before our first weekend service was to begin, we decided to cancel the video. This is just one example of what we call a *creative cramp*. This particular creative cramp occurred in the midst of a crucial capital campaign. Isn't it funny how cramps occur at the worst possible time?

Cramps hurt. Cramps can be debilitating. They can slow you down for a short period of time or they can be a symptom that exposes a major injury. After a rigorous workout, I'll often experience cramping in one or both of my legs. Some of these cramps can be so severe as to prevent me from walking.

The same thing happens to all of us in the creative realm. Every creative person will experience cramping. Anyone who exercises their muscles experiences cramping. As a result of these cramps, those of us who are engaged in creative leadership could become paralyzed from achieving our purpose. It's as if we are paralyzed from moving creatively.

When a cramp happens, you have two options for treatment: rub the cramp and attempt to temporarily soothe the pain or stretch out the muscles and keep going. As a creative leader, you have to ask yourself some tough questions: Will I continue to splash in the soothing shallows of sameness, or will I risk riding on the crest of creativity? Will I opt for temporary relief from the pain, or will I stretch out the cramp and keep going? If you're serious about taking that plunge, be aware of the creative cramps that can cause damage in the church if that creativity is misused or mismanaged. With that in mind, let's consider several key principles to help you manage the creative cramps.

Content Dictates Creativity

God is a God of order, and the Bible is a book of order. If we desire to mimic God's creative genius, we have to realize that our creativity must emerge from order, not chaos. Too many people are looking to jump on the creative bandwagon without realizing this important distinction: You don't start with creativity; you start with God. He alone is the Author of creativity. Remember, everyone reading these words is a creative genius. The question, then, is not, How can I become creative? but, How can I unleash the creativity that's already present inside me?

The church should be the most creative entity in the universe, because it's the place where the children of our Creator are united to express their love to Him. But that charging ship called creativity must always be controlled by the rudder of timeless biblical truth. In other words, the truths in Scripture should drive our creativity; creativity must not drive the biblical message. Biblically driven teaching is given to us by Christ and His apostles. And creativity is a vehicle to communicate this timeless truth into forms that capture the imagination and hearts of our audiences.

Therefore, we must be willing to trash a creative idea if it does not help people better understand God or the Word of God. For this reason, I try very hard not to make reference to an R-rated movie or cultural situation that is explicitly immoral or causes a member of my audience to stumble. You simply cannot mix a biblical message with a cultural message that is obscene or immoral.

Along with the Bible, your weekly message should drive your creative content. Present a unified or holistic message. Let the music and drama set up the message, helping the audience see the truth come to life. Don't confuse or distract your audience from the message that God has given to you that week. If a video or drama does not underscore the theme of the service, then it's just a prop and should be removed.

Every so often—usually after a particularly multisensory weekend—we go back to the basics with a simple, low-key service. A basic chips-and-salsa service will not only make the more innovative and creative services stand out, but will also teach our audience to experience God's truth without the bells and whistles of modern technology. Without balance, we can lose perspective and fall into creative overload, effectively wearing too much dangling jewelry that detracts from an attractive outfit. Again, use your entire creative team to strategically plan a holistic service. The more diversely talented people you have in the mix, the more chances you have to plan dynamic services that honor God and keep you from overaccessorizing.

I live in the Dallas–Fort Worth area—home of the Dallas Cowboys, real cowboys, big hair, and Texas flair. Accessory overload is at an epidemic level in the metroplex. Just a quick glance in a local restaurant or shopping mall will reveal outfits with too many necklaces, bracelets, belts, and bags. I've learned that sometimes the best fashion advice is learning what not to wear.

Likewise, the key to a great worship service is all about choosing the right accessories. Too many watches, gold chains, and clashing colors will not get your people where you want them to go. In fact, they will actually distract your people from the message. The answer is not more videos, louder music, and better singers. Though all of these elements can have an important role in reaching our culture, we must exercise caution when we use any of them. If it's too flashy, our people may miss the essence of the gospel. If we're not careful, we can easily become prop-, video-, drama-, or music-driven.

Biblical content must inform our creativity. Similarly, our weekly message must drive the creative content of each service. At Fellowship Church, we've found that our audience responds best when there is one central message highlighted and underscored by each element in our worship service. Don't fall into the temptation of allowing the authority of Scripture to be overshadowed by lesser elements, as creative as they may be.

Excellence Doesn't Equal Expense

Creative cramps can easily occur in the financial realm. Don't believe that you have to be a big church with a big budget to be successful as a creative leader. You have more resources than you realize right where you are. A smaller church can use its intimate setting to really maximize the creative potential. Since the audience can typically distinguish a small object or photograph in the hands of the speaker, a bigger or more elaborate visual is not necessarily a better one. Small churches also have less complicated audio-visual systems in place. We have experienced many headaches when we've had to delay the beginning of our service or revamp a song or drama that didn't fit as well as we planned. Small churches are much more able to shift on the fly without major disruptions. For these reasons and more, I would say that the smaller church actually has some distinct creative advantages over a larger church.

Regardless of size, every church can be excellent. A lot has been said and written about excellence in ministry, but it boils down to basically two extremes. On one end of the continuum is the "keep-it-real" crowd that strives to be authentic and free-flowing in their execution. Unfortunately, that can often be a disguise for laziness. Under the guise of "keeping it real," some have chosen consistency and predictability over creativity and effectiveness. On the other end of the continuum is the regimented, production-crazed crowd who has gone so far as to discourage the coughs of the audience in their service script. Our challenge is to find that happy medium.

One important caution in the financial realm relates to technology. Technology is either a tool or a tail. It has incredible potential to be used as a tool to leverage some great things for God's kingdom. We have recently been able to use technology so that my weekly message can appear simultaneously to four separate campuses at the same time. In a sense, my ministry potential has quadrupled because of technological breakthroughs. But technology also has the potential to be the tail that wags the dog. And that dog can quickly turn into a pit bull that seizes your discretionary dollars.

It's tempting to try and keep pace with our culture by acquiring the newest, hottest thing out there. Every time you consider investing in the latest technology, ask yourself, Who are the toys really for? You don't have to buy all of the high-end gear to be cutting edge. Some of the best videos we've done were shot with just one camera. In fact, in the early days, we rented cameras. Most of the finest creative elements in our worship services have emerged with minimal expense, but they have been delivered with maximum impact. You'd be amazed what you can do with a team of committed people who are passionate about showcasing the hope of the gospel. Obviously a church in today's culture needs to consider technology in the annual budget. However, make sure you research creative alternatives before you write a check.

Creativity Is Tethered to Tension

If you've ever taken any physics classes or fallen off your bike, you know that motion causes friction. This reality couldn't be truer in the church world. The essence of creativity is change, and people don't like change. Most people are comfortable with their friends, their seats, their classroom, and their way of doing things. Creativity upsets this entire equilibrium.

Pay attention to what people have to say and evaluate their suggestions honestly. But don't allow their fear of change to cause you creative cramps. Don't get discouraged by criticism. If you cower in the face of conflict, your creative potential will be undermined and your church will pay the price.

A close friend of mine who pastors a church in Florida told me about all of the creativity and positive change that was occurring in his church. He shared with me about a young man who had grown for several years under his leadership. One day, this young man walked up to my pastor friend and said that he was leaving the church. He said, "It's just changed too much. It's not the same church it was when I became a Christ follower."

My friend looked at this man in disbelief and said, "You know, we changed a lot to reach you. And now you're telling me you're not willing to change to reach the next group?"

Creativity is a long-term investment. If your top leaders are not totally committed to the vertical vision, then fear of friction will dismantle this God-given virtue. At Fellowship, we do not value upsetting people, but we do value upsetting their equilibrium to challenge them for spiritual growth. Studies have shown (and our church has proven) that creativity can change lives. To be sure, creativity must be biblically driven and it must honor God. However, when we have our people off balance, we have a great potential to catch them off guard with a powerful punch from the pages of Scripture.

Over the years, we've had many people question our leadership when change caused friction in their lives. We did the best we could to explain our reasoning but never detoured from our course of creative leadership. It is very tempting to want to please people, but leaders often experience leadership cramps when they allow their vision to be compromised to appease a few negative people. Once the vision goes horizontal, disaster will follow.

Creative Thinking Is Draining

Creativity is a thrill ride; it turns a boring routine into a challenging adventure. But at the same time, creativity is draining. The process of implementing a creative idea takes an enormous amount of time, thought, and energy. For me, there is nothing that is as demanding as thinking creatively. It's easy to keep complex ideas complex. It doesn't take much effort to quote highbrow theologians or Hebrew word studies from the pulpit. However, it does require commitment and a tireless work ethic to take the truth of God and communicate it simply. Isn't that what Jesus did? Don't be disheartened when you get weak in the knees and feel burned out from creative thinking. It will happen. But if you discover the catalysts that take you to creative heights, you can get back on track.

One critical component to keeping the creative juices flowing is to take regular, strategic breaks. My best ideas always occur during rest breaks. Have you ever wondered why you have these incredible ideas while playing golf or singing in your shower? For others, these ideas really fly when they are fishing at a stream or driving in their car.

It's during these down times that the *theta waves* —the brainwaves most responsible for creative thinking—are hitting the coastline of your consciousness. On the other hand, theta waves shut down when you are under pressure. Not surprisingly, theta waves are most active in the minds of children. To help these brainwaves really thrive, we have to check out of the adult world and its hectic schedule from time to time and engage in some childish recreational activities.

Discover the environments and activities (for me, it's fishing) that help your creativity soar then integrate them into your regular routine. What does it for you? Once you figure this out, you will rediscover the joy of creative thinking and leading your church to new frontiers.

Another critical element to beating the creative drain is to be consistently inconsistent in your planning. Believe it or not, it is possible to get stuck in a rut, even when you think you are being creative. Looking back, I can see various points in our ministry where we thought we were being creative but were actually floundering. After playing the same style of music in the same way in the same order every week, we landed in a creative rut. What was once innovative became predictable and stale. Innovation is all about being consistently inconsistent, which means that you need to keep people wondering what's coming next.

Remember that predictable communication leads to low connection between a speaker and his audience. Creative leaders break out of their mold, keep things changing, and have people on the edge of their seats waiting for the next message from the Lord.

Keep the Home Front at the Forefront

Creative ministry is demanding. And because this demand will never subside, you must make a commitment to protect the priorities and boundaries you've set up regarding your family and your work. Your pursuit of excellence in the creative church can become so all-encompassing that you abandon your marriage and family in the process. Your wife and kids will end up as casualties of mismanaged ministry. It's happened to too many of our peers. Don't let that happen to you.

I learned early on that delegation was the key to keeping my family priorities straight. Basically, I had to do those things that only I could do and delegate the rest. That was necessary for me, and it is for you as well because there is one thing we cannot delegate—time with our families. I tell the people in my church, "Unfortunately, I'm not able to know all your kids' names. I won't know your dogs' names. I'm not going to be able to attend every soccer game or graduation. I just can't meet personally with everyone." When I say that and follow through with my time commitment to my family, I am modeling the priority of the family. And that's the greatest message I will ever preach. My family doesn't care about my sermons or how many people attend Fellowship Church. They want to see me hanging out with them at home. They want their dad. And they want their dad to be there for Mom.

We have to show our families that they are not competing with the church. Too many kids feel that they are getting the leftovers from their dads in the ministry. Too many wives feel as though they are sharing their husbands with the entire church. Here's one specific way you can protect your family: Unplug yourself from technology.

As much as I love my cell phone, I have to make a conscious effort to turn it off once I come home or else I'll have it stuck to my head all night. Lisa has enforced a new rule in our house to combat this problem. She makes me stay in the car and finish my phone call before I'm allowed to come through the front door. We also disconnect our home phone periodically when life is getting hectic. One line remains open for emergencies, but only three people from the church have this special number.

The television is another vandal that can eat away time with your family. Not only does it offer more junk than useful information, but it also takes you away from good conversations with teachable moments. Basically, living life more simply is a great way to show your family that you are truly home. I'm not just talking about being physically present. I'm talking about being there in mind, body, and spirit.

I have a passion for helping people, especially other pastors, keep balance in their life. I challenge parents to keep their marriage and family a priority—first the marriage, then the kids. The greatest gift we can give our children is a great marriage. When we do that, everything else in the family will fall into place. We must constantly work at keeping balance between our work, our marriage and family, and our church involvement. For the pastor, the line between church involvement and work is often blurred, because those two worlds are one and the same. But even for pastors, I believe the biblical priority list is first, a personal relationship with God, then marriage, then the children, then church activities as a family, and finally, our work.

One of the biggest problems facing the evangelical church is the sad reality of divorce among Christians. I'm convinced that modeling a great marriage is the best way to turn the tides of divorce in the church today. We have to model a great marriage for our church and for our kids, who are watching our every move. Thursday night is an oasis for Lisa and me because it is our regular date night. We guard this night very jealously because it is the one time of the week we tear away from work and our kids to be alone. We celebrate that my weekly sermon is finished and that we get to rekindle our romantic flames. As I tell my congregation, what you used to get your wife is what you use to keep your wife. Don't ever stop romancing your spouse.

In the early days, when our kids were small, they would cry at the door when we'd leave them for our weekly date. That was difficult, but it's far better to have your kids crying at the door than crying at divorce court. If you don't protect this sacred time alone, everything and everyone will swallow it up. When we model this commitment to our kids, we are showing them that Mommy and Daddy are the leaders. The kids don't run the show; the parents do. We're also showing our teenage daughters what to look for in a godly husband and providing a godly example for our son as he matures.

Another way to model a great marriage is to always paint your spouse in a good light. Sometimes it's tempting for a speaker to share everything that is going on in their life; and obviously, that's needed to build authenticity between the speaker and his audience. However, you must make private decisions about what you will share in public. Don't ever let your wife hear you criticize her in front of hundreds of people. And screen all stories with your wife first (thereby avoiding the temptation to tell embarrassing stories in public—I've been guilty of that in the past, and believe me, it's not pretty).

As for the kids, I believe that quality time emerges from quantity time. You cannot make up for eleven months of neglect in a two-week vacation. Forget it. A positive and negative aspect of pastoral ministry is that your weekends are taken. The positive side is that you can schedule other kid times during the week that are probably unavailable for the nine-to-five crowd. On the other hand, the ministry can take away some great weekend time. For this reason, we have our staff take off one weekend per quarter to spend with their families. This time does not count as vacation time, but is a compensation for all the weekends they sacrifice for the church.

As a pastor, you have to plan strategic absences. It is wise to be away when most of your people are also absent, such as Thanksgiving weekend, the two weekends after Christmas, spring break, and a few weeks in the summer. My absences allow us to develop other speakers in our church and give people a fresh voice to listen to. It's a win-win.

Speaking of being strategically absent, make sure you maximize your vacation time with your family. Just like you don't want to double-date on your one night a week with your spouse, you don't want to take people on vacation with you. When generous people in your church offer their cottage or lake house for you and your family to enjoy, they sometimes mean that they will be joining you. Because the ministry is so demanding, you can't afford to have a "vacation" with non-family members. You need that time to rest and rekindle family connections.

A final comment is to guard the negativity you allow into your house. The ministry can be full of negative people, so be careful to keep your dinner table from becoming a place for harboring resentment and anger. Your kids are watching everything you do and say. We implemented a ten-to-one rule for this very reason, trying to tell ten positive stories about life change for every negative story from the life of our church. It is natural to want to hash out your hurt feelings, but these hurt feelings can easily turn dinnertime into bittertime. My wife has been so good to capture teachable moments when a negative comment comes into our family. Instead of responding in anger, we teach our kids to love people and to know that God is in control of everything. Though it is not easy to model the love of Christ when the emotions are running hot, it helps our kids see that the local church is a powerful agent of change, not negativity.

Turning people into full-court followers of Christ is a daunting task of tremendous challenges—some of which you may not have realized yet. Do yourself a favor: Take each challenge as it comes and don't worry about what's around the bend. Be prepared and be aware that challenges will come, but also have faith that God will give you the strength and grace to deal with each one when it surfaces in your ministry. When I think about what we've overcome at Fellowship over the past fifteen years, it's staggering. I suspect the same is true in your church. We make it through those times because we focus on keeping the vision vertical.

The ultimate meal deserves the ultimate presentation. And by managing the creative cramps, we have the ability to turn a bland, tasteless presentation of the Bread of Life into a colorful, multisensory experience that motivates and inspires people to take the Bread, eat it, and invite others to the meal. That's what the church is all about. Controlled creativity helps make that a reality in your church and mine. Not only will our church benefit from our creative commitment, but our family will also know that they are our first priority, the object of our greatest commitment toward creativity.

Time to stop working on this chapter now. I just spoke with my son on my cell phone. He had a great day and wants to tell me about it. So I'm going to talk to my son and give him a big hug. See ya later.

Of making many books there is no end, and much study wearies the body.
ECCLESIASTES 12:12

CHAPTER 10

Three Things They Didn't Teach Me in Seminary

When Lisa and I were married more than twenty-five years ago, we knew we wanted to have children and raise a family. We were two young people in love, feeling excited and a little bit scared about entering this next phase of our lives together. But we both came from very supportive families who loved us and brought us up in good Christian homes. We had read a couple of books. We had heard James Dobson and others speak on the family many times. We even attended a parenting seminar or two. So when Lisa was pregnant with LeeBeth, the first of our four children, we thought we were ready to rock and roll with the family band. We thought we knew the score on this parenting thing.

We didn't.

Nothing could have prepared us for the reality of parenting. No book. No speech. No seminar. Not even our great upbringing clued us in to the constant challenges of being a leader in the home.

> *I don't know the key to success, but the key to failure is trying to please everybody.*
> BILL COSBY

The same was true of becoming a senior pastor in a church plant. Watching top Christian leaders in action didn't prepare me. Learning leadership skills in various ministry positions didn't prepare me. Seminary provided me with great knowledge, but still didn't prepare me. There is only one way to learn to navigate the challenges of church leadership—by doing it.

The following pages represent the sobering facts of ministry that hit me square in the jaw when I began working as a senior pastor. Those who have been involved with a church plant know these sobering realities better than anyone. Church planters have to start at the ground level, cultivating leaders, building the vision, and raising important resources from day one. I hope my post-seminary, on-the-job education will help you understand and overcome the greatest challenges facing you and every church leader.

It Takes Super-Sized Cash to Finance Ministry

You can't go to a drive-through restaurant these days without being asked one particular question after placing your greasy order: "Do you want to super-size that?" (Thankfully, for our health's sake, this option is slowly being phased out because of a revealing documentary released in the past couple of years.)

But despite the connotations to the fast-food industry and its very questionable contributions to our overall health, church leaders need to get in the habit of asking this same question with the goal of motivating people toward greater spiritual growth through giving. People come to our churches week in and week out with their tithes and offerings. It's the pastor's responsibility to say, "Do you want to super-size that?" We must challenge our people to super-size their tithes and offerings to the greatest thing going and growing, the local church. This reality ambushed me as I left the safe haven of the seminary halls. What I discovered is that *it takes super-sized cash to finance ministry*. As point people, we have to say, "Don't you want to super-size that offering?"

For many of our regular attendees at Fellowship, the offering is a novel concept. Almost 50 percent of them came from an unchurched background, so the idea of tithing is even more foreign. All of our people, regardless of their church background, need to be challenged in managing the resources God has given to them. We do it for a spiritual reason (we're commanded to tithe) and for a practical reason (the work of ministry is not cheap). Whether your budget requires thousands, tens of thousands, hundreds of thousands, millions, or tens of millions, this mandate and responsibility does not change.

As I interact with pastors around the country or at our own Creative Church Conference at Fellowship, I am frequently asked about what has changed the most as Fellowship has grown. My answer is always the same: "My leadership style hasn't changed much. Our commitment to creativity hasn't changed. Our work ethic hasn't changed. What has changed the most is having to say no more often and having more zeroes behind everything."

Your values should not change. Your work ethic should not change. What should change is your numbers and range of influence. Your people need to understand the resources required—the mean green necessary—to provide the ultimate presentation of the Bread of Life so that lives can be changed. I recently told a group of pastors at one of our Total Access Conferences that we speak of millions of dollars now instead of the thousands or hundreds we used to talk about. But it's all relative. And regardless of where you are as a church (numbers-wise), it's all important—you just add more zeroes as you grow.

I have argued that creativity must remain a constant. As God blesses your creative efforts, your need to raise super-sized cash will remain a constant as well. And if you are the senior pastor, you are also the chief fund-raiser—like it or not. If you are thinking, "Well Ed, it's a God thing. I mean, God does it. Not me, right?" you're right—God does it. But God uses leaders like you and me to cast the vision, go for the ask, and close the deal. We've got to be serious about fund-raising if we say we're serious about reaching this culture for Christ.

Find, Develop, and Challenge People with the Gift of Giving

I'm sure you have already discovered that most people need an invitation to become a part of the life of your church. Most people will not just show up for your praise team or greeters' ministry out of the blue. Your best children's teachers don't fall from the sky. It just doesn't work that way. You must keep your eyes open for these talented and committed people who can add vitality to your ministry. It takes a strong and committed leader to invite the uncommitted to be an integral part of carrying out your vision. It is the same way with developing givers in your church.

About a year and a half ago, we were preparing to take our annual beach retreat with our youth ministry. A lot of kids and even some leaders needed money to go on this trip. I stood up in front of our people and announced, "If you want to give some scholarship money, if your heart really pounds for those kids who need the Lord, then I want you to step up and give to make this happen." Now, we do a lot of special offerings throughout the year, but I did challenge the people specifically for this need.

The Tuesday after that particular weekend, our chief financial officer called me and said, "Ed, I want you to know that someone gave a generous gift to our church for this beach retreat." She then told me this person's name.

"Is this person even a member or a part of Fellowship Church?" I asked.

"I've never heard of him in my life," she replied.

Wow, I thought, *this person's given a generous check and he's not even a part of our community! I'm going to get to know this person.*

So I called him that afternoon and scheduled a lunch the following week. I met this guy for lunch, and as we started talking, I realized he was not even a believer. God then gave me the awesome opportunity to lead him into a personal relationship with Christ. And during our time together, I did some reconnaissance work. I found out that this person had the unmistakable gift of giving.

The most amazing part of this encounter was what this brand-new believer said to me: "Ed, you mean everybody doesn't give ten percent to Fellowship Church?"

He couldn't believe that everyone wasn't as committed as he was to give back to the local church. If only we had a million more givers like this in our churches! I told him that he was unique. I told him he had the gift of giving.

Over the ensuing months, I took a couple of fishing trips with him. During the last eighteen months, he has been the largest donor at Fellowship. I cannot begin to tell you the gifts he's given us. He's done well financially. But many others in our church have done much better than he has. The difference is that he is exercising his gift of giving.

One of our responsibilities is to find and cultivate these people. We must pray for them and use discernment to cultivate these giving champions to carry out the vision. Some of these people will say, "Well, all I can do is make money and write checks. It doesn't seem like that big of a deal." Obviously, I'm quick to encourage them that this gift is essential to the ministry of the local church. We have other people who can sing, others who can teach, and others who serve brilliantly to meet the needs of our people. However, you and I both know that we need those gifted men and women who can write those checks. Encourage them to keep working. Encourage them to use their God-given gift to make money and use it to bless their local church. The ministry requires money and lots of it. I can't say it any plainer than that.

Don't Play Nerf Ball with the Church about Giving

Do you remember playing with Nerf balls when you were a kid? Those soft, low-impact balls made playing indoors a nonissue—nothing got broken and you were off the hook with Mom and Dad. But too often we take the same approach with the church. We take a low-impact, soft-sell approach to stewardship. We don't want to offend anyone or "break" anything, so we take the easy way out. We play Nerf ball with the church.

For the first four or five years at Fellowship Church, I worried about talking about money. I thought I might upset our people and turn off the seekers. I wish I could have those four or five years back to make up for those missed opportunities to teach on this subject. As I've matured as a leader and speaker, I've realized that pastors should talk about money all the time because Jesus talked about money all the time. He talked about money more than prayer, heaven, or hell. That means that we cannot be shy when it comes to talking about dollars and cents.

Even seekers know it's not free to run a church. You've got to remind them and tell them within the context of biblical teaching about financial concepts. But I would also challenge you to talk about money, specifically in at least one series a year. When it comes up, don't shy away from the topic. Say "Hey, if you're a believer, this is what Jesus has to say about your money. God's given you your stuff. But in reality, it's not your stuff; it's His stuff. And He tells us right off the top to bring ten percent of our money to Him as a minimum worship requirement."

Also, talk about money with creative illustrations that will help your people connect emotionally with this important principle. We have to move the heart as well as the mind to motivate our people to step up and give to the local church. The following is one of my favorite illustrations I've used over the years:

Awhile back I took my family to a high school football game. During the middle of the third quarter, one of my twin daughters asked for some money to buy some candy. Normally I don't buy a lot of candy for my kids, but I handed her a $5 bill and told her she could have some. She made her way to the concession stand and came back with a package of Skittles. As she was eating the Skittles, I asked, "Landra, can I have a few Skittles?"

She looked at her Skittles, then looked back at me and said, "No!"

Landra didn't understand several realities. Number one, she didn't understand that if had I wanted to, I could have forcibly taken the Skittles from her and eaten every one myself. She didn't realize the strength I have.

Number two, she didn't understand that I was the one who actually bought them for her. I paid for them with my money.

Number three, she didn't understand that if I had wanted to, I could have bought her so many packages of Skittles that she couldn't even eat them all.

The same realities apply to our lives as well. God has given all of us some Skittles. He looks at you and me and he says, "I'd like some Skittles. Would you give me some Skittles? I just want a few back."

But many of us defiantly say, "No, God! They're mine." And God says again, "Can I have some Skittles?"

But we still respond, "No. They're mine."

Like my daughter Landra, many of us don't understand three things. Number one, if God wanted to, He could take all of our Skittles from us. We forget that He's much stronger than we are.

Number two, we fail to realize that God is the one who gave us the Skittles in the first place.

And number three, if God wanted to, He could rain so many Skittles on our lives that we wouldn't know what to do with them all.

I've used that same illustration a couple of times in messages on giving and am amazed at how such a simple story about my daughter's Skittles has impacted so many people spiritually, emotionally, and practically. After I used it for the first time several years ago, I received a letter in the mail.

Dear Ed, recently you talked about giving. You talked about how your stuff comes from God and belongs to Him. You told an especially entertaining story about one of your daughters and her refusal to share with you the Skittles that you just bought for her. That was probably one of the most moving illustrations I've ever heard about giving back to the one who's given it all to you. Thanks for sharing that.

We truly thank God for everything and have enclosed an offering. The Skittles we are joyously sharing are enclosed inside the bag. Please use it in whatever way you feel will best serve the Lord through Fellowship.

Inside the envelope was a bag of Skittles, and in that bag was a check for $80,000. Don't ever underestimate the power of a great illustration!

People Give to Vision, Not Need

If people gave to the neediest organizations, the neediest organizations would have the most money. The reality is that people give to vision, not need. People like being a part of something successful—an organization that has purpose, clear direction, and a compelling vision. People always need to know where you are taking them. They will forget the vision if you don't remind them of it over and over again. You cannot communicate the vision of your church too much. It simply isn't possible.

During one series on vision, we were in a building campaign for our campus in Grapevine. We called the campaign "Get in the G.A.M.E." *G* stood for *generosity,* the *A* for *attitude,* the *M* for *ministry,* and the *E* for *eternity.* We talked about getting off our rears, getting out of the stands, and into the game. We challenged our people to get plugged into the ministry. And during the course of the series, we signed up several thousand new volunteers to the ministries at Fellowship.

Essentially, I asked people to quit eating for free at Fellowship Church. There were too many attendees showing up for the meal but not doing anything to serve. I challenged them to serve and I challenged them to give. We related our campaign to a sports analogy because Dallas is a big sports town. We knew people could identify with that.

We recruited an all-pro quarterback living in the area to help promote this campaign. We did a very funny video where this quarterback threw passes to one of our founding members. What made it funny was that the two players had little in common: one was an all-star NFL quarterback and the other was a middle-aged pastor. We used the classic NFL theme music to complement some very creative writing, trying to show that if "you got game," you are not sitting on your rear; you are on the playing field. The playing field means you are actively serving the ministry and giving regularly. It was a very effective illustration of our vision. The video and campaign helped show our people what could be by painting an exciting picture of the future.

Hire a Mountain Guide

At certain times, the financial mountains are so high and so big in your church that you'll have to hire a mountain guide. I'm talking about contracting with a consultant to make it happen for you.

I know many churches have planned and executed capital campaigns without the help of a consultant and that's fine. But over the years, we've found a consultant extremely helpful, particularly during our major campaigns. And I would highly recommend this for you and your church. Thankfully, we have had someone on our board of trustees who has done all of our fund-raising projects for us.

We've done four different campaigns here at Fellowship Church. The first one we did was when we were just four or five years old. We were in rented facilities at the time and were trying to buy some land to build our own building. We called the campaign, "Build the Vision." This was our first attempt at launching a campaign of this scope and size. We were growing rapidly and had a huge mountain to climb. So, we felt strongly that we needed a mountain guide, a fund-raising expert to come alongside us and show us the best way to achieve our goals.

We felt a great sense of urgency because we were rapidly outgrowing the high school and theater we were currently using. We knew it was God's timing to move forward with a building program. And we also knew that a lot was riding on the campaign. We could not afford to mess this up by trying to do it on our own. So, with the help of this consultant, Paul Gage of the Gage Group, we presented the vision clearly to the church and told them it was time to "Build the Vision."

The great thing about Paul is that, as a longtime member, he understands the vision of our church, our unique style, and our commitment to creativity. As a result, each of the campaigns he has overseen has been tailor-made for Fellowship Church. Consultants are valuable also for the freedom they provide to your leaders. If we had been in charge of this building campaign, it would have pulled us away from the weekend priority and the overall vision for the church. Consultants free you up to do what you do best. I say that with a major caution! Be sure the consultants you use add real value to your vision. Don't get duped by consultants who charge a lot of money and do very little real work. Oftentimes, in various ministries, your staff knows more than some of these consultants do, so use discernment as to when and how you hire outside help. Get references—don't use consultants who haven't been referred to you.

Our second campaign was also highly effective. We had moved

into our existing building in Grapevine by the skin of our teeth. We certainly didn't have any funds left over for a parking lot. When we did some initial research, we discovered that adequate parking would cost us several million dollars. Our church was already leveraged to secure the land and build our first building, so we again asked Paul to help us create a one-year campaign called "Pave the Way." Part of the campaign included a pretty powerful illustration from the stage. We drove a car on the stage and said, "It's not just about cars. It's about people . . . and *every* parking place is an opportunity for someone to hear the life-changing message of Christ." We even had the car out in the foyer area for several months with a big sign on it. You couldn't move around our facility without being reminded of our Pave the Way campaign. Our vision was everywhere.

Again, that's why casting the vision creatively and consistently is so critical. Creativity was used to paint a picture of thousands of cars filling up our parking lot and thousands of people streaming into our worship center. Our people could feel the excitement and responded immediately. They could see their neighbors and coworkers lining up to enter our parking lot. When you move the heart, transformation takes place. Within the year, we had achieved our goal and paved our parking lot.

Driving a car on the stage is pretty out there, but it not only captivated the attention of our people, it became the buzz around the Dallas–Fort Worth area. "You know that church that drives the car out on the stage?" Excitement is contagious. That buzz brought many new people into our building for the first time just to see how wheels-off we can be.

One thing we've learned here at Fellowship Church is to structure our campaigns based on the size of the church and the size of the project. Throughout our history, we've had a three-year campaign, a one-year campaign, a campaign that had an "end of year" emphasis, and a two-year program.

That means that you have to look at your numbers carefully. Know your growth rate, your current offering totals, and your anticipated needs. If your church is growing quickly and your people are giving consistently, you might be able to go for a shorter campaign. Can you break up a potentially long campaign into shorter phases? It's not always necessary to pump that three-year traditional campaign that every church seems to love.

Ultimately, you need to be committed to creativity as you plan your campaigns and be very flexible. A word of caution: always ensure that you are meeting your most critical needs in your church as you advance with any campaign. What are those needs? You will decide, but be sure to guard your weekend services and your staff needs as two critical examples.

No Matter What You Do, People Will Bolt on You

Unfortunately, one of the realities of infusing creativity into your leading and preaching is that some people will grow uncomfortable and leave your church. Remember how I said that motion causes friction? Well, it is discouraging to think that the same element that brings vitality and new people to your church is the same thing that can bring frustration and desertion. Even more discouraging is that it's often the founders or charter members who are the first to leave, because founders get funky when they see things changing. It's the small-fish-in-a-big-lake theory.

When you have a small, stagnant pond, the two-pound bass is big. When your pond becomes a lake, the two-pound bass becomes just another fish, and he doesn't like it. But if you commit to creativity and the changes it brings, the short-term conflict you experience will be bumps on the road to great heights and long-term health.

No matter what you do, people will bolt on you. I don't care if you can preach like Bishop T. D. Jakes, lead like Bill Hybels, or sing like Bono from U2; people will leave your church.

Another surprising phenomenon is that you will grow as much through subtraction as through addition. Does that sound strange? I never heard this point in seminary or in the numerous leadership conferences I've attended through the years. However, every time someone has left Fellowship Church and gotten involved in another local church, God has replaced them tenfold. Sometimes we think, "Oh, they can't leave! They're so key." But just watch and see how God replaces them with new faces as long as you remain committed to your God-given vision. Yes, sometimes it was hurtful and disappointing when certain people left our church, but God used those times to grow our church.

Some people just won't connect with your vision for the local church. No matter how many questions you answer or how clearly you communicate your vision, some people just can't buy into what you're doing. And that's OK. These people can be a great asset in another place. Don't be afraid to encourage them to attend another local church that does connect with them. You will free them up to bless another church with their service, and you will free up some space in your own church to minister to the people God has brought to you. Then you'll see how you can grow through subtraction.

Some people get mad, some people whine, others are downright negative. Beware of divisive people; they want to divide and separate. If you aren't careful, they will divide your staff and mess you up.

Why People Leave

I've polled pastors and leaders from across the country from smaller churches, larger churches, church ministries, and other ministries. And here's what folks say across the board when they leave the church.

It's Not Deep Enough. My brother Ben is a writer and a radio talk show host. He also is a singles pastor. After speaking at a service one night, a guy walked up to him and said, "Ben, I enjoy Second Baptist Church and all, but the messages you've been giving lately are just not deep enough." Ben looked at him and said, "Well, I don't know about you, but I'm still working on 'Love thy neighbor as thyself.'" Now that's what I call deep!

A couple of years ago we took our management team white-water rafting. While we were going through a dangerous part of the Snake River in Colorado, we had an expert river guide with us. The guide didn't inject a lot of confidence into us when he told us that many people had drowned in that area in the last few years. Sure enough, about a minute after we took a picture of our team happily paddling down the rapids, Mike, our children's pastor, was catapulted into the white water. This was a serious situation.

Our guide dug his paddle in the frigid waters, turning the life raft around, back toward Mike. Our guide then called out to Mike, who was surrounded by the angry rapids in frigid temperatures. "Hey Mike, I want to talk to you about the original Greek for the word *paddle*. I also want to give you a quick synopsis of the historicity of white-water rafting."

Obviously our guide didn't say that! Our guide looked at all of us and said, "Guys, throw out the life raft. Guys, extend your paddle." What did we do? We rescued Mike.

For far too long, the church has been talking about the Greek word for paddle and the historicity of rafts while people have been drowning around us. What is depth? Is depth talking about Greek and Hebrew or talking about history?

Yes, there's a time and a place for all of this as we teach the Bible. But the local church is first and foremost a place for rescue, not a lecture hall. We've been given a mandate to rescue people, to change their lives by the power of God. When I hear "It's not deep enough," it tips me off that this person is not yet in tune with the purpose of the local church.

It's Too Big. When our church grew from 150 to 250, some people said, "It's just getting too big. I don't see you as much as I used to," or "I remember I used to know everybody," or "Now I have to sit out in the hall or in the overflow area."

You could call this founder's syndrome. You could call it the small-fish-in-a-big-lake theory. I was considering these kinds of comments one August evening while driving past Texas Stadium. Tens of thousands of people were walking into Texas Stadium with a spring in their step and a twinkle in their eye because they were going to see the Cowboys play a preseason game. They walked half a mile in the Texas heat, packed in like sardines as they filed toward the stadium for cramped, overpriced seats to sip flat beverages and eat cold hot dogs.

Quite frankly, they were heading to a worship service. They had the right response, but the wrong god. These were the same type of people who whine and moan and groan if they have to walk the length of a football field to worship in a church. They'd say, "I can't believe this, can you? The parking lot's packed. This is crazy; it's just too big."

I mean, have you ever met a serious shopper who said, "You know, I don't like malls because they're just too big." That's hilarious. I believe that a growing church is a biblical church. Check out the Book of Acts, particularly chapter 2. The first church grew by 3,000 in a day. That's a reflection of the power of God and the awesome potential for the Bride of Christ.

A growing church is a blessing for several reasons. First, a growing church is a reflection of heaven. Have you ever thought about it like that? Heaven is not going to be a holy huddle of a half-dozen homogeneous people. It's not going to have a million Eds or millions of you. The Bible is quite clear that heaven is going to be packed with people from every tribe, every tongue, and every nation. Heaven is not going to be small, and it's not going to be dull.

Another benefit of a growing church is the wide range of ministries involved in a growing church. Think about the ministries in your church. As it grows, there tend to be more and more ministry opportunities. That's a good thing.

How about a large relational base? Isn't that a good thing? If you are single, it's an incredibly good thing! It also helps you as you try to encourage seekers to check out your church. A growing church helps break people away from the holy-huddle mentality. As new people become a part of the community, it becomes harder and harder to protect their church "turf."

Another obvious benefit is that it is an amazing opportunity to showcase the gifts of your people. A growing church has access to more people to pool their diverse resources for the glory of God. With access to more people, more diverse gifts can be leveraged for the kingdom. Everyone has a place to minister in a growing church. With a greater access to a diverse group of gifts, you'll find that it will perpetuate excellence. And this excellence will perpetuate growth for your church.

It Has Too Little Accountability. Who are you accountable to? (We touched on this in chap. 7 on staffing.) Have you noticed that there are some accountability assassins running around? When people ask you who you're accountable to, do you know what they're saying for the most part? They're saying, "I want you to be accountable to me." They don't really love you; they want to control you.

As for accountability, I'm all for it. However, accountability is relational, not critical. Accountability does not mean that you open your life up and give the public total access. That does not equate to accountability. We have a board of directors that signs off on every check to keep us accountable. They can fire me if they so choose, and they also keep us accountable in legal and ethical areas. However, in the end, I believe every dynamic church needs to be staff-led. I'm not talking about zero accountability. I'm saying that your staff needs to be able to carry the ball to the hoop unobstructed.

We've got to have accountability. That is a biblical concept.

However, it's got to be relational. We've got to free up leaders to lead, because every great staff has been given a vertical vision. The problem is that vision vandals come in and test your commitment so that your vision will go horizontal. If they can get you to focus on them or others in your church, then they have gotten you to take your eye off the prize. Please don't be tempted to abandon your God-given vision. If you want to impact the world, you must have God's fingerprints all over your ministry because you have leveraged everything to achieve the vision He has given you. I hope this thought will free you up to fight for your vision. In a sensitive and godly way, you must defend your vision so that you can be accountable to God one day with complete integrity.

It's Too Entertaining. Now and then, people say this about Fellowship Church. We often counter, "Too entertaining? Didn't Jesus hold His audiences spellbound?"

I want you to look at the word *entertaining*; it means to capture and hold someone's attention for an extended period of time. The church better be entertaining. I mentioned earlier how we made a play on this word. We say Fellowship Church is "Innertainment for the Heart." We had better be in the entertaining business if we want to capture people's attention and ultimately capture their hearts.

Consider these objections by bolters: the church is/has not deep enough, too big, too little accountability, too entertaining. There's a common thread here. Have you picked it out? The answer is that they're "me-istic" statements. "It's not deep enough for *me*. It's too big for *me*. I want you to be more accountable to *me*. It's too entertaining for *me*."

We're not afraid to tell any of our potential members who are considering membership that our church is not for everybody. Fellowship Church is not the perfect church. (We tell them not to join the perfect church because they'll mess it up.) We are not trying to dodge questions or concerns. We are, however, serious about keeping our vision vertical. We address the concerns of our members sensitively, but we do not allow negative people to deter us from the vision that God has given to us.

This can be easier said than done. It is during these times that you need that relational accountability with your staff, so you aren't tempted to allow your vision to go horizontal. Ensure that your staff sticks up for one another, watching each other's back. The vision for Fellowship Church belongs to every member and particularly, every staff member at Fellowship Church. It is up to all of us to work together to keep our vision vertical. That is why I am so freaky about loyalty. Loyalty gives your vision strong legs to stand firm and resist the storms that will come. It keeps your vision vertical.

Dealing with Negative People

What do you do about negative people? I've had a little fun and spoken in hyperbole about some of the criticisms I've faced over the years, but I need to keep my sense of humor in this area because criticism hurts. I know I'm not perfect. I know that I'm as likely to mess up as the next guy. But let's face it: ministry is demanding enough without having to face insensitive critics. Please use my experience to help you deal with these inevitable naysayers.

Pray and Stay above the Fray. If you don't pray and stay above all of the negativity, you'll be sucked into the current of criticism. Remember our boy Nehemiah? (I've written an entire book on the leadership principles of Nehemiah entitled *High Definition Living.*) Nehemiah did the impossible. He was on the wall and he had some sidewalk supervisors who tried to get him down off the wall. What did he do? He didn't mudsling with them. He stayed on the wall. He talked to them. But you have got to stay above the fray and pray. Don't chase down every negative person. Don't fall into the trap of believing that you can change them. The only way they're going to change is if they have a burning bush experience.

Now, that's not 100 percent true. But 95 percent of the time, if someone talks to you about the objections I just mentioned, you are probably not going to persuade them otherwise. More often than not, they are negative people who don't connect with your vision. This is your opportunity to ask them to plug in at another church. The older I get, the more I am able to discern negativity with the red flags that the Holy Spirit puts in my spirit.

A funny thing that will happen with negative people is that they will often come back. Some who left us early on have come back and are now plugged in. Maybe they needed some time. Maybe they realized through trial and error that this is where God wants them to be. This is another reason why you have to keep that vision vertical. If some negative people are going to come back anyway, why should you change your vision to try to keep a few negative people from leaving? It doesn't add up. All that communicates is that you are more concerned about pleasing men instead of pleasing God.

Do the Math and Clear the Path. Secondly, do *the math and clear the path.* Think about the vision vandals mentioned in Numbers 13–14. Remember those twelve spies that were sent to scope out the land of Canaan? Well, ten of the twelve spies became the first vision vandals. God told them that He was giving them the land, but these ten spies returned and scared the people from seizing the Promised Land. Caleb and Joshua were the two people who stood up for God. Just two of the twelve stood up for God. Caleb was willing to believe God. He silenced the people before Moses and said that they should go up and take possession of the land with the power of God behind them.

When do you confront someone who is negative? You confront them when it affects your relationship with God, when it affects your God-given mission in life, or when it affects your family. Other than that, pray about it; but don't mess with negative people. You don't have to return every angry call, every e-mail, and every negative letter. More often than not, it's better to ignore them than respond to angry people.

Keep in Mind Who's Behind. Satan is the major force behind negativity. Satan works negativity so hard because he knows the kind of difference-maker you are and he knows your potential. He knows the power of division in the local church. Remember that Satan is also called the Antichrist. What did Christ pray for on the cross? He prayed for unity. The Antichrist is all about opposing the things that are most near and dear to the heart of God. He knows the power of discouraging a vertical vision. That's why he's picking on you. The spiritual intensity is amazing. Usually, when the temptation is turned up, especially around our church, I always say, "God, thank you for this opportunity to build my trust in You." It deepens my faith, because I know that just around the corner, we're getting ready to receive so much blessing that we won't even be able to handle it.

When Satan attacks, he is tipping his hand off to the fact that you are about to receive a new blessing from God. Maybe you will experience growth. It may be that He is going to give you new opportunities to influence your community for Christ. Whatever it is, God will turn the trial into growth.

Here's the bottom line, though. It hurts me when people leave. I'm guessing that it will hurt you too. We are human and it hurts us when people bolt and abandon our vision. Negativity is so discouraging for a leader and it doesn't get easier to handle over the years. But God is faithful and will continue to grow your church if you remain faithful to the vision He has given you.

In closing out our discussion of dealing with negative people, be sure to respond properly. Ask yourself if there is any truth to what they're saying. In your prayer time, ask God if there is any truth to their questions or concerns. Sometimes it is during these times that the Lord is trying to soften your heart to allow for personal growth. When it comes time for someone to leave, challenge them in a good way to get involved somewhere else. Bless them and release them to another ministry. Tell them to get plugged in somewhere else. Don't be afraid to "share the wealth" with other churches in your area. And finally, remember that damaged people damage people. Look behind the hurtful things they say; you'll often find someone with a lot of hurt or grief in their own life. Pray for their healing wherever they may go.

As Blessings Increase, So Do Temptations

I caught a tarpon in Florida a few summers ago. One day, a fishing guide took me out and we saw all these tarpon cruising around. I cast a fly to the tarpon and the tarpon ate it. The tarpon was so big that he didn't even know he was hooked for awhile. He was just swimming along like a happy tarpon. And then, all of a sudden, he felt the sting of that hook in his mouth. He went nuts, jumping and flopping around. I was tethered to this fish for over an hour. He wore me out. It was such a battle that I wanted to mount the fish; but I released it and had a replica made so I could remember the mammoth struggle.

I want to talk to you about temptation in this last section, because temptation is a lot like fly fishing. As blessings increase, the hook of temptation becomes more of a constant in our lives. The real problem is that temptation is customized to our weaknesses. So whatever weakness that you might have, Satan knows how to exploit it. He is crafty at tying flies, because he is a master angler. And don't think he's not angling for you right now. He will tie a tasty fly to match the kind of fish he is after, just like a great fishermen. Maybe he'll put a little red on his fly to make it look like an injured fish. Maybe he'll put a little yellow on there for some contrast. It's a scary thought to think that Satan is tying a fly right now to entice you in your weaknesses.

What area in your life and ministry is he most likely to exploit? He cinches down his fly and looks at it with pride. The hook is really disguised well. He ties it to his fly rod and he looks at you and he looks at me. He's a master angler. He's been fishing for thousands of years. And he loves to go after leaders; those are his prized possessions. And he casts and he waits and he waits. You can't see the hook; it could be that attractive co-worker or a member of the opposite sex in your church, maybe it's that Web site that pops onto your screen, or the thought that pops into your head. It could even be as simple as distracting a leader from his main mission, his "M.O." Whatever it is, he's after you.

Remember Your M.O.

Remember your M.O. and hold on tightly. As I've already said, our M.O. is "It's the weekend, stupid." So goes the weekend, so goes Fellowship Church. So goes the weekend, so goes your church. "Well," you might say, "what about discipleship? What about small groups?" Hey, if the weekend isn't going right, you don't have discipleship and your small groups won't be thriving.

It is so easy to get fragmented, isn't it? Because one of the ways he tempts us is by distracting leaders from passionately pursuing their vision. Satan's trophy room is incredible, because he's reeled in some serious spiritual giants. Think just for a moment about the people that he's reeled in and are mounted on his wall. Unlike me, Satan does not practice catch and release, does he? He plays for keeps.

Where are you being tempted? What do you do if you're tempted? Remember that James 1:13 says, "When [you're] tempted," not "If." We're all going to be tempted. James 1:14, "But each one is tempted when, by his own evil desire, he is *dragged* away and *enticed.*" Those two terms are fisherman's terms. They mean, literally, to lure a fish from cover. Satan is the master at matching lures to the catch he is after. Temptation, like an angler's fly, is often disguised.

Remember the Greatness of God

What do you do when you're tempted? First of all, you remember the greatness of God.

Texas has real cowboys. I'm talking about Copenhagen-dipping, Coors-sipping, Wrangler-wearing, truck-comparing cowboys. They're always talking about trucks. "Jimbo's got a three-quarter-ton truck. Billy Bob's got an F-350 one-ton truck."

One day I asked one of these rugged guys about trucks. "What does that mean, 'a one-ton truck'?" I found out that it is the weight that the frame of the truck can withstand under pressure.

See Psalm 139:15: "My frame was not hidden from you when I was made in the secret place." God knows our frame. He knows the temptation load you and I can carry. So remember how great God is. Don't jump in to get some quick satisfaction. Don't dive into the deep end to satisfy a God-shaped need. That's a quick fix, but it will only numb you. Remember the greatness of God and fall into His arms. Remember, He will never put you in a situation that is beyond your ability (in Christ) to endure.

Look Past the Bait

I've seen a tarpon that weighed more than 100 pounds. You know how that tarpon became so big? He watched a lot of flies go by. As I told you earlier, when that tarpon hit the fly, he didn't know he was hooked.

A lot of people have taken the bait of temptation and they're swimming around, ignorant about the hook stuck in them. But one day, boom! You will feel the sting of the hook. You will jump and thrash around when you know you're caught.

A fish like the one I caught can kill people if it jumps in the boat; it can knock people off of the boat. Sin is the same way. It can hurt and maim innocent bystanders. We see carnage like that all the time in our churches and ministries. Look past today's fix and consider where that sin will lead.

Remember the Seasons

When is the best time to catch tarpon? If in Boca Grande, Florida, it's in the months of May, June, or July. You'll find them there by the thousands. But if you go in the winter, your chances are slim to none. We have to realize that temptation is only for a season. It will subside and then it may come back stronger. It's very important to realize that.

We've talked a lot about creative leadership; and hopefully, you are beginning to see the benefits of infusing creativity into your entire organization. Don't let this chapter weaken your resolve to become a more creative leader. Remember, if creative leadership were easy, everybody would be doing it. You've probably heard the saying, "Everything worth doing is worth doing well." I might add that everything worth doing is worth the commitment to make it happen.

Allow God to use the unique person He formed long ago in innovative and amazing ways. You cannot even dream of where this journey will take you if you commit to your vision and to creative leadership. Mimic the creative character of God. Despite all of my leadership experience growing up in a pastor's home and the opportunity to attend seminary, there's just nothing like the real thing. Understanding these three principles about finances, managing negative people, and the reality of temptations will carry you to greater heights in your pursuit of leadership that is infused with creative energy.

Creative Q & A: Section 4

Q: How do you balance your personal life with such a large ministry?

A: As mentioned earlier, the greatest message I will ever preach isn't going to be in front of a crowd of thousands. It's not even going to be delivering the gospel at Christmas or Easter. The greatest message I will ever preach is the one that I live out in front of my wife and children. It's what I model day in and day out for my family.

And because of that fact, I have to keep a very close eye on the balance between work and home. If I'm not making that strategic time for my family; if I'm not living out God's Word for my wife and children by making them a top priority, then I'm not going to be effective anywhere.

Balancing family life with the ministry is a difficult task, especially when so much of a pastor's personal life *is* the ministry. It's something that I have struggled with, studied, and spoken about several times over the past fifteen years. I feel so adamant about getting this across that I've written a book, *Kid CEO*, to help people manage the difficulties of balancing life's priorities. And we always address personal topics like this at our leadership conferences (C3) every year.

One of the most dangerous possibilities in the ministry is the potential for the church to seductively become a mistress for pastors and leaders. If you hope to be a creative, innovative, and effective leader, it's vitally important to take time away from work. Make your family a higher priority and spend strategic time with them. If you don't, your creativity is going to hit a wall. You're going to burn out and break down. And your family is going to feel the brunt of that burnout just as much as you will. So take some time away from the church and give it to your spouse and your kids.

Your children don't care that you're a pastor or that you have a message to deliver on Sunday. All they care about is whether you were at their baseball game or piano recital. Remember the list of priorities that God has placed in your life: Christ follower first; spouse second; parent third; worker fourth. Don't change the order God has set.

Another essential element in balancing your personal life and the ministry is to keep the negative aspects of leading a church from crossing your family's boundaries. In other words, paint a positive picture of life in the ministry.

Say you have small children. As the pastor or leader in the church, you get in the habit of coming home and complaining about all the negativity you had to deal with that day. You start exposing the dark underbelly of the church to your family, because after all, there is a negative side to the ministry. But as you continue that trend, and as your children grow, they can begin to develop a negative view of the ministry. They hear only the negative, so they think it is all negative. Don't let that happen.

As the leader of the church and the leader in your home, it is vital that you paint the ministry in a positive light for your family. You can't teach your kids to be positive unless you're positive yourself.

I'm not saying that you have to paint a false picture of the church for your family. Doing that can cause more harm down the road. Don't sugarcoat everything. You can talk about bad things sometimes but do it in a way that shows all that God is doing in your ministry. Tell stories of life changes, of miracles for the people the church prayed for, of how something negative can be used by God for a positive outcome.

My mind rushes back to a situation in my own family a few years ago. My wife and I had been talking about how God had brought a friend of ours to the church. But we also knew that her husband was not a believer. So we talked about it openly with our family. We didn't sugarcoat the deal and tell our kids that everything was OK, because it wasn't. Someone's eternity was still up for grabs. So we talked honestly about how we needed to pray for God to work on that man's heart. And in talking about that negative situation in a positive light, our children saw where God could work. And they began to pray for him. They would come up to Lisa or me and ask, "Is Mr. So-and-So a Christian yet?" Three months later they were still praying and asking, "Is he a Christian yet?"

Don't hide your family from everything going on in the church. But don't fully expose them to the dark underbelly of the ministry. Let your family be aware of what is going on and let them see the positive life-change stories in your church, because that will teach your children about the great things God does through the church. And it will teach them that the church isn't just where Mommy or Daddy works.

Christ said in Matthew 6:33, "But seek first his kingdom and his righteousness, and all these things will be given to you as well."

Again, our relationship with Christ should be the number-one thing in our lives. After that should come our relationship with our family. Then comes our work. This hierarchy goes for pastors and church leaders too. Yes, we are in ministry, but that is our career. At the end of the day and at the end of our lives, we need to see that we had the right priorities in the right places. And it all starts with God.

Q: You've said, "It takes super-sized cash to run the church." Isn't that a contradiction from your earlier statement, "You don't need a lot of money to be creative"?

A: Let me clarify this point—the creative process is not dependent on money, but the work of the ministry is. I said earlier in the book that you don't have to have a lot of money to be *creative*. And I stand firmly behind that statement. Some of the most creative ideas we've ever had have been the least expensive.

However, there is an important reality that many pastors fail to realize. A successful ministry takes an enormous amount of resources. It doesn't matter if you have 10 or 10,000 people in your church—it takes a truckload of cash to drive the church.

Pastors (and I'm speaking from personal experience here) often do not realize the amount of money it takes to run a church. They are not taught the business side of the ministry in school— an oversight that often leads to big problems years down the road. Then, when it comes time to talk about the mean green, they shy away from it.

Pastors are not trained to talk about money. Most of us don't want to talk about money. We're afraid it will drive people away. Sure, we all talk about money while we're in the midst of a building campaign, but what about the rest of the time? The truth of the matter is that it takes money to operate a church, just like any other organization.

Don't feel ashamed or embarrassed to talk about the very thing Jesus talked about more than almost any other subject. All too often we act like money is evil. But the Bible clearly tells us that the *love* of money is evil—not money. So don't be afraid to say the word *money* in church. It's not a curse word!

People know that buildings don't build themselves. They know that electricity in the church costs just as much per hour as it does in their homes. They know that mission trips don't pay for themselves and that insurance policies aren't complimentary gifts for the church. And they also know that Pastor Jones doesn't work for free. (Hopefully, anyway!) And although it's very apparent that he loves what he does and that he'd do it without a salary if he could, his children still need to eat and he still has bills to pay. People know it takes money to run a church.

Where we fall into a trap is when we finally do talk about money, we go to the congregation and beg them to give. We plead and grovel with them to give enough money for us to be able to build this building or start this program. The problem with that is people don't give to need. If that were true, the poorest and most rundown venues would have the most money. People give to vision. So talk about money. But don't do it pessimistically or with your hands out. Don't say, "Oh, please give to this cause. We desperately need you to contribute!"

Instead, be excited in sharing what God is doing in your church. Put some emotion into it and be cheerful. Second Corinthians 9:7 says, "God loves a cheerful giver." Let your people be cheerful about giving. And remember, the way to gain cheerful givers is to talk enthusiastically about money and the opportunity that the people have to be a part of fulfilling God's vision for your church.

"Come, follow me," Jesus said,
"and I will make you fishers of men."
MATTHEW 4:19

CHAPTER 11

Go Fish!

while back, a friend of mine invited me to a fishing lodge on Andros Island. This Bahamian island is in one of the remotest areas in the Western Hemisphere. It also happens to have some fantastic saltwater fly-fishing. If you haven't figured this out by now, I love to fish. You might have missed that fact somehow in our journey—maybe you were just skimming the book (shame on you)—so I thought I'd remind you of my great love for fishing.

I also want to infect you with that same excitement for the sport of fishing. So, before you close this book on creative leadership, I want to do for you what my friend did for me. I want to invite you to go on a fishing trip with me.

We've looked at many different elements of creativity—the foundation, payoff, environment, staffing, communication, team-planning, and even the downside. But as we conclude this book, keep your eyes on the motivation behind all of those elements. What is at the heart of all the creative thought, planning, and implementation that we go through week in and week out?

The answer—you guessed it—is *fishing*.

Leaders don't force people to follow—
they invite them on a journey.
CHARLES S. LAUER

Creativity, in and of itself, is just an exercise in trying new things. The Christian leader has a higher calling, a greater purpose, and a deeper passion than simply trying new things for the fun of it. As Christian leaders, we are creative for the same reason Christ was creative. We are fishermen. Millions of lost fish are at stake. And it takes a lot of creative casting to attract those fish.

So in this chapter, we're going on a fishing trip to discover what sets the creative *Christian* leader apart from the rest. We'll look at the creative "fisheristics" that make our leadership challenge unique. I've got my gear and all my flies are tied, so let's go fishing.

That's exactly what Jesus told a bunch of first-century fishermen in Matthew 4:18–19: "As Jesus was walking beside the Sea of Galilee, he saw two brothers, Simon called Peter and his brother Andrew. They were casting a net into the lake, for they were fishermen. 'Come, follow me,' Jesus said, 'and I will make you fishers of men.'"

This is a fascinating passage. Jesus was bringing His key players into His life and ministry to be His inner circle, His management team. Jesus, being God in the flesh, could have chosen anyone. He could have picked people from all different walks of life. He could have chosen a bunch of farmers. He could have chosen a bunch of soldiers. He could have chosen a bunch of physicians or accountants. He could have chosen a bunch of attorneys, but we would still be in court (only kidding; my best friend is a lawyer).

So whom did Jesus choose? He chose fishermen. Of the twelve disciples, why would He choose seven fishermen to stand with Him through the most critical moments in His life and ministry?

The answer is essential for discipleship as well as for leadership. We need to understand why fishermen were essential to Christ's mission and, thereby, essential to the mission of the church.

Let's talk "fisheristics"—characteristics that we all need in the most powerful purpose in life—that of being a fisher of men. As leaders, we need to remember that fishing for men is our primary motivation for the ministry. And we must model fishing for our staff members and the Christ followers in our churches. Our churches should be great fishing holes that rescue fish from the muck and bring them safely into the freshwater.

What a powerful purpose! Jesus told a bunch of fanatical fishermen, "Hey, follow Me. I'll make you fishers of men." He didn't say, "I'll make you catchers of men." Our job is to cast into the deep waters. The Master Fisherman does all the catching. All He tells His followers to do is fish. Just fish.

Fisheristic 1: Fishermen Have "Reel" Purpose

Fishermen use reels to bring in the catch of the day. Leaders in the business of catching fish need to understand the "reel" purpose for life and for our ministries. The reason God does not zap us to heaven the moment we commit our lives to Christ is because He wants us to bring as many people as possible into heaven with us.

We all have specific local bodies of water that God has given to us. He wants us to fish. He also wants us to train up new fishermen to cast into the inlets and coves that we may have missed. He'll do all the catching. All He wants us to do is fish. Our purpose is not a larger ministry for our kingdom, but a larger population in God's kingdom.

Creative leadership will help attract fish, but we must remember why we are trying to attract fish in the first place. We've got to understand and own this amazing and powerful purpose because when we get it down, it will lead to the next powerful fisheristic.

Fisheristic 2: Fishermen Have "Reel" Passion

When we have "reel" purpose, we'll have "reel" passion. When I take first-time fishermen out in a boat, and they feel the tug of the fish on the line, they experience the excitement. They feel the passion coursing through their veins. They say to me, "Man, I've got to reel this fish in! This is cool! I've got to get 'em!" They are passionate.

Do you remember the old Schlitz Beer commercial? Remember the guy would say, "You only go around once in life, so you better go for all the GUSTO!" Here's another one from McDonald's. "You deserve a break today!"

Now, why do we remember that? Do you know why? It's because those companies have hired creative advertisers and artists and paid them millions of dollars to enhance their product. They are successful because they pass their passion on to their consumers. Their enthusiasm is contagious, and as a result, we remember their commercial jingles. These companies are peddling bitter beer and fat-laden hamburgers. As Christian leaders, we have a much better message to offer.

Jesus was a passionate fisherman. He was passionate about connecting lost people to the hope of the gospel. He was passionate about the kingdom of God. His passion was so contagious that it spilled over to the disciples, who literally gave their lives to carry on His message of hope and love. Committed Christ followers today carry on the message of the gospel because of the passion that was shared by pastors and other great leaders in former generations.

Think with me about the Great Commission. In Matthew 28:19, Jesus said, "Go." What part of *go* do we misunderstand? Go and do what? "Make disciples of all nations." His ministry lasted a little more than three years. He knew that He only had about thirty-six months in the public domain. What did He do? He picked fishermen. Why? Because life is too short not to fish. Then three years later, right before His ascension, what did He say? "Go into all the world. Preach My gospel and welcome new fish into the family of God through baptism."

Look at the bookends of Christ's ministry. His first and last words were all about action and sharing the gospel. They were all about fishing. In the beginning of His ministry, He said, "Come." *I want to train you to be fishermen.* Then at the end He said, "Go."

I want you to take what you've learned and go fish. His use of the word *go* means "as you are going; as you are living your life." Just as Christ's disciples came to Him and learned how to fish for souls, we are teaching others to do the same through our churches and our ministries.

Christ was passionate then and is passionate now. You can feel His passion. So once we understand the powerful purpose, we will have this "reel" passion. We are passionate about our purpose to be active fishermen.

Here's something that we often miss as leaders. And when we miss this, everything is out of whack. Most of our people see the gospel as "God and me" instead of as "God and the world." They think, "It's all about me. What makes me look good, what helps my self-image, what feeds me. It's all about me and my deal and my growth and my maturity. Me, me, me, and my, my, my. It's just God and me."

Creative leaders must continually remind people in their ministries that the gospel is not about God and me. Biblical Christianity is about God and the world. Scripture reads, "For God so loved the *world*," and "Go unto all the *world*." If our churches are not white-hot with passion for reaching those outside of ourselves, then we are missing the major thrust of Christianity. We are totally missing the boat. If the church is all about me and my, then it will turn from a fishing entity that is focused on lost fish to a private swimming pool in a marina where all the fish gather together to hang out. This is not the picture Christ had in mind.

Christianity is unique. It separates itself from every other world religion because Jesus tells us that we need to get outside of ourselves and think about the world. That is when we are truly fulfilled. When I get outside of myself, I can think about others. Then guess what happens? That's when Ed's needs are met. But when Ed gets selfish and whiny and worries about me and mine, I have missed the good news. The good news is outward-focused. Forgetting that fact is where a lot of our churches get tripped up.

Passionate fishermen will go anywhere for new fish, not just to their favorite fishing holes. Fishermen will slather on the sunblock. They will go into mosquito-infested areas, enduring all kinds of nasty weather to get the fish. Fishermen have to go where the fish are.

That's why creative leadership is so huge. It helps connect our purpose to our passion. When we understand the staggering numbers of lost fish at stake, we will do everything in our power to think and minister differently to fulfill our mandate as pastors and Christian leaders. We must know our purpose and have the passion.

Fisheristic 3: Fishermen Are "Reel" Optimists

Great fishermen also need optimism to be successful. They're always saying, "We'll get 'em tomorrow. Didn't catch 'em today, but I'm telling you, tomorrow, man," or "In that next spot, that next cove, or that next flat, we're going to catch 'em."

If we are going to truly impact the world for Jesus Christ, we have to meet the fish where they are. You have to think like a fish to be successful. We have to think and know how people away from the Lord are going to feel, what they are going to say, and how they are going to react to the good news.

Many people don't want to get dirty or wet or slimy when they go fishing. They say, "Man, I don't want any part of that. It would be much easier for us to kick back in an air-conditioned house right now." Christians who are truly fishers of men are not worried about getting a little slimy; they are willing to try some different things—different flies, different lures, or whatever it takes to catch the fish. When we miss the fish in one area, we don't pack our bags and go home. We say, "We'll get 'em next time. The next cast, or in the next flat, is where I'm going to catch the big one."

Christian leaders should be the most optimistic people in the world. We are not peddling beer or burgers; we are offering people the lifeline that will connect them to a holy God. Again, we are just asked to cast. He does all the catching. So be optimistic.

Comfort doesn't cut it in God's economy. When I look at the people who have dropped by the wayside at Fellowship Church in the last fifteen years, it is usually because they sought their own comfort above the church's mission. We do not want a comfortable church. A comfortable church is not a biblical church in my mind.

We don't worry about comfort and, because of that, I believe Fellowship Church is one of the most unselfish churches I have ever seen. We are a church that challenges people. We will get in their face—close enough to smell their cologne and coffee breath. We get between people and their makeup to challenge them to get out there and fish. But we do it in a positive, life-affirming way. Our goal is not to scare people into fishing; it is to motivate them to join us in this great biblical sport.

As leaders, we've got to be optimistic. We've got to brave the elements to reach the fish. We've got to commit to creativity so we can reach lost fish with new lures and casting techniques. Sometimes we will catch fish, sometimes we won't. But you know what? We don't worry about catching fish. Again, all we're supposed to do is fish.

Fisheristic 4: Fishermen Have "Reel" Persistence

Great fishermen are also going to have "reel" persistence. I've been with a lot of incredible fishermen over the years, and every one of them is persistent. I almost used the word *patient,* but I didn't. People say to me, "Well, Ed, it's cool that you like fishing, but I don't like to fish because I'm just not that patient." But fishermen are not that patient. We are persistent, but we are not very patient as a rule.

Being persistent relates to action and intentionality. You never give up on finding those fish. And when you are persistent, guess what? You are going to see great things. You are going to see fish rescued from the muck and mire. You are going to have story after story in your life where people were cast to, reeled in, and caught by the grace and the power of God. And here's a straight fact about fishing. If you don't have any good, recent fish stories, you are spending too much time in the marina.

I think about some fishermen I've met who have caught some incredible fish over the years. They love to tell people their fishing stories. I think if someone is truly a follower of Christ, and they are a fisher of men, they will also have fishing stories about how God used them to reach people for the kingdom. If I don't have very many recent fish stories, then I'm probably not doing much fishing.

You know what great fishermen do? Great fishermen just keep on casting; they keep on working. They know they are not going to attract every soul to the bait, but they have incredible faith in the power of God. They know that He will catch the fish if they continue to cast. At Fellowship Church, we have many people who show up and just nibble a little bit but don't take the bait. That's between them and God. But God reaches a lot of them through our continual commitment to creative casting. Just because I have lost some fish along the way doesn't mean that I stop fishing.

Challenge yourself, your staff, and your church with this question: Do you have any recent fish stories of how God used you in His redemptive plan in your body of water? Maybe some of you can name names as you read this and can recall some great fish stories over the years. But if it's been awhile, then something is wrong. If you've been spending too much time in the marina, you won't have any new stories. Let me encourage you to go after the lost fish and allow God to grow those little guppies into mature marlin. Remember what Christ said: "Go fishing."

Our time is short. James 4:14 says that our lives are just like a mist. So life is too short not to fish.

Fisheristic 5: Fishermen Have a "Reel" Partnership

We've got to have "reel" partnership. Many times when I fish, I use the services of a fishing guide. A guide puts me in the right place to do some fishing. The guide allows me to experience the thrill of catching fish. Ultimately, I have no control over whether that fish is going to grab the bait, but I have the best chance of reeling it in when I'm with an experienced guide.

I've had the opportunity to fly-fish with an outstanding guide named Prescott. We like to search for a very elusive fish called a permit. The permit is the trickiest fish to catch in saltwater, specifically shallow saltwater. A permit is a pretty large fish, a bulky fish. They also happen to be one of the smartest fish out there. I've been saltwater fly-fishing for twelve years, and every year I try to go somewhere and fish for a permit. Over the years, I've gone to Belize, Honduras, Mexico, and the Bahamas. Many people fish for twenty years and never hook a permit.

I've been very fortunate, though, to hook permit on a couple of occasions, and I know the only reason is because I follow the advice of my guide, Prescott. When Prescott and I are looking for permit together, I always do better when I do exactly what he says.

The same is true with our ultimate Guide. When we do what the ultimate Guide (our heavenly Father) says, He is going to transform our fishing techniques and our creative leadership.

We have a tendency, though, to do our own thing and make our own cast, don't we? It's a natural urge we must fight all the time. So often, the Lord shows us the people to talk to and the people to help. He puts them on our heart, and sometimes we respond to His promptings. Other times, we miss out because we are thinking about ourselves. We may be trying to build our kingdom, do this deal, make this amount of money, or chase that opportunity, instead of being sensitive to what the Lord is saying.

The picture of a fisherman and a guide is very similar to the reality of the local church. At Fellowship Church, we know that we are partners with the Lord in catching and training fish. We've got to listen to Him. We have the awesome privilege of partnering with the ultimate Guide in accomplishing His great purpose for the church and our individual lives.

It takes a team effort and a real commitment to innovation to catch fish. As we partner with the Lord Jesus, we are able to do what it takes to catch fish. We partner not only with the Lord Jesus, but also with our teammates in the local church. The local church is the hope of the world. Jesus instituted and anointed one organization to carry out His great mission—the local church. And we should partner with our own teammates and with other local churches to get the word out.

Practice Catch and Release

When I fish, I don't keep the fish I catch. If I were starving, it'd be another story. But 99.9 percent of all the fish I catch, I let go. I reel them in and let them go. Do you know why I let them go? Because when I let them go, they get big and strong and I can catch them again. They are going to feed on all the smaller fish or crabs or plankton in the ocean. I also know that they will reproduce and make babies. Then the babies will grow up bigger. I do that for the ecosystem so that there is a healthy body of fish in the water.

As Christian leaders, we should be into catch and release. As God catches those people and brings them into the family of God, we release them into ministry. They become part of that healthy ecosystem called the church.

A healthy church is a healthy body of water. A healthy church does not have a bunch of big fat marlin swimming around in it. That is not a healthy church. That is a stunted church that is sadly out of balance. I've already mentioned what I believe a healthy church looks like. It has three types of people—three types of fish—inside its walls. It's got some fish that are lost and heading to hell. They are stuck in the mire and mud on their way to hell. If you lead a church and there are not a bunch of hell-bound people attending, you should restructure your leadership efforts. Without hell-bound seekers, the church is not a biblically functioning community.

The second group of people you should find is baby fish. They have recently been born again into the family of God and are little babies in their faith. They are like little guppies saying, "Yippee, I'm part of this local church. This is cool! Yay! I'm in a new swimming hole." They are probably going to be the most excited and passionate people in your church, and you need to capture their enthusiasm and get them plugged into the life of the church.

Then you have the third group—a bunch of big fat marlin—the mature believers. If the big fat marlins are doing their jobs, then they are going out and inviting their hell-bound friends to come to church. In turn, the hell-bound friends are becoming baby believers and eventually growing into mature marlin. That is the healthy ecosystem for the church that the New Testament describes.

Go Fish!

People often ask me, "Ed, why is Fellowship Church so exciting? I've never been to a church like it. It is so enthusiastic." Do you know why? It's very simple. We have adopted God's purpose—not mine, not yours, not the staff's—God's. We go fishing and we are very passionate about it. We don't allow mission drift and neither should you. Also, we are very persistent. We keep on fishing. Everything we do is about creatively casting the hope of the gospel. Everything we do has a hook in it. Every song, video, and activity has a hook in it. All of our ministries have the hook of the gospel in them. If something doesn't, we throw it out. Because of this commitment, we know we are partnering with the Spirit of the Lord, and we believe He is empowering us to do some serious fishing.

Let me ask you a question: Is your church committed to this kind of fishing? Are you willing to do whatever it takes to reach the lost fish out there, even if it means dismantling a ministry or worship style? All I can do is tell you what God has done for Fellowship Church. It is a complete and total God thing. It's a miracle of the grace and the mercy of our fanatical fishing Guide. We are in partnership with Him.

The apostle Paul understood this principle intimately. In 1 Corinthians 3:6–7 he said, "I planted the seed, Apollos watered it, but God made it grow. So neither he who plants nor he who waters is anything, but only God, who makes things grow." This verse could revolutionize your ministry. When we realize that we are partners with God, we won't get trapped trying to build our kingdoms. When we realize who our Guide is, we cannot fail.

When God wants to grow a bunch of mature fish, He looks for the most fertile body of water around. Why has Fellowship Church grown from 150 to more than 20,000 in fifteen years? Is it because of marketing? Is it because of the contemporary music? Is it because of casual dress? Are you kidding me? It's all about God! He is the one. I believe the reason He has chosen to bless Fellowship Church is because we understand His narrow purpose and try to play it out with passion, optimism, and persistence, never forgetting that we are in partnership with Him.

You have got to love to fish as a Christian leader. Think about your local church. Reflect upon your own salvation. Don't ever forget the miracle of the grace of Christ in your own life. Now think about the people who have been reeled in by the grace, mercy, and power of God. Think about how you can partner with the ultimate Guide to catch them and release them, so they can grow and mature into big, fat, honking marlin. When we realize the miracle of our own salvation, we will be passionate about welcoming others into the family of God.

What about you? Do you know your ultimate purpose as a leader? Are you passionate about unleashing creativity to be the leader God has made you to be? All it takes is one creative image or creative drama to connect a lost person to the hope of the Creator. One innovative building campaign could help attract thousands of new people to the family of God. Are you willing to do whatever it takes to be a fisher of men, women, students, and children? Remember, God is the One who catches the fish. But He calls us to cast our lines and nets into the water to join His fishing expedition. He has wired all of us with a unique blend of creativity that He is just waiting to use to draw people to Himself. Life is too short not to fish. Jesus does the catching; all we have to do is be willing to brave the elements and use our God-given creativity as we cast for hopeless fish heading for a Christless eternity.

I press on toward the goal to win
the prize for which God has called me
heavenward in Christ Jesus.

PHILIPPIANS 3:14

Is It Worth It?

As we end this book, the journey toward creative leadership is not over. We're just entering the first stretch of a long and amazing race. And there are going to be many, many times along the course of that demanding journey when you begin to wonder, *Is it worth it? Is it really worth all the effort?*

There's no doubt that creativity is demanding, but I hope this testimony from a man in our church will help you see that the creative process is worth every sacrifice, every drop of sweat, and every ounce of energy you expend.

> I have one sister and two brothers. Gary, the youngest of our family, is a pilot. [He] had never really seen the need for a personal relationship with Christ. He had a chance to fly down one weekend and participate in a weekend service at Fellowship. It just happened to be a service where Ed was talking about fly-fishing, and my brother loves to fly-fish.
>
> My wife and I were both sitting there with Gary and, as every word was spoken, as it came out, we were in our seats thinking, "This is for Gary." We were really amazed and just blown away by God's sovereignty and how He was speaking directly to Gary through Ed's talk.

We looked at him every once in awhile and we could see his lip quivering a little. And he's not an emotional guy at all. As he sat there, it's like God just took him and began peeling away at his heart, just one layer at a time, one layer after another. And by the end of the service, he had given his life to Christ.

Gary mentioned right there that he'd love to have the actual fly that Ed tied. I knew how important that was, so I came back the next day, talked to one of the pastors on staff, and told them a bit about the story and what happened to him. And Ed was nice enough to give me the actual fly. My wife and I took it, mounted it, and sent it to Gary. Now he's got it hanging over his fireplace. For him, it's a constant reminder of how God hooked him that day.

I'm ready to go fishing. Are you with me?

Appendixes

NOTE: The following appendixes are black-and-white representations of full-color print pieces. For a fuller picture of what we do at Fellowship Church, please visit www.creativepastors.com. Print kits, which include bulleting graphics and presentation slides, are now available for many of our teaching series.

APPENDIX 1A

*Easter
Invitation
tear-out
cards*

(front)

2005 Easter Service Times

Saturday, March 26   5:00pm
Sunday, March 27   9:30am
    11:15am
    1:00pm

fc fellowship|church
P L A N O

6400 Ave. K • Plano, TX
972-471-5700
www.FellowshipChurch.com

- 4 identical services
- Excellent children's programs
  available at each service

2005 Easter Service Times

Saturday, March 26   5:00pm
Sunday, March 27   9:30am
    11:15am
    1:00pm

fc fellowship|church
P L A N O

6400 Ave. K • Plano, TX
972-471-5700
www.FellowshipChurch.com

- 4 identical services
- Excellent children's programs
  available at each service

2005 Easter Service Times

Saturday, March 26   5:00pm
Sunday, March 27   9:30am
    11:15am
    1:00pm

fc fellowship|church
P L A N O

6400 Ave. K • Plano, TX
972-471-5700
www.FellowshipChurch.com

- 4 identical services
- Excellent children's programs
  available at each service

2005 Easter Service Times

Saturday, March 26   5:00pm
Sunday, March 27   9:30am
    11:15am
    1:00pm

fc fellowship|church
P L A N O

6400 Ave. K • Plano, TX
972-471-5700
www.FellowshipChurch.com

- 4 identical services
- Excellent children's programs
  available at each service

APPENDIX 1B

*Easter
Invitation
tear-out
cards*
(back)

*Christmas
Direct Mail
piece with
die-cut*

(front—unfolded)

Experience a Christmas Eve that can change your life

Join us Friday, December 24th at 3:00pm and 6:00pm

Two identical community-wide services that will be memorable for the entire family.
(Free event. Free parking)

PRESENTED BY:

fc fellowship|church

2450 Hwy 121 N • Grapevine, TX 76051 • 972.471.5700
www.FellowshipChurch.com

Celebrate Christmas Eve with Fellowship Church at the American Airlines Center

I-35 at Victory Ln, just north of Downtown Dallas.

Check out FellowshipChurch.com for additional details and directions

NEW LOCATIONS

January 16th, Fellowship Church will open two new convenient locations, Fellowship Church Plano and Fellowship Church Uptown. Both will provide creative worship environments for adults and children.

Fellowship Church Plano
Strategically located in North Dallas, the new 100,000 square foot campus is just off I-75 between Spring Creek and Legacy.
(see map on back)
Service Times:
Sundays,
9:30am & 11:15am

Fellowship Church Uptown
Conveniently located by West Village in the North Dallas High School.
(see map on back)
Service Times:
Sundays,
9:30am & 11:15am

FELLOWSHIP CHURCH

FC offers, bible-oriented, contemporary worship services that are alive with energy and creativity. Excellent childcare, exciting children's and student ministries are available as well as programs for singles and married adults.

Fellowship's Grapevine campus is located in the heart of the DFW Metroplex, at the intersection of Hwy 121 and I-635, just north of DFW Airport.

Service Times:
Saturdays, 5:00pm & 6:30pm
Sundays, 9:30am & 11:15am

Senior Pastor: Ed Young

*Christmas
Direct Mail
piece with
die-cut*

(*back—unfolded*)

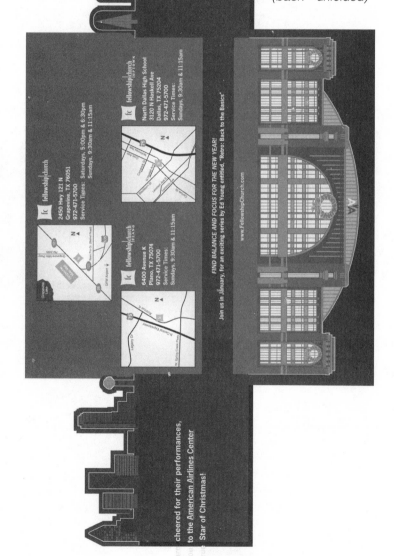

In an arena where superstars are cheered for
Fellowship Church invites you to the Ameri
to celebrate the True Star of Chri.

ʃc **fellowship church**

2450 Hwy. 121 N
Grapevine, TX 76051
972-471-5700
Service Times: Saturdays, 5:00pm & 6:30pm
Sundays, 9:30am & 11:15am

ʃc **fellowship church** PLANO

6400 Avenue K
Plano, TX 75074
972-471-5700
Service Times:
Sundays, 9:30am & 11:15am

ʃc **fellowship church** UPTOWN

North Dallas High School
3120 N Haskell Ave
Dallas, TX 75204
972-471-5700
Service Times:
Sundays, 9:30am & 11:15am

FIND BALANCE AND FOCUS FOR THE NEW YEAR!
Join us in January for an exciting series by Ed Young entitled, "Retro: Back to the Basics"

www.FellowshipChurch.com

cheered for their performances,
to the American Airlines Center
Star of Christmas!

APPENDIX 3A

"Retro" Series Graphic
(Worship Guide Cover and PowerPoint Slide)

APPENDIX 3B

Satellite Campus Promotion
(on the inside of the Worship Guide)

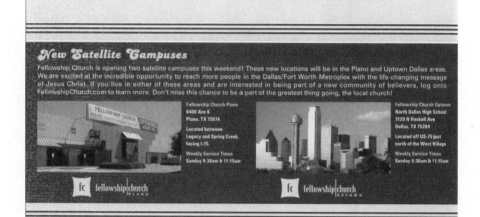

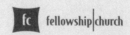

APPENDIX 4A

"Tri-God" Series Graphic
(Worship Guide Cover and PowerPoint Slide)

APPENDIX 4B

Hard-copy Invitation to Baptismal Celebration during "Tri-God" Series

Special Baptismal Celebration

after the weekend services July 12 & 13

Name: _____

Day Phone: _____ Evening Phone: _____

Email: _____

Age Group: (please check one)

❑ Child/Youth (age_____)

❑ Adult

I would like to be baptized on: (please check one))

❑ Saturday, July 12, 7:30pm

❑ Sunday, July 13, 12:30pm

Someone from our office will contact you prior to your baptism to answer any questions you may have and to give you additional information about this service.

Please use the back of this form to write your story about how you became a Christ-follower.

Please place completed form in offering bag or bring it by the Guest Services Kiosk in the Atrium.

"Multiple Choice" Series Graphic
(Worship Guide Cover and PowerPoint Slide)

APPENDIX 5B

Example of Guest Registry Form

(Tear-out section of Worship Guide and PowerPoint slide during the "Welcome" portion of the service)

GUEST REGISTRY
FELLOWSHIP CHURCH, EST. 1990

FORM NO. **01/17-18/2004**
TO REORDER CALL: 972-471-5700

• Use Pen or No.2 Pencil   • Make dark marks   • Erase completely to change

Mr/Mrs/Ms   LAST NAME   FIRST NAME   M.I.

EMAIL   BIRTHDATE(S)

ADDRESS   CITY

STATE   ZIP   HOME PHONE#   WORK PHONE#

OCCUPATION/PLACE OF EMPLOYMENT

THIS IS MY:
○ 1st time   ○ 2nd time   ○ regular attendee

I/ WE ATTENDED:
○ Sat. 5:00pm   ○ Sun. 8:30am   ○ Sun. 11:15am
○ Sat. 6:30pm   ○ Sun. 9:45am

○ I'm praying to establish a personal relationship with Christ.

MY AGE GROUP:
YOUTH:
○ Jr. High (6th-8th)   ○ Sr. High (9th-12th)

SINGLES:
○ 18-27   ○ 27-35   ○ 35-45
○ 45 & BETTER

MARRIED ADULTS:
○ 20s   ○ 30s   ○ 40s   ○ 50s   ○ 60s

Children's names & birthdates: _____
_____
_____

SCHEDULE ME FOR THE NEXT:

Baptism:
○ Wed., Feb. 4   ○ Sat., Feb. 21   ○ Sun., Feb. 22

Newcomers Membership Class:
○ Sat., Jan. 31, 6:30pm   ○ Sun., Feb. 1, 9:30am   ○ Sun., Feb. 1, 11:15am   ○ Thurs., Feb. 5, 6:45pm

E2: Spiritual Growth Classes
Experience   ○ Feb. 12, 19, 26 - 7:00pm
Excel   ○ Feb. 5, 12, 19, 26 - 7:00pm

Discover Your Design:
DYD(cost: $20)   ○ Thurs., Feb. 5, 12, 19, 26

Kid Faith: Basics for Kids:
○ Sat., Jan. 31, 6:30pm   ○ Sun., Feb. 1, 11:15am   ○ Thurs., Feb. 5, 6:45pm

I WOULD LIKE MORE INFORMATION ON:

○ How to establish a personal relationship with Christ   ○ How to join Fellowship Church

○ Preschool   ○ Children   ○ Jr. High   ○ Sr. High   ○ Singles   ○ Athletics   ○ Greeters
○ Missions   ○ Women's   ○ Men's   ○ Married Life   ○ Special Needs   ○ HomeTeams
○ I would like to volunteer in the _____ ministry.

"Thread—Tailor Made" Sermon Mind Map (front)

(color highlighting not shown)

A

INTRO: TAILOR MADE VIDEO.

HOW DO YOU LIKE THIS JACKET? IS THIS THING AWESOME OR WHAT? IF IT FITS PERFECTLY, I HAVE TO ADMIT THAT THIS JACKET COST QUITE A FEW PENNIES... BUT IT WAS WORTH IT. BECAUSE AFTER ALL, YOU ARE WHAT YOU WEAR, RIGHT?

I KNOW NOT EVERYONE BUYS NEW CLOTHES FOR EASTER (AS I SAID IN THE VIDEO), BUT I NEVER DID GROWING UP. BUT HOW MANY OF YOU—BE HONEST—HOW MANY OF YOU HAVE A NEW OUTFIT ON THIS EASTER? EASTER KIND OF BRINGS OUT THE FASHION FANATIC IN ALL OF US. DOESN'T IT? WE HAVE THIS PASSION FOR FASHION.

ILLUS: EVER SINCE I CAN REMEMBER, I'VE BEEN INTO FASHION. EVEN WHEN I WAS A LITTLE KID, MY MOM TOLD ME I'D CHANGE MY CLOTHES TWO OR THREE TIMES A DAY. IN THE SIXTIES YOU COULDN'T BUY PANTS WITH STRIPES DOWN THE SIDE, SO I ASKED MY MOM TO SEW THEM ON FOR ME. I WANTED TO HAVE NUMBERS ON MY CLOTHES AND MY MOM, BEING AN ARTIST, WOULD PAINT NUMBERS ON MY SHIRTS FOR ME. IN FACT, I'VE BEEN TOLD THAT WHEN I WAS BORN I CRIED AND CRIED. THE DOCTORS COULDN'T FIGURE OUT WHY I WOULDN'T STOP CRYING. FINALLY, THEY FIGURED IT OUT. IT WAS BECAUSE MY DIAPER AND BOOTIES DIDN'T MATCH.

THAT LAST PART...

DIFFERENT KINDS OF CLOTHING FOR DIFFERENT THINGS. WE HAVE FORMAL WEAR, CASUAL WEAR, BUSINESS CASUAL, WEDDING CLOTHES AND CLOTHES. AND THEN YOU HAVE ALL OF THE SPORTSWEAR: FISHING, BICYCLING, BASKETBALL, SURFING, TENNIS, GOLF.

C

THREAD: TAILOR MADE — MARCH 25–27, 2005

...KEY TO ATONE FOR THE SINS OF MAN TO COVER THAT... TO CLOTHE THEM...GOD WAS GIVING THEM A SIGN AND HIS... CLOTHE THEM...

PURSUE THE CLOCK FORWARD SEVERAL THOUSAND YEARS TO ANOTHER GARMENT... A BABY WAS BORN IN A MANGER IN A SMALL TOWN OUTSIDE OF JERUSALEM CALLED BETHLEHEM AND WAS WRAPPED IN SWADDLING CLOTHS—ANOTHER GARMENT...

IF YOU DID SOME STUDY AND YOU LEARNED ABOUT TRAVEL DURING THE ANCIENT DAYS, YOU WOULD SEE THAT OFTEN MEN AND WOMEN WOULD WEAR SHAWLS WHEN THEY WOULD TAKE A TRIP. BECAUSE MORE OFTEN THAN NOT THEY WOULD BE WALKING. WELL, THESE DEATH SHAWLS WERE LIKE WALKING CASKETS. OFTEN, WHEN SOMEONE WOULD DIE, WHEN THEY WOULD CLOCK OUT, OTHERS PEOPLE WOULD DIG HOLES FOR THE DEAD PERSON, WRAP THEM IN THE DEATH SHAWL, BURY THEM AND THAT WAS IT. MANY PEOPLE BELIEVE THE DEATH SHAWL... TO WRAP JESUS IN WERE ACTUALLY HER OWN... THIS WAS ANOTHER FORESHADOWING OF THINGS TO COME.

THE CHILD GROWS UP AND WEARS ANOTHER GARMENT—A PURPLE ROBE. SOLDIERS THEN THEY THROW A MOCK ROYAL ROBE—A PURPLE ROBE—ON HIM AS THEY ABUSE HIM AND TORTURE HIM. HE DIES A CRUEL DEATH AND IS WRAPPED IN GRAVE CLOTHES—ANOTHER GARMENT...

D

ALL OF THESE GARMENTS ARE MADE... THEN CHRIST BURSTS FORTH FROM THE GRAVE... RESURRECTION! LEAVING THE OLD GRAVE GARMENT... BEHIND. BREAKING THE POWER AND THE PENALTY OF SIN AND DEATH FOREVER!

T.S. WHAT WOULD HAPPEN IF WE COULD SEE WHAT WE'RE REALLY WEARING. IF WE COULD SEE PAST ALL THE THREAD OUTFITS, PAST ALL THE STUFF, AND SEE WHAT WE LOOK LIKE BEFORE GOD? GOD DOESN'T LOOK ON THE OUTSIDE. THE TRUTH IS, AS NICE AS WE LOOK ON THE OUTSIDE, ON THE INSIDE OUR LIVES SORT OF LOOK LIKE THIS JACKET I'M WEARING. YOU MIGHT BE SAYING, "WELL, ED, HOW CAN YOU SAY THAT?"

GOD IS HOLY AND HIS STANDARD IS PERFECTION. IN OTHER WORDS, HIS GARMENT IS WITHOUT WRINKLE OR STAIN. IT'S PERFECT. WE'VE ALL SINNED AND WE'VE ALL CUT UP THIS JACKET. THIS TAILOR MADE SUIT THAT GOD HAS FASHIONED FOR US. JESUS, AND ALSO I AM A SINNER AND... ANYTHING THAT YOU DO OR... DO THAT IS NOT FOR THE GLORY OF GOD... GIVING IN TO ANGER, DISRESPECTING OTHERS, MARITAL INFIDELITY, SUBSTANCE ABUSE, LUST, SHADY BUSINESS DEALS, CHEATING AT SCHOOL, LYING, GIVING BACK TO GOD (MISMANAGING YOUR MONEY), LYING, GIVING SELFISHNESS AND GREEDY HATE.

AND THIS JACKET REPRESENTS WHAT OUR BEHAVIOR, OUR SIN HAS DONE TO OUR LIVES. WE HAVE RUINED OUR SUIT WITH SIN. OUR LIVES ARE TATTERED, TORN AND... FILTHY... AND NOW WE HAVE NOTHING TO OFFER GOD ACCEPT OUR FILTHY RAGS.

ISAIAH 64:6... "ALL OF US HAVE BECOME LIKE ONE WHO IS UNCLEAN, AND ALL OUR RIGHTEOUS ACTS ARE LIKE FILTHY RAGS."

OUR SIN HAS MESSED UP THIS TAILOR MADE COAT. OBVIOUSLY, THAT'S NOT THE ORIGINAL INTENT O THE DESIGNER. THE ORIGINAL INTENT OF THE TAILOR WAS FOR IT IS THING TO BE WORN AND TAKEN CARE OF. BUT I AM FREE TO DO WHAT I WISH WITH THE GARMENT, AND I CHOSE TO CUT IT UP. GOD'S ORIGINAL DESIGN WAS FOR ME NOT TO DO THAT. BUT I DID THAT. I HAVE THIS NATURE TO SIN. THAT'S BEEN GIVEN TO ME BECAUSE ALL OF US COME FROM A CROOKED FARMER AND A DRUNKEN SAILOR. THE CROOKED FARMER IS ADAM. THE DRUNKEN SAILOR IS NOAH.

EVEN THOUGH WE ARE SINNERS, GOD LOVES US. GOD SENT JESUS CHRIST TO DIE A HORRIBLE DEATH ON THE CROSS. ALL THE WORST GARMENTS WE CAN'T EVER WORN HE WORE ON THE CROSS ON OUR BEHALF. WE CAN'T GO TO GOD ALONE. JESUS IS OUR GO-BETWEEN, AND THAT'S GOT THE STORY OF EASTER.

T.S. LET'S GET BACK TO THIS JACKET. THIS JACKET REPRESENTS OUR SIN. OUR SIN STAIN. OUR SIN MAKES THE GARMENT IMPERFECT. IT DOESN'T MEASURE UP TO THE DESIGNER'S STANDARD. EVEN IF THERE IS JUST ONE THREAD OUT OF PLACE.

[NEXT PAGE]

B

LOOK, TOO. AT ALL THE DIFFERENT FASHION TV SHOWS AND FASHION MAGAZINES. THERE'S AN ENTIRE CABLE NETWORK ORBITING AROUND WHAT WE WEAR. WE ARE, AS A SPECIFIC SPECIES. WE HAVE AN INNATE INTEREST IN CLOTHING. YOU MIGHT SAY WE HAVE A THING FOR THREAD. AFTER ALL, FASHION ALL COMES DOWN TO A SINGLE THREAD...

WOULDN'T IT BE FASCINATING TO SEE ALL THE THREAD THAT WAS USED TO MAKE THIS JACKET? THAT WOULD BE PRETTY CRAZY, WOULDN'T IT. TO SEE ALL THAT THREAD AND ALL THE STUFF THAT WENT INTO MAKING THESE CLOTHES. THEN SOMEONE DESIGNS SOMETHING LIKE THIS COAT, THEY PUT EVERYTHING INTO IT. IT'S A REFLECTION OF WHO THE TAILOR IS.

PUT THE SHREDDED COAT BACK ON AND READ THE FOLLOWING SCRIPTURE VERSES.

GENESIS 3:21, "THE LORD GOD MADE GARMENTS OF SKIN FOR ADAM AND HIS WIFE AND CLOTHED THEM."

PSALM 139:13, "FOR YOU CREATED MY INMOST BEING; YOU KNIT ME TOGETHER IN MY MOTHER'S WOMB."

LUKE 2:12, "THIS WILL BE A SIGN TO YOU, YOU WILL FIND A BABY WRAPPED IN CLOTHES AND LYING IN A MANGER."

JOHN 19:2, "THE SOLDIERS TWISTED TOGETHER A CROWN OF THORNS AND PUT THEM ON HIS HEAD. THEY CLOTHED HIM IN A PURPLE ROBE."

JOHN 19:23, "WHEN THE SOLDIERS CRUCIFIED JESUS THEY TOOK HIS CLOTHES, DIVIDING THEM INTO FOUR SHARES, THIS GARMENT WAS SEAMLESS, WOVEN IN ONE PIECE FROM TOP TO BOTTOM."

JOHN 20:6-7. "THEN SIMON PETER... WENT INTO THE TOMB. HE SAW THE STRIPS OF LINEN LYING THERE, AS WELL AS THE BURIAL CLOTH THAT HAD BEEN AROUND JESUS' HEAD. THE CLOTH WAS FOLDED UP BY ITSELF, SEPARATE FROM THE LINEN."

...DO WE HAVE A DESIRE FOR CLOTHES? FOR THAT MATTER, WHY ARE WE AWARE THAT WE NEED CLOTHES AND THAT WITHOUT CLOTHES WE'RE NAKED?

WE'RE THE ONLY SPECIES THAT HAVE THIS YEARNING, THE WHOLE CONCEPT OF NAKEDNESS IS UNIQUE TO HUMAN BEINGS. ANIMALS, FOR EXAMPLE, DON'T KNOW THEY'RE NAKED. I'VE NEVER WALKED UP TO MY GIANT BULL MASTIFF AND SAID, "HEY, PUT YOUR PANTS ON!"

WHEN ADAM AND EVE SINNED, THEY GOT THE THREAD BETWEEN THEMSELVES AND GOD. FOR THE FIRST TIME THEY REALIZED THEIR NAKEDNESS. THEIR PHYSICAL NAKEDNESS, THOUGH, WAS JUST A... THAT EXISTED ON A DEEPER LEVEL... SPIRITUAL NAKEDNESS. SO, IN THEIR SHAME, THEY LEAVES TOGETHER IN... TO COVER THEIR NAKEDNESS.

A FASHION, THE ENTIRE UNIVERSE HELD ITS BREATH TO SEE WHAT OUR HOLY GOD WOULD DO. GOD TOOK THE FLOOR OF THE EARTH. THE ANIMAL AND SPILL ITS BLOOD... FIRST ATTEMPT TO COVER MANKIND'S FIRST... THEY TOOK OUT A SKIN... MADE ANIMAL SKINS FOR ADAM AND EVE... THIS BEGAN THE CRUEL DEATH AND IS WRAPPED... THAT IT TOOK THE SPILL...

"Thread—Tailor Made" Sermon Mind Map (back)

(color highlighting not shown)

[Section E]

DON'T WANT CHRIST WOVEN THROUGH EVERYTHING IN OUR LIVES BECAUSE IT MIGHT BE UNCOMFORTABLE OR INCONVENIENT. THERE'S A LACK OF TRUST.

SO, THAT'S WHAT WE'RE GOING TO LOOK AT OVER THE NEXT SEVERAL WEEKS. WHAT DOES IT REALLY MEAN TO BE CLOTHED IN CHRIST? HOW ARE YOU WEARING THIS TAILOR MADE JACKET?

WHEN WE TRULY BECOME CLOTHED IN CHRIST, WE TRADE THE TORN JACKET FOR A NEW ONE. EPHESIANS 4:24 SAYS: "PUT ON THE NEW MAN WHICH WAS CREATED ACCORDING TO GOD, IN TRUE RIGHTEOUSNESS AND HOLINESS." AND HERE'S WHAT WILL HAPPEN WHEN WE PUT ON CHRIST AND WEAVE HIM INTO EVERY AREA OF OUR LIVES. IT WORSHIPS WITH HIM ... THE SIGNS OF OUR RELATIONSHIPS WITH OTHERS. IT REMOVES THE SHOTS AND WORRY ... THE STRESS AND FEAR, AND THEN IT GIVES US THE SUPERNATURAL ABILITY TO SEE THE TAPESTRY OF LIFE FROM GOD'S PERSPECTIVE.

I WANT YOU TO TAKE THE THREAD THAT YOU WERE GIVEN WHEN YOU WALKED INTO THE WORSHIP CENTER, AND I WANT YOU TO ASK THE PERSON SEATED NEXT TO YOU TO TIE IT AROUND YOUR WRIST. THIS THREAD REPRESENTS THE THREAD THAT IS CHRIST THAT IS ... EVERYTHING. THIS REPRESENTS THE FACT THAT WHAT NEEDS TO BE WOVEN INTO EVERY ASPECT OF OUR LIFE AND MINE AND AROUND EVERYTHING ... THE WELL ... AND WE'RE GOING TO TALK ABOUT ... THE BEAUTY AND THE JOY OF THAT NEXT WEEK.

AS YOU WEAR THIS THREAD THROUGHOUT THE SERIES IT WILL BE A CONSTANT REMINDER THAT JESUS IS THE THREAD THAT CONNECTS THE DISCONNECTED FABRIC OF OUR LIVES. AND WHEN YOU ARE CLOTHED IN CHRIST—THE ULTIMATE TAILOR MADE GARMENT—I GUESS YOU COULD SAY ... THE CLOTHES REALLY DO MAKE THE MAN. BEGINNING REMEMBER. IT'S ALSO ABOUT HOW ARE YOU WEARING HIM?

[Section F]

DISCONNECTED FABRIC OF OUR LIVES. THIS PLAN WOULD MAKE US INTO WHOLE ... BEINGS. IT WOULD MEND ... THE BROKEN THREAD CAUSED BY SIN. IT'S SEWN ... HERE FROM THE OLD TESTAMENT SACRIFICAL SYSTEM TO, ULTIMATELY, THE SACRIFICE OF JESUS PAYING THE PRICE ON THE CROSS FOR ALL OF OUR SINS.

WE'VE GOT TO UNDERSTAND SOMETHING—OUR SAVIOR IS A MASTER TAILOR. CHRIST IS THE COMMON THREAD IN OUR LIVES. AND GOD WANTS TO SEW OUR LIVES BACK TOGETHER WITH THE THREAD OF CHRIST. HE WANTS YOU ... TO BE TAILOR MADE. NOTHING IN THIS WORLD WILL EVER ... US. WE WILL NEVER BE ABLE TO RECONNECT THE DISCONNECTED FABRIC OF OUR LIVES UNTIL WE UNDERSTAND THE COSMIC CONNECTION THAT HOLDS EVERYTHING TOGETHER.

ILLUS: DID YOU WATCH THE OSCARS WHERE ALL THE CELEBRITIES AND STARS WERE BEING INTERVIEWED? THEY WERE ASKED ONE QUESTION. ... WHO ARE YOU WEARING?

I HAVE TO ASK YOU THE SAME QUESTION TODAY. I SAID EARLIER THAT YOU ARE WHAT YOU WEAR. BUT IT'S NOT REALLY ABOUT WHAT YOU ARE WEARING, IT'S ABOUT WHO YOU ARE WEARING? AND SOMEDAY IN ETERNITY YOU'RE GOING TO STAND IN FRONT OF GOD AND HE'S GOING TO ASK YOU THE SAME QUESTION: WHO ARE YOU WEARING?

THERE'S ONLY ONE DESIGNER LABEL THAT REALLY FITS. JESUS IS PERFECTLY, AND THE ... GARMENT IS JESUS. ... WHEN HIS THREAD SURROUNDS US.

WHEN YOU PUT ON A PIECE OF CLOTHING, YOU DON'T PUT IT HALF WAY ON AND THEN WALK AROUND. YET, MANY OF US ARE FRANTICALLY TRYING ON ALL THESE OTHER GARMENTS AND THEY DON'T FIT ONLY ONE IS TAILOR MADE.

ILLUS: THIS JACKET WAS MADE FOR THE WAY MY I STAND AND CARRY MY SHOULDERS. IT WAS DESIGNED BASED ON THE FACT THAT I WEAR ... WATCH ON MY WRIST. IT WAS DESIGNED WITH ... MOVEMENT IN MIND. (MOVE AROUND A LOT) IT WAS MADE TO ACCOMMODATE THE EXACT ... OF MY CHEST AND MY ARMS AND MY WAIST.

GOD HAS A TAILOR MADE GARMENT FOR YOU, RIGHT HERE ... JESUS IS THE GARMENT. HE IS THE THREAD THAT HOLDS OUR LIVES TOGETHER. HE IS THE ULTIMATE JACKET THAT COVERS OUR SIN FOREVER. GOD HAS NEW THREADS FOR YOU AND ME AND THEY ARE THERE FOR THE TAKING. ...

... THAT'S WHAT EASTER IS ALL ABOUT. ... JACKET ... BUT JESUS CHRIST PAID FOR IT ALL. HE PAID THE ULTIMATE PRICE FOR YOUR SINS AND MINE. AND WE ARE RESCUED THROUGH THE POWER OF HIS RESURRECTION. THAT'S WHAT EASTER IS ALL ABOUT. THAT'S WHAT WE'RE CELEBRATING TODAY: THE FACT THAT WE CAN BE CLOTHED IN CHRIST AND MADE CLEAN, RIGHTEOUS AND HAVE OUR SINS WASHED AWAY.

I HAVE TWO QUESTIONS TO ASK YOU. ... ARE YOU CLOTHED ...? MAYBE YOU HAVEN'T MADE THE CHOICE TO PUT ON CHRIST. I WANT YOU TO KNOW THAT YOU CAN—TODAY, NOW. MAYBE YOU'RE ASKING, "HOW" [SINNER'S PRAYER]

[Section G]

THAT'S WHY IT'S GRACE, AND HIS MERCY IS SO AMAZING. BECAUSE GOD OF THE MAKER—AND HIS PLAN INTO ACTION. A PLAN TO RECONNECT. ... IS WITH GOD, TO ALLOW US TO STAND IN HIS PRESENCE ONCE AGAIN—A PLAN TO ... THE FABRIC OF LIFE AND PROVIDE THE ULTIMATE WARDROBE FOR US. GOD HAS ... DESIRED EACH OF US AND PICKED OUT THE PERFECT ... FABRIC AND STILL FOR US. HE HAS PUT ... PUT THEM ON. AND CHRIST PAID FOR IT ALL! ALL WE HAVE TO DO ... WE EITHER PUT THEM ON OR NOT. WE EITHER GET DRESSED OR NOT.

ROMANS 13:14. "RATHER, CLOTHE YOURSELVES WITH THE LORD JESUS CHRIST, AND DO NOT THINK ..."

GALATIANS 3:27. "FOR ALL OF YOU WHO WERE BAPTIZED INTO CHRIST HAVE CLOTHED YOURSELVES WITH CHRIST." ... GOD HAS THIS MASTER DESIGN. THIS MASTER PLAN THAT WE ARE CELEBRATING TODAY—A PLAN TO ... THE ...

IF YOU'RE SITTING THERE COUNTING THE EASTER LILLIES AND SAYING TO YOURSELF, "I'VE ALREADY ACCEPTED CHRIST, THIS ISN'T FOR ME", MY SECOND QUESTION IS FOR YOU. ... AREN'T WEARING CHRIST. YES, YOUR SALVATION IS SECURE YOU'VE ACCEPTED CHRIST'S GIFT OF FORGIVENESS. BUT YOU AREN'T WEARING THE JACKET THE WAY IT WAS DESIGNED TO BE WORN.

- STRAIGHT JACKET—GOD—LEGALISTIC
- CASUAL GOD—TOSS GOD OVER OUR SHOULDER, NON-COMMITTAL
- COAT CHECK GOD—FOR WORLD-WIDE EMERGENCIES
- SUNDAY BEST GOD—LOOK GOOD ON ... WEEKENDS BUT THE REST OF THE WEEK IS WHIFFS OFF
- DISS GOD—ANGRY AT GOD SO WE TOSS HIM ASIDE AND TRAMPLE ON HIM
- PIMP GOD—USE GOD TO GET WHAT WE WANT
- CAMO GOD—PUT A CAMO JACKET OVER HIM AND HIDE THE LIGHT FROM OTHERS

YES, YOU MAY BE CLOTHED IN CHRIST, BUT LOOK AT HOW YOU TREAT THE JACKET. MANY OF US WEAR THE JACKET THE WAY WE WANT TO, NOT THE WAY GOD HAS DESIGNED. WE DON'T WANT TO WEAR HIM FULLY. WE PUT ON CHRIST THE WAY WE WANT. WE PICK OUR CLOTHES ON ANY GIVEN DAY—BASED ON HOW WE'RE FEELING AT THE MOMENT. WE ...

APPENDIX 7

"Juicy Fruit—Faithfulness" Sermon Mind Map (handwritten format)   *(color highlighting not shown)*

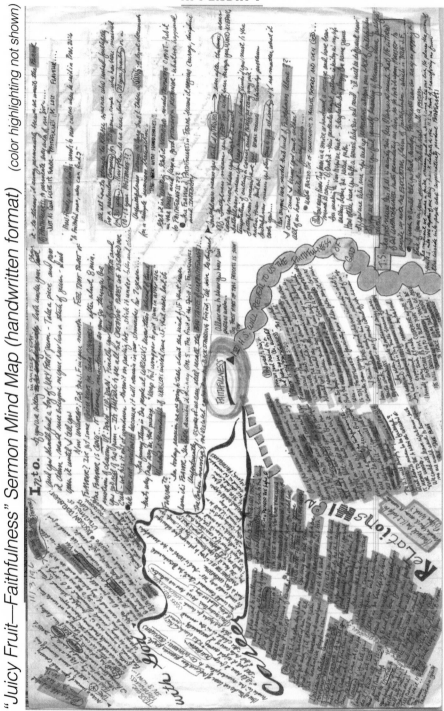

APPENDIX 8A

"In the Zone—Creature from the Cash Lagoon"
Sermon Notes (p. 1)

IN THE ZONE : CREATURE FROM THE CASH LAGOON
DECEMBER 11-12, 2004

PLASTIC PEOPLE EATER

The Average Household Has More Than $8400
In Credit Card Debt
(Min. Payments) – 25 Yrs To Pay Off,
Spending Total Of $24,000 At 18% Interest
Americans Get 50 Unsolicited Credit Card Offers Each Year.
Americans Have Over 1 Billion Cards
Credit Debt 735 Billion About 31% Higher
Than It Was 5 Years Ago

PROVERBS 22:7
"... the borrower is servant to the lender."

VIDEO: "NY AT TIMES SQUARE"
   CUE: Warning: Overuse Can Be
         Hazardous To Your Personal Wealth! **[GO]**

BUDGET BOOGEYMAN

BLUE-LIGHT
KEEP-UP, ONE-UP, SHOW-UP
SAVE IT-BLOW IT ALL

PROVERBS 27:23-24a
[23] "Be sure you know the condition of your flocks,
   give careful attention to your herds;
[24] for riches do not endure forever,"

"AL" – The Average American Child

VIDEO: "Creature From The Black Lagoon -Dying"
   CUE: "...You Know What Happened
         To The Creature?" **[GO]**

APPENDIX 8B

"In the Zone—Creature from the Cash Lagoon"
Sermon Notes (p. 2)

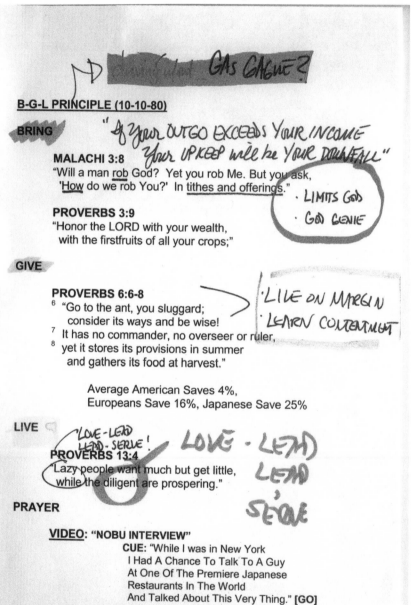

B-G-L PRINCIPLE (10-10-80)

BRING

"If your OUTGO EXCEEDS YOUR INCOME
Your UPKEEP will be YOUR DOWNFALL"

MALACHI 3:8
"Will a man rob God? Yet you rob Me. But you ask,
'How do we rob You?' In tithes and offerings."

· LIMITS GOD
· GOD GENIE

PROVERBS 3:9
"Honor the LORD with your wealth,
with the firstfruits of all your crops;"

GIVE

PROVERBS 6:6-8
6 "Go to the ant, you sluggard;
consider its ways and be wise!
7 It has no commander, no overseer or ruler,
8 yet it stores its provisions in summer
and gathers its food at harvest."

· LIVE ON MARGIN
· LEARN CONTENTMENT

Average American Saves 4%,
Europeans Save 16%, Japanese Save 25%

LIVE

LOVE - LEAD
LEAD - SERVE!

LOVE · LEAD
LEAD
SERVE

PROVERBS 13:4
"Lazy people want much but get little,
while the diligent are prospering."

PRAYER

VIDEO: "NOBU INTERVIEW"
CUE: "While I was in New York
I Had A Chance To Talk To A Guy
At One Of The Premiere Japanese
Restaurants In The World
And Talked About This Very Thing." [GO]

APPENDIX 9

"In the Zone" Series Graphic
(Worship Guide Cover and PowerPoint Slide)

APPENDIX 10A

*Tear-out Christmas Invitation
inside Worship Guide (front)*

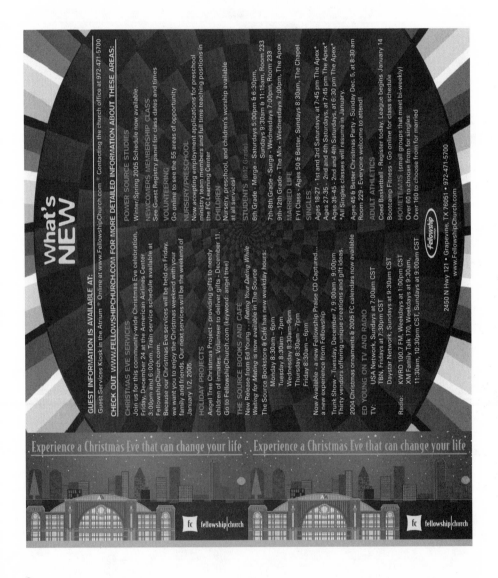

APPENDIX 10B

Tear-out Christmas Invitation inside Worship Guide (back)

Celebrate Christmas Eve with Fellowship Church
at the American Airlines Center

Join us Friday, December 24th at 3:00pm and 6:00pm

Two identical community-wide services that will
be memorable for the entire family.

(Free event, Free parking)

VISIT FELLOWSHIPCHURCH.COM FOR DETAILS, DIRECTIONS AND TRAIN SCHEDULE

2450 Hwy 121 N • Grapevine, TX 76051 • 972-471-5700 • www.FellowshipChurch.com

Celebrate Christmas Eve with Fellowship Church
at the American Airlines Center

Join us Friday, December 24th at 3:00pm and 6:00pm

Two identical community-wide services that will
be memorable for the entire family.

(Free event, Free parking)

VISIT FELLOWSHIPCHURCH.COM FOR DETAILS, DIRECTIONS AND TRAIN SCHEDULE

2450 Hwy 121 N • Grapevine, TX 76051 • 972-471-5700 • www.FellowshipChurch.com

This WEEKEND

This weekend we're continuing a series called "In The Zone." God wants all of us to reach our full potential. I'm excited about this series because I believe it will teach us how to make that a reality in our lives. We will discover some powerful biblical principles about what it means to live a life blessed by God. So, make it a priority to be here over the next several weeks and you will find out how to live a life in marked contrast to those around you - *in the zone.* ●

Senior Pastor, Ed Young

FIRST TIME VISITORS

Welcome to Fellowship Church. If this is your first time to worship with us, we're especially glad you're here today. Please take a moment to fill out the guest registry in the worship guide, then tear it out and drop it in the offering bag when it is passed later in the service. This will allow us to answer any questions you might have about all of the incredible things happening here at Fellowship.

YEAR END REVIEW

2004 was a year of tremendous impact, growth and life-change at Fellowship Church.

• 2409 joined Fellowship and 2154 were baptized.

• Planning has begun to open satellite campuses in Plano and Dallas in January 2005.

• Our radio and television show reached more viewers and listeners than ever before, with the addition of the USA Network and 90 million viewing households.

• 650 churches have partnered with Fellowship Connection.

As the end of the year quickly approaches, your joyful and gracious involvement through year end giving is vital to the ministry of Fellowship Church.

You can participate in giving though a number of ways. Whether it is by cash, check, stocks, bonds, mutual funds or online, we will provide you with a record of your giving for tax purposes. Deductions for 2004 are allowed for charitable contributions if given by December 31. For more information, log onto our website at www.FellowshipChurch.com (keyword: giving). You can call our business office at 972-471-6709 from 8:30am - 5:00pm if you have any questions. Thank you for your continued faithfulness to Fellowship!

CHILDCARE

Parents, we encourage you to take advantage of our safe and secure state-of-the-art children's facilities during our weekend worship services. Our trained staff and loving volunteers will provide your children with an environment where they can learn about God's love in an age-appropriate way. For our kindergarten through 5th graders, we have designed a dynamic and energetic children's appropriate service they will love. However, if you feel it necessary to take your children ages 5 and younger to our adult worship service, we will provide a family friendly environment designed just for you in Room 232. Our helpful ushers and greeters will assist you in locating any of the children's areas and Room 232.

In The ZONE

WEEKLY SERVICE SCHEDULE

Saturday - 5:00pm & 6:30pm, Sunday - 9:30am & 11:15am

First Wednesday - January 5, 7:00pm

First Wednesday of each month - praise music, prayer and communion

APPENDIX 11

"Character Tour" Series Graphic
(Worship Guide Cover, PowerPoint Slide,
and Video Opener for Sermon Series)

ED YOUNG

PASTOR. Ed Young is a pastor, author, and speaker with a passion for communicating God's unchanging truth through culturally compelling and creative teaching methods. He is the founding and senior pastor of Fellowship Church, one of the ten largest churches in America. Located in the heart of Dallas/Fort Worth, Texas, the church's main campus sits on 141 acres just north of DFW Airport. The church also operates three satellite campuses: one just north of downtown Dallas, one in the northern suburb of Plano, and the other north of Fort Worth near Alliance Airport.

Ed comes from a solid family of leaders. Born in Raleigh, North Carolina, to Dr. Ed and JoBeth Young, Ed has been in and around Christian ministry and church leadership his entire life. His father is a prolific author and the senior pastor at Second Baptist Church in Houston, Texas. His brother, Ben, is both a celebrated author and speaker who serves as a senior associate pastor at Second Baptist. And Ed's youngest brother, Cliff, is the lead singer of the popular Christian band Caedmon's Call. Ed earned his bachelor's degree from Houston Baptist University and a master of divinity degree from Southwestern Baptist Theological Seminary in Fort Worth, Texas. Later in his ministry, he also was awarded an honorary doctorate from Dallas Baptist University. He worked for several years as an associate pastor at Second Baptist. Then in 1990, he was called to lead a church start in Irving, Texas. Ed and a core group of 150 members began what was known then as the Fellowship of Las Colinas. Upon its move to permanent facilities in Grapevine, Texas, in 1998, the church changed its name to Fellowship Church and has grown to an average weekly attendance of more than twenty thousand people.

AUTHOR. Ed is the author of nine books:

Six books on Christian living:
- *You! The Journey to the Center of Your Worth*
- *Kid CEO: How to Keep Your Children from Running Your Life*
- *Know Fear: Facing Life's Six Most Common Phobias*
- *The Creative Marriage: The Art of Keeping Your Love Alive*
- *Rating Your Dating While Waiting for Mating*
- *Fatal Distractions: Overcoming Obstacles That Mess Up Our Lives*

Three books on Leadership:
- *The Creative Leader: Unleashing the Power of Your Creative Potential*
- *High Definition Living: Bringing Clarity to Your Life's Mission*
- *Can We Do That? 24 Innovative Practices That Will Change the Way You Do Church*

Two of Ed's books, *High Definition Living* and *Know Fear*, are also available in Spanish and Korean. *Kid CEO* is available in Korean.

Ed has also written a forty-day study based on his book *Know Fear*, as well as many small group Bible studies based on his teaching series.

CONFERENCE SPEAKER.

Ed hosts an annual church leadership conference held at Fellowship Church's Grapevine campus called C3—the Creative Church Conference. Each year, thousands of pastors, leaders, and teachers come to C3 to learn how to effectively implement creativity in their own ministries. The general C3 conference is held in January every year, and the C3 children's conference is held in October. In addition, regional C3 conferences are offered throughout the year at various locations around the U.S.

Ed is also frequently invited to speak at other church leadership conferences including:

- The Team Church Conference
- National Outreach Convention
- WillowCreek Resource Challenge Conference
- WillowCreek Teaching and Preaching Conference
- Liberty University Super Conference
- Granger Innovative Church Conference
- Church on the Cutting Edge Conference
- Beyond All Limits Conference
- Young Catalyst Conference
- Southern Baptist Convention
- Southern California Evangelism Conference

BROADCASTER.

Ed Young Ministries is a weekly television program shown on USA, Daystar, TBN, the Church Channel, and PAX stations nationwide. It is also aired on CNBC–Europe and the Australian Christian Channel.

Ed's radio ministry is broadcast daily in major metropolitan areas throughout the United States, as well as on XM Satellite radio.

MENTOR TO CHURCH LEADERS.

Ed has reached out to pastors and leaders around the world by creating a resource Web site called CreativePastors. com. CreativePastors provides thousands of ministry and leadership resources to help churches better communicate the life-changing message of Jesus Christ in creative and compelling ways.

As a part of CreativePastors, he produces a monthly leadership CD entitled *Leadership Uncensored* that deals with the real-life, day-to-day challenges of leading a church. This series has been one of the most requested resources on CreativePastors.com.

Ed also meets with pastors several times a year through a limited-attendance conference called Total Access—a program that allows church leaders a first-hand and in-depth look at the leadership structure and creative programs of Fellowship Church and its affiliated ministries.

More information about Fellowship Church, CreativePastors,
the Creative Church Conferences (C3), and Ed Young TV and Radio
is available on www.EdYoung.com.